W9-AOH-650

André Gide, Updated Edition

Twayne's World Authors Series

French Literature

David O'Connell, Editor

Georgia State University

TWAS 86

André Gide, Updated Edition

Thomas Cordle

Duke University

Twayne Publishers • New York
Maxwell Macmillan Canada • Toronto
Maxwell Macmillan International • New York   Oxford   Singapore   Sydney

Twayne's World Authors Series No. 86

André Gide, Updated Edition
Thomas Cordle

Twayne Publishers   Maxwell Macmillan Canada, Inc.
Macmillan Publishing Company   1200 Eglinton Avenue East
866 Third Avenue   Suite 200
New York, New York 10022   Don Mills, Ontario M3C 3N1

Library of Congress Cataloging-in-Publication Data

Cordle, Thomas, 1918–
      André Gide / Thomas Cordle. —Updated ed.
          p.   cm. — (Twayne's world author series : TWAS 86)
      Includes bibliographical references and index.
      ISBN 0-8057-8283-4
      1. Gide, André, 1869–1951—Criticism and interpretation.
   I. Title. II. Series.
   PQ2613.I2Z6153   1993
   848'.91209—dc20   92-28708
                                                  CIP

The paper used in this publication meets the minimum requirements
of American National Standard for Information Sciences—Permanence
of Paper for Printed Library Materials. ANSI Z3948-1984. ⊚™

10 9 8 7 6 5 4 3 2 1 (hc)

Printed in the United States of America

E.B.C.
In memoriam

Contents

Preface

Gide was 30 years old when the nineteenth century reached its end. A substantial part of his work, some 10 books, was in print before 1900. He was nearly 50 when the Europe that we know today emerged from the debris of the First World War. Born during the Franco-Prussian War, he grew up in a France that continued to taste the humiliation of defeat even after the International Exposition of 1878 had shown her definitive resurgence as a first-class power. He belonged to that brilliant generation of artists and intellectuals who were implicitly charged with the redemption of their country's greatness. His early manhood coincided with that period of wealth and stability known as "La Belle Epoque," of which his contemporary Marcel Proust has left an imperishable portrait in *A la Recherche du temps perdu.*

Gide was very much a man of that fin de siècle. He enjoyed the social status and wealth that a mass of paintings, books, and plays have led us to regard as its outstanding attributes. Objectively he was a product of that era. His books, however, reveal hardly anything at all about it. Their settings are spare and remote from the center of pleasure and power. It is true that, in subtle and uncontrollable ways, they speak of the advantages of wealth and class, but they do so without the unquestioning complacency that lends so much exotic charm to Proust's pictures of Paris and the Norman coast. In Gide privilege is revealed more for what it is in reality: an instrument of power and coercion. And Gide's style, so lean and direct, so uncluttered of metaphor, is the antithesis of that richly ornamented period that is so marvelously reflected in the opulent images of Marcel Proust.

Gide was not, to be sure, alone in refusing to depict in his stories the ease and grace of La Belle Epoque. His close friends Paul Claudel and Paul Valéry rejected their world even more bluntly than he. Claudel went literally to the ends of the earth to get away from it, and the plays he wrote while in his 20s are filled with rebellion and anarchy. Valéry remained in Paris, but he withheld his poetic voice for 20 years while he devoted himself to the study of mathematics, logic, and other forms of abstract thought. During the First World War, however, he returned to poetry and thereafter led a life and produced works that contain many reflections of the charmed world of his youth. Claudel remained forever an outsider to the secular world that he had repudiated, but he made another kind of peace with orthodoxy through his submission to the Roman Catholic church, which was one of the pillars of that stable order against which he had earlier revolted.

Gide's refusal to find satisfaction in his surroundings was less blatant than that of Claudel and Valéry, but it was just as certain and far more lasting. He never embraced anything in that enchanting order and instead remained estranged from it to his end. It was as if he had known its fragility and falsity from the start. "As if," yes; but in fact not so. Gide's moral perspicacity did not come directly from his observation of the world. Rather, it was a product of his heroic efforts to understand and master his own intimate turmoil and division. It took him considerable time to perceive with clarity the part played in that inner drama by the culture in which his life was immersed. When that perception came, his genius as the foremost dissenter of his time was born, and from book to book he elaborated on that theme over a period of some 50 years.

Nevertheless, during all that time, the vital energy of Gide's work, its passionate drive, continued to derive from the internal dialogue initiated by the bewilderment and frustration of his childhood and by his herculean efforts to cope with that legacy. All his work, as he wrote in a passage of his *Journal* that I have chosen as the epigraph for the body of this book, was "intimately motivated." It is a work whose sources are in the author's psyche, and for that reason it is preeminently a "psychological" work. The external world is not entirely absent from Gide's early stories and plays. But it appears as a stylized world whose essential function is to be a symbolical representation of his psyche. Gide often turned to Greek myths and to the histories and parables of the Bible to find an adequate and appropriate expression of his own dilemmas. His extraordinary ability to see the connection between his consciousness and those ancient stories is one of the most arresting aspects of his genius. In this creative process there was a reciprocal enrichment: Gide saw his personal problems more clearly in the light of old myths, and at the same time he gave a fresh, new, and warmly human interpretation to these often obscure old stories.

Furthermore, the psychology that Gide exposed in his books was not the classical psychology of the passions and the sentiments, but rather the new psychology of the unconscious that was later to be articulated by Freud and his school. Long before he had heard of Freud—indeed, before the publication of Freud's seminal work, *The Interpretation of Dreams* (*Die*

Traumdeutung, 1900)—Gide had discovered in his own inner life the preponderant role of dreams, fantasies, symbolical acts and objects, and irrational impulses, and from his first book onward he used these phenomena as devices to reveal character and promote action in his stories.

I have essayed in chapter 1 to analyze Gide's private history in such a way as to bring into relief the passions that moved him to write stories and plays about his interior conflicts. Gide's memoirs of his first 25 years, *Si le Grain ne meurt (If It Die)*, are the primary source for this analysis. His record of the psychic traumas of his early years and of his subsequent efforts to reorder his life without doing further violence to himself is one of the great documents of the twentieth century. Progressing from frustration and apathy to courage, insight, and understanding, it is a tale of overcoming that spares nothing and no one in its quest for truth and wisdom.

The first and most powerful forces that directed Gide's life and shaped his work were the erotic drives that were born of his relations with his parents in infancy and early childhood. This part of his history is exceptionally complex. Narcissism, pederasty, Catharism, the climactic developments in this drama, provided him with the great themes of his imaginative work. Gide's erotic character was also complicated by the culture of French Calvinism that he imbibed from his parents. It endowed him with a reverence for the gospel and a love of virtue and restraint that remained with him throughout his life. It also gave him an enemy whom he blamed for much that he found amiss in himself and in the world.

In the three chapters that follow my introductory analysis of Gide's personal history I have examined almost every piece of his poetic work. I have devoted a separate commentary to each book with the aim of preserving the particular tone and ensemble of aesthetic means that characterize it. From myth to parable, from intimate journal to history and realistic narrative, Gide cast his work in all the great modes: pastoral, romance, irony, tragedy, comedy, humor, all of which flowed from his extraordinary mind with apparent ease and naturalness. His diary informs us over and over that it was this differentiation of tones that he as an artist sought most ardently and laboriously. It is the hallmark of his literary genius.

At the same time, there are large changes of outlook in Gide's long career that must not be ignored, and for that reason I have divided his work into three periods, each distinguished by particular external influ-

ences and by his attitude toward himself and his role in the world. When
Gide began writing he was a neurotic adolescent. He fell under the spell
of Stéphane Mallarmé and the group of symbolist poets who surrounded
him. Their influence Gide gladly accepted. Their aesthetic of timeless-
ness, remoteness from the problems of real life, and elevation of language
and vision is abundantly manifested in the books that he published
between 1891 and 1897; and in truth something of its presence can be
seen and felt throughout his entire career.

Three great events in Gide's life that occurred in 1895 (his encounter
with Oscar Wilde in North Africa, the death of his mother, and his
marriage to his cousin Madeleine Rondeaux) spelled the beginning of a
new order of freedom and triumph that demanded a more personal and
more emotional form of literary expression. He abandoned the symbolists and adopted Goethe as his guide and model, initiating the period of
his most powerful work. It lasted until the First World War. I have
called it a "romantic resurgence."

The daily horror of the war of 1914–18 and a serious crisis in his
relations with his wife in the latter year chastened Gide's spirit severely,
and in response to his altered state of mind he muted the strident
individualism of his work and turned to a critique of the bourgeois
society that he knew well from experience but had largely neglected until
then. There is a distinct loss of energy after this transformation, but it is
compensated in no small measure by the deeper and broader understanding of humanity that the work conveys. Gide had achieved a certain
wisdom after his early years of neurotic uncertainty and his long period of
rebellious assertion. Not surprisingly, he became one of the most influ-
ential and sought-after men in Europe during the 1920s and 1930s. He
was a beacon to the younger writers of those years and a powerful voice in
the defense of culture and democracy.

Gide's poetic work, viewed as a whole, contains the history of French
literature from 1890 to 1950. At every stage of that history Gide was in
the vanguard proposing new directions and new models to the young
writers of the time. He made several important contributions to the body
of symbolist literature, but as early as 1895, in *Paludes*, he ridiculed with
a devastating humor the effete tone of the symbolist literary discussions.
At the very beginning of the twentieth century he revitalized with new
insights the psychological novel, a genre that belongs essentially to
France. In 1909 he was one of the founders of *La Nouvelle Revue française*,
whose declared aim was to encourage new departures in writing. (The
editorial board of the magazine rejected Proust's *Du Côté de chez Swann* in

1913 on the grounds that it belonged too much to the past.) With *Les Caves du Vatican* in 1914 Gide revived the novel of adventure and struck a creative spark in the mind of a new generation of writers that included not only the surrealists but Montherlant and Malraux. Gide was not the first to rediscover the novel of manners after the war, but *Les Faux-Monnayeurs* was, in 1926, an important venture into that genre that dominated the literature of the twenties and thirties. That novel's formal innovations are still regarded as revolutionary.

It is important to observe, however, that Gide's art, in spite of its novelty and originality, was always driven by his need to express, in the form of an idea, his most intimate feelings about himself and his relations with those nearest him. The form is dictated by the idea and is always secondary to it. Gide's presence is so vital and so commanding in each book that one must look a second or third time to see his role in the literary history of his time. He did not hesitate in his final poetic work, *Thésée*, to revert to a narrative form and a subject that were characteristic of his symbolist period.

Finally, a note about the book that follows: in spite of the existence of excellent English translations of the entire work of Gide, I have preferred to refer always to the most accessible French edition and to offer my own translation of passages quoted from it.

Acknowledgments

Acknowledgment is hereby made to the following publishers for permission to quote from copyrighted material:

Editions Gallimard (Paris)
André Gide. *Divers* (1931). *Oeuvres complètes* (15 vols., 1932–39), Vol. 1 (*Les Cahiers d'André Walter*), Vol. 3 (*Philoctète, Lettres à Angèle*), Vol. 6 (*Feuillets*), Vol. 11 (*Dostoïevsky*), Vol. 13 (*Journal des Faux-Monnayeurs, Feuillets*), Vol. 15 (*Feuillets*). *Théâtre* (1942) (*Saül, Le Roi Candaule*). *Littérature engagée* (1950). *Journal, 1939–1949; Souvenirs* (1954) (*Et nunc manet in te*). *Romans, récits et soties; Oeuvres lyriques* (1958) (*Le Traité du Narcisse, La Tentative amoureuse, Le Voyage d'Urien, El Hadj*). Jean Delay. *La Jeunesse d'André Gide* (2 vols., 1956–57).

Alfred A. Knopf, Inc.-Random House, Inc. (New York)
André Gide. *Strait Is the Gate* (1924), tr. Dorothy Bussy. *The Vatican Swindle* (1925), tr. Dorothy Bussy. *The Counterfeiters* (1927), tr. Dorothy Bussy. *The School for Wives* (1929, 1950), tr. Dorothy Bussy. *The Immoralist* (1930), tr. Dorothy Bussy. *Two Symphonies* (1931), tr. Dorothy Bussy. *If It Die* (1935), tr. Dorothy Bussy. *The Journals of André Gide* (4 vols., 1947–51), tr. Justin O'Brien. *Fruits of the Earth* (1949), tr. Dorothy Bussy. *Two Legends: Theseus and Oedipus* (1950), tr. John Russell. *My Theater* (1951), tr. Jackson Mathews. *So Be It, or the Chips Are Down* (1959), tr. Justin O'Brien.

New Directions Publishing Corporation (New York)
André Gide. *Marshlands and Prometheus Misbound* (1953), tr. George D. Painter.

Martin Secker and Warburg Limited (London)
André Gide. *The Journals of André Gide.*

Chronology

1869 November 22: André Paul Guillaume Gide, only child of Paul Gide and Juliette Rondeaux, is born, in Paris. Father (b. 1832), a professor in the Law School of the University of Paris, was descended from an old Huguenot family of Uzès (Gard). Mother (b. 1835) belonged to the wealthy proprietor class of Normandy.

1877 Suspended from school for masturbation; threatened with castration: anxiety and guilt.

1880 October 28: father dies. Severe anxiety forces withdrawl from school, departure from Paris, treatment for nervous disorders.

1882 Discovers aunt's adultery and the shame and heartbreak it causes his cousin Madeleine; vows to devote his life to curing her distress.

1887–1889 Rejoins his class in school. Friendly rivalry with Pierre Louÿs. Passes baccalaureate exams. Plans to write a novel. Asks Madeleine to marry him; she refuses.

1891 *Les Cahiers d'André Walter* (anonymous). Louÿs presents him to Mallarmé and Hérédia. Madeleine again refuses to marry him. *Le Traité du Narcisse.* Meets Oscar Wilde.

1892 *Les Poésies d'André Walter* (anonymous).

1893 *Le Voyage d'Urien. La Tentative amoureuse.* In October departs for North Africa. Homosexual experience with an Arab boy.

1895 *Paludes.* Returns to North Africa; meets Wilde and Alfred Douglas; has homosexual contacts with young Arabs. May: mother dies. October: marries Madeleine Rondeaux.

1897 *Les Nourritures terrestres.*

1899 *Le Prométhée mal enchaîné. Philoctète. El Hadj.*

1900 *Lettres à Angèle, 1898–1899.*

1901 *Le Roi Candaule.*

1902   *L'Immoraliste.*

1903   *Saül. Prétextes* (critical pieces, including *Lettres à Angèle*).

1906   *Amyntas.*

1907   *Le Retour de l'Enfant prodigue.*

1909   Foundation of *La Nouvelle Revue française* (N.R.F.) under direction of Jean Schlumberger, Jacques Copeau, André Ruyters, with active collaboration of Gide, Michel Arnauld (Marcel Drouin), Henri Ghéon. *La Porte étroite.*

1910   *Oscar Wilde.*

1911   *Nouveaux Prétextes. Isabelle. C.R.D.N.* (anonymous; limited edition; first version of *Corydon*).

1912   *Bethsabé.* Jury duty, Court of Assizes, Rouen.

1914   *Souvenirs de la Cour d'Assises. Les Caves du Vatican.*

1917–1918   Vacations with Marc Allégret, in Switzerland (August 1917), in England (summer 1918). Learns upon return that Madeleine has burned all his letters to her. Profound distress.

1919   *La Symphonie pastorale.*

1920–1921   *Corydon* (anonymous; limited edition; complete version). *Si le Grain ne meurt* (limited edition). *Morceaux choisis.*

1922   *Numquid et tu . . . ?* (anonymous; limited edition; religious reflections dating from war years).

1923   *Dostoïevsky.* Birth of Catherine Gide, daughter of Gide and Elizabeth van Rysselberghe (daughter of his long-time friends M. and Mme Théo van R.).

1924   *Incidences. Corydon* (commercial edition).

1925–1926   Travels in Congo and Chad. *Les Faux-Monnayeurs. Si le Grain ne meurt* (commercial edition). *Journal des Faux-Monnayeurs. Numquid et tu . . . ?* (commercial edition).

1927–1928   *Voyage au Congo. Le Retour du Tchad.* Gide's exposés lead to parliamentary inquiry into activities of companies holding concessions in Equatorial Africa.

1929   *L'École des Femmes. Essai sur Montaigne.*

1930   *Robert. La Séquestrée de Poitiers. L'Affaire Redureau, suivie de Faits divers.*

1931   *Oedipe. Divers.*

1932   *Oeuvres complètes* (interrupted by war in 1939 at Vol. 15; contains works up to 1929).

1934   *Perséphone.*

1935   *Les Nouvelles Nourritures.*

1936   *Geneviève.*

1932 1936   Political activity: attacks capitalism and supports social policies of communism and U.S.S.R.; antiwar and anti-Fascist meetings and publications; goes with Malraux to Berlin to intercede for release of Dimitrov et al. (1934); opens 1st International Congress of Writers for the Defense of Culture (1935); at invitation of Soviet government visits Russia, delivers funeral oration for Gorky in Red Square (summer 1936). *Retour de l'U.R.S.S* (1936) and *Retouches à mon "Retour de l'U.R.S.S."* (1937) reveal disillusionment with Russia, provoke rupture with Communists.

1938   Death of Madeleine Gide.

1939   *Journal 1889–1939.*

1940–1945   Retires to south of France. Resigns from N.R.F. under collaborationist direction of Drieu La Rochelle. Tunis and Algiers (1942–45). *Le Treizième Arbre* (in *Théâtre*, 1942). *Interviews imaginaires* (1943).

1946   *Thésée. Journal 1939–1942. Le Retour.*

1947   Nobel Prize for Literature. *Et nunc manet in te. Théâtre complet* (8 vols., 1947–49).

1948   *Les Caves du Vatican* (farce in three acts).

1949   *Robert, ou L'Intérèt genéral. Feuillets d'Automne.*

1950   *Journal 1942–1949. Littérature engagée.*

1951   February 19: Gide dies in Paris.

1952   *Ainsi soit-il, ou Les Jeux sont faits.*

Chapter One
The Gidean Personality

No work has been more intimately motivated than mine—and whoever does not see that has little insight into it.[1]

Neurotic Narcissus

A work of great power imparts unfailingly to the life that engendered it a tone of destiny that is altogether different from that of biography in the ordinary sense. The most commonplace events in the life of a genius are incommensurable with the events of other men's lives. The work, shedding its magical radiance upon its own obscure birthplace, lends to every moment of the human existence from which it has emerged a significance of awesome proportions.

We commonly say that art owes its being to a transformation of the real. We should not forget that the work, once it has come into being, in turn transforms that same reality out of which it was made. This must in fact be the true end of art and the reason for its being: not to be something in itself, but by the force of its vision to remake what already is—and to begin with, the life of its creator.

Viewed without reference to his future work, the first years of Gide's life are a grim tale of frustration and incomprehension. One cannot contemplate his reiterated efforts to dominate his circumstances and find satisfaction in them without experiencing to some degree the futility of his gestures. Those early failures and disappointments are redeemed, and in a perverse sense justified, by the books that Gide wrote from his twentieth year onward. Literature was for him primarily a way of putting things to rights in the world. "Things are perpetually in disequilibrium," he wrote near the beginning of his career. "Equilibrium is perfect 'health.' . . . The work of art is an equilibrium outside of time, an artificial health."[2]

Dr. Jean Delay, who has written what is to date the most complete and authoritative biography of Gide (which stops, however, with Gide's twenty-fifth year), summarizes, toward the end of the two-volume work, in the blunt, elliptical style of the medical "history" the first 25 years of his subject's life. No sort of account is better calculated to bring out the "coefficient of adversity" in Gide's circumstances. It is not so much the incidents themselves that strike us as their shattering effect upon Gide's psyche and their reverberation in his later life:

Age 25, writer, unmarried. Nervous temperament. Emotive constitution. Prot-estant middle-class milieu. Only son. Father died at age 47: pulmonary tuber-culosis. Mother died at 60: cerebral hemorrhage.

Anxiety neurosis in childhood. Predisposition to nervous disorders. Noctur-nal terrors, insomnia, anxiety crises, muscular agitation. Highly suggestible. On pretext of illness, part real, part put-on, avoided going to school, where he felt out of place. Suffered from feeling that he was different from others. Precocious masturbation having caused suspension from school at age 9, medical consulta-tion: threat of castration. Anxious struggle against masturbation. Feelings of guilt and inferiority. No close friendships. Raised by virile, authoritarian, puritanical mother, both respected and feared, who became sole authority after premature death of father. Father left upbringing of son to his wife. Family influences almost exclusively feminine.

At 13 discovers suffering of first cousin, two years older than he, a pure and pious girl, distressed by her mother's adultery. Beginning of a compassionate love of mystical character. Transformation of behavioral patterns. Becomes very religious, very studious. Extraordinary taste for reading. Birth of literary voca-tion: at 15 keeps a private diary. Confirmation. Mystical and poetic exaltations. Relapses into onanism. Doubts, scruples, obsessions, fundamental ambiguity. Describes struggle between "angel and demon" in first book, written at 20. Pedophilic visions. Fear of prostitutes, compared to "acid-throwers."

At 21, in spite of maternal opposition, asks his cousin to marry him: refusal. Frequents fashionable literary milieus. Meets aesthetes; writes a *Narcisse*. His comrades make fun of his puritanism and his timidity. At 23 calls himself "completely virgin and depraved." Still loves his cousin, who continues to refuse marriage. Excused from military service on account of frail constitution and uncertain lungs. Great moral crisis in which are mingled vast philosophical, religious, and aesthetic considerations and an evident desire to be freed of maternal authority. With a friend of his own age, also timid and inexperienced, sets out on a long trip. Intends to "become normal."

At 24, in Algeria, mild pulmonary tuberculosis. One pedophilic experience, then experiences with a prostitute of Biskra. In process of renormalization when his mother arrives. Tears, supplications, promises. Later attempts paralyzed by emotional inhibition. Consults Andreae in Geneva: pulmonary condition satis-factory, but nervous overstimulation. Hydrotherapy and winter cure in a Swiss resort. Works, but is obsessed with desire to go back. Second trip. Begs mother and cousin, whom he still wants to marry, to accompany him: refusal. Meets in

Algeria two homosexuals, notorious proselytizers: Wilde and Douglas. Pedo-philic relations with young Arabs, celebrated lyrically: in fact, mutual mastur-bation. Excesses. Exaltations. Revolt against mother and morality. Decides to declare himself a homosexual and an immoralist. . . .

Return to France. Mother no longer opposed to marriage. Condemnation of Wilde by the courts. Death of mother. Confused emotions. Moral crisis. A few days later, engagement. Seized by scruples, consults physician and asks two questions relative to the possibility of giving up homosexual habits and to his aptitude for marriage. . . . Physical examination negative, but signs of pre-disposition to nervous disorders. Primary and secondary sexual characteristics normal.[3]

Dr. Delay's intention in writing this case history was to allow the facts of Gide's early life to speak for themselves and to re-create, without interpretation or added emphasis, the constant state of mental distress and disorder in which Gide lived during his entire childhood and youth. The terse style of the medical notation renders admirably the sense of a fatal progression from one disaster to another. Sometimes the notes are too brief to convey all the horror and pathos of the child's situation. In general the notation is too laconic and too "objective" to reveal the subject's unrelenting efforts to overcome despair and to create, within his particular circumstances, a life of satisfaction and joy.

It is precisely Gide's genius—"genius" in the sense that Sartre gave that word when he said that it "is not a gift but a way out that one invents in desperate cases"[4]—that is both revealed and obscured by this record of his "medical" history. There is in fact little of a medical character in it. For the most part it is an *ethical* history, a record of the encounters of Gide's ego with the wishes and determinations of others. The motif—or motive, since in this case they are the same—that runs through the entire history is love. Religiousness, poetic creation, rebellion, and protest appear in their turn as the personality of the subject matures, but they emerge always in relation to the primary erotic drive. The first meaning-ful experience of Gide's life was one of frustrated love. Everything that he did after that, and most of what he wrote, can be interpreted as a protest against that injury or an attempt to compensate for it.

No doubt every human personality has as its nucleus a reason of this sort, born of the encounter of its blind, groping will and the specific objects of the world. Rarely, however, do we see this so clearly and forcefully as in Gide's case. The basic event of his early life was a rebuff. The symptoms of distress that it produced in his mind and body show how painful the experience was for him. His protest against being deprived of love was that "precocious masturbation" cited in the medical history. On the first page of the memoirs that he wrote when he was 50, Gide said that this act was present in his life as far back as his memory reached (*J-S*, 349). That amounts to saying that it was the first act of his conscious life, his first deliberate effort to reckon with his situation in the world. The world's response was terrible: exclusion, condemnation, and the threat of mutilation.

The erotic impulse thus refused and condemned had nowhere to go but inward. The next phase of Gide's life was narcissistic. He became reticent and withdrawn—or, as he put it, "stupid." His preferred day-dreams of that period present a consistent pattern of destructive wishes directed against himself. He delighted in scenes of disorder and breakage and was enchanted by a story of George Sand in which a little boy is transformed into an oak branch as he floats in the water.

The death of his father, which occurred when Gide was just 11, produced a powerful perturbation in the child's psyche. He was immediately assailed by headaches, insomnia, loss of appetite, fatigue, prostration, and uncontrollable agitation of the limbs. His father's death, coming at the moment when he was beginning to relive his infantile struggle for the possession of his mother, had probably produced in him a great upsurge of joy and relief—which he then had to repress because of the dreadful sense of guilt it brought with it. He may even have felt responsible in some measure for the death, because he had wanted his father to disappear.

Gide found himself, at the onset of puberty, in that situation of exclusive intimacy with his mother that he had desired as a child. She, legitimately concerned by the condition of his nerves, had withdrawn him from school and was seeking in every way possible to restore him to health. He recovered fairly soon from the most disquieting physical symptoms of the neurosis. The restoration of order in his psyche was a longer process. It extended, by the shortest reckoning, to his seventeenth year, when he finally rejoined his class in school. These years of acute emotional disturbance gave to Gide's personality an expression that changed very little during the rest of his life. The actions of his later years and the strategies of his novels and plays are, in the last analysis, reenactments of the drama of his childhood. The oedipal situation, with its components of desire, frustration, and guilt, implanted in him a dependence upon the maternal figure, and an accompanying rancor toward her, that became the fundamental theme of his psychic life. When he was past 50, Gide wrote the following lines in his memoirs:

I think that one might have said of my mother that the qualities she loved were not those possessed by the persons upon whom her affection weighed, but rather those that she wished to see them acquire. At least I try to explain to myself in that way the ceaseless labor that she undertook upon other people; upon me in particular; and I was to such a degree exasperated by it that I no longer really know whether my exasperation had not finally destroyed all the love I had for her. She had a way of loving me that sometimes could have made me hate her and that set my nerves on edge. (*J-S*, 608)

Gide's mother had been dead more than 25 years when he wrote these words; yet her power to arouse ambivalent feeling in him was unchanged and undiminished.

Tristan and Corydon

The first great step in Gide's psychic restoration was the resolve that he made at age 13 to love and protect his cousin, Madeleine Rondeaux, for the rest of his life. "I had until that moment wandered aimlessly," he later wrote. "Suddenly I discovered a new orient in my life" (*J-S*, 434). His love for her was extremely complex. She was, on the one hand, a hurt child in whom he could see something of his own childhood injury. They had both been wounded by the discovery of adult sexuality—even though the circumstances of the discovery were very different. In seeing Madeleine's distress, Gide relived his own pain, but this time it was happening outside of himself, in another person, and he was able to respond to it with understanding and sympathy. It was as if he were coming to the aid of the hurt child that he had once been, the child whom no one had understood or succored. Madeleine's plight allowed him to release those feelings of pity and indignation that he had been compelled to choke back some years before.

More important than compassion, however, is the degree of dependency that we see in Gide's love for his cousin. She was older than he and was very grave and mature in her bearing. She was said to resemble his mother, though her photographs reveal a considerably more delicate and feminine physique than that of Mme Gide. Gide decided very early that he must marry her, and thereafter no refusal deterred him. Madeleine was terrified of marriage, but she finally yielded, moved less by Gide's suit than by the deathbed wishes of his mother. They were married five months after her death.

It was not until 1949, more than 10 years after Madeleine's death, that he disclosed the secret that some intimates had long suspected: their life together had been without sexual relations. The medical consultation that Dr. Delay records at the end of Gide's medical history was without avail. His love for Madeleine was of the type that does not admit sexual expression. Everything in his early history points to the conclusion that Gide had invested in Madeleine his frustrated love for his mother. Their life together was a recapitulation, on improved terms, of the oedipal situation that had caused him such great distress when he was a child.

The substitution of Madeleine for his mother was perhaps an unconscious act to begin with, but in his later years Gide became fully aware of its significance. In his last work, a short memoir entitled, *Ainsi soit-il, ou les Jeux sont faits* (1952), he related how, in his dreams, their faces were often confused: "The outlines of the faces are not sharp enough to keep me from shifting from one to the other; my emotion remains keen, but what causes it is vague. Moreover, the role that one or the other plays in the dream's action is about the same, that is to say an inhibitory role, which explains or motivates the substitution" (*J-S*, 1216).

It must be said that, for Gide, love and marriage were not the mere repetition of the oedipal situation, but rather its overcoming. His love, he felt, was simply too fine and too elevated to be defiled by carnal pleasure. This illusion was the greatest and most important creation of his life. It liberated him to a great extent from the crippling guilt of his early adolescence. His constant devotion to the ideal of purity that he saw embodied in Madeleine redeemed the impurities of his own flesh. He had in a sense rediscovered the Catharist ideal of chastity in love and had thus transformed himself from a guilty Oedipus to a triumphant Tristan.[5]

The expression of love that Gide discovered in North Africa when he was 24, and to which he remained committed for the rest of his life, was at the other pole from his love for Madeleine. His chaste devotion to her had grown out of the inhibition, and then the sublimation, of a prior love for his mother. His homosexual adventures were, on the contrary, indulgences in sensuality. The desire that led him to this particular pleasure was likewise rooted in his early years. It was a manifestation, in vaguely socialized form, of the autoerotic fixation that had characterized his sexuality since childhood. His confessions on the subject reveal that his homosexual experiences were always essentially narcissistic. His contacts were furtive and brief, without resumptions or repetitions. His partners in these episodes were not persons that he loved, but casual substitutes for his own body, the object to which his desires had long before been diverted.

Pederasty, as opposed to onanism, held a great advantage for Gide. It could be openly avowed. Though his own society was rigorous in its condemnation of the practice, it had been honored and cultivated in Greek and Roman antiquity and was still sanctioned by Arab and Indian cultures. In declaring himself a pederast, Gide struck a defiant and rebellious public posture, but it was a posture that held no guilt or shame for him. Pederasty became a screen for autoerotism, just as his Catharist marriage became one for the Oedipus complex. By adopting the role of the pederast, Gide transformed the neurotic Narcissus of his childhood and youth into a tender and candid Corydon.[6]

Erotic dualism was a fundamental postulate of Gide's psyche. The great enterprise of his youth was that of turning his neurotic fixations into ethical acts. He succeeded by putting on the masks of Tristan and Corydon. His problem for the rest of his life was to maintain these illusions and to keep peace between them. Gide was neither an authentic Catharist nor an authentic pederast. Catharism was, in his life, nothing more than a conscious fiction that he used to screen out his mother fixation. Classical pederasty was, except for one relationship of his middle years, a fiction too. It was assumed by him as a way of justifying the occasional acts of pedophilia that autoerotic fantasies inspired in him. The underlying complexes—narcissism and mother fixation—were always ready to emerge and destroy the ethical fictions through which he projected his personality into the world of others.

Furthermore, the erotic motives represented by Tristan and Corydon were radically contradictory. Their very coexistence was a manifestation of Gide's ambivalence. His long struggle to overcome that ambivalence is projected into his literary fictions in the form of conflicts between the two kinds of love that divided his erotic nature. These are, typically, mortal engagements in which one love defeats and suppresses the other.

The history of Gide's literary work is very largely defined by the growth and transformation of his erotic nature. The work of his youth expresses primarily the self-absorption, the anxiety, and the frustrations of the Oedipus-Narcissus complex. With the creation of the ethical figures of Tristan and Corydon in his mature years, his complexity turned from weakness to strength. The books of his later years (after 50) reveal the collapse of those great illusions and the return of the original complex. This regression was enlightened, however, by the very deep understanding that Gide had by then gained of his own personality.

The Poet

The roles that Gide played as a poet and an artist bear a structural resemblance to his erotic roles. His stories contain at once the truth of his nature—his desires, inhibitions, joys, and hatreds—and a mythological interpretation of it. By infusing his personal poetry into an ongoing cultural dialogue, and by presenting his impulses under the masks of legend and romance, Gide turned his complexity into a paradigm of the human condition. This creation has to be regarded, with respect to its source, as an illusion, but it is the sort of illusion that conveys the only truth we possess about the conflicts in us between nature and culture.

In this work of literary creation it is inappropriate to speak of self-delusion, as I did in describing Gide's erotic relations. Writing was for him a searchingly conscious process in which personal truth and cultural myth complemented and modified each other. Writing was the means through which Gide finally liquidated the contingencies of his past and transformed his being into a complex of purposes.

The fundamental defect of his psyche was the fixation upon his person that endowed him, in effect, with a self and a double, with two characters and two sets of feelings. His inner division was so profound that, as a child, he thought there was a second reality quite apart from the familiar reality of every day and the world of dreams that he entered at night (*J-S,* 362). In his adult years, he articulated this feeling as a lack of contact with the surrounding reality, but his childhood sense of things was really closer to the truth. He had been so violently severed from his infantile desires and satisfactions that it was as if he had left that self behind him and had become another being in another world. His unconscious will to destroy the superfluous double is disclosed in the fantasies of self-dissolution that he entertained as a child.

At puberty Gide's duality resolved itself into two movements that alternately governed his outlook and his activity. In the phase of self-love, he was inhabited by a sense of power, election, and vocation. The contrary mood of self-hatred was characterized by physical torpor and malaise and by feelings of shame and inadequacy.

This division might have continued to torment Gide without relief if he had not discovered the therapeutic exercise of writing. When he was 14, his tutor (rather unaccountably) put into his hands the *Fragments d'un Journal intime* of Henri-Frédéric Amiel.[7] Amiel, a Genevan professor, was, like Gide, shy, anxious, and ambivalent. By recording and analyzing the play of his feelings in a diary, he had found that he could achieve a kind of integration of the rational and irrational movements of his consciousness. Following the example of Amiel, Gide began to write a diary, "out of a need to give form to a confused inner agitation" (*J-S*, 506). The diary was not primarily a literary form in Gide's hands. It was a mirror in which he contemplated and arranged the projected expressions of his personality. It was the counterpart of the mirror on his desk in which, he said, "I contemplated my features tirelessly, studied them, educated them as an actor would do, and sought on my lips, in my eyes, the expression of all the passions I wanted to experience. . . . In those days, I could not write—and I was about to say, think—it seemed to me, except in front of that little mirror. . . . Like Narcissus, I leaned toward my image; all the sentences that I wrote at that time are somewhat bowed by that fact" (*J-S*, 514).

The diary led Gide, via a natural gradient, to fiction. His first published work, *Les Cahiers d'André Walter* (1891), consisted in large part of pages extracted from it. His subsequent introduction of imagination into the activity of writing marked an important advance, for it effected the integration of the introspective consciousness of the diarist with its double in the unconscious. Speaking of an early work, *La Tentative amoureuse* (1893), Gide wrote: "I tried to indicate the influence of the book on him who writes it, and during the very writing. For in coming out of us, it changes us, it modifies the progress of our life. . . . The subject acting is self; the thing retroacting is a subject that one imagines. It is then an indirect method of action upon oneself that I have given there; and it is also quite simply a story" (*J*, 40–41).

By giving to his impulses and resistances the status of imaginary objects, and by turning their sterile conflicts into symbolic actions involving strategies and outcomes, Gide transformed his opaque self-absorption into a hierarchy of personal values.

The countermovement of self-hatred found two very different kinds of expression in Gide's writing. The first is to be seen in the images of cruelty, violence, and death that occur in all his imaginative works. These images are directly related to the sadomasochistic fantasies of destruction and dissolution that began with the repression of love in his childhood. They afforded him a symbolic catharsis, a way of destroying repeatedly both the guilty, unhappy shadow in his psyche and the obstacles that stood in the way of his desires.

The other mode of self-destruction in his works is less violent but in a sense more radical, more thoroughgoing. As a young writer, he found himself capable of a complete emotional and intellectual abdication in the presence of the thoughts and feelings of others. He prized this "unknown resonance" as "the best thing in him" and attributed the relief he felt in it to a reaction against his excesses of introspection.[8] In truth, it was not a reaction, but a reassertion of the will to subjugate and mortify his guilty being. That was why it brought him relief.

Ambivalence, inconstancy, dividedness: these neurotic weaknesses of his childhood became, with the discovery of the diary, sources of poetic energy. "The true artist," Gide said in his lectures on Dostoyevski, "is always half-unconscious of himself, when he is producing. He does not know exactly who he is. He comes to know himself only through his work."[9] Gide's work is as deeply motivated by the need to see himself in a projected form and to realize through the agency of the story a resolution of the conflict between the opposed voices of his psyche as it is by the need to justify through myth and illusion his special erotic tendencies. The energy present in the tension of dividedness became, as he advanced in age and in artistic power, an advantage and a value, instead of the crippling handicap it had been in his youth. A "loose leaf" inserted in his *Journal* following the year 1923 contains a character analysis that could well be his own:

I have never been able to give up anything; and defending in myself at once the best and the worst, I have lived drawn and quartered. But how can I explain that this cohabitation of extremes in me did not engender anxiety and suffering so much as a pathetic intensification of the sentiment of existence, of life? The most contrary tendencies have never succeeded in making me a tormented being, but rather a perplexed one—for torment accompanies a state that one would like to get out of, and I did not want to escape what implemented all the potentialities of my being; that *state of dialogue*, which for so many others is just about unbearable, because for me necessary. Because, for those others, it can only impede action; whereas, for me, far from leading to sterility, it invited me, on the contrary, to the work of art and immediately preceded creation, led to equilibrium, to harmony. (*J*, 777–78)

The Catharist

The basic erotic and poetic schemes of Gide's life were conceived to repair the injuries his psyche had suffered through the repression of love in his childhood and the guilt provoked by the return of the same desire in his adolescence. They have no other source than his relations with his mother and father. No matter how complex the symbolic forms he later dressed them in, there is always in these schemes an underlying simplicity of purpose that discloses the original source. The *power* of Gide's work derives in a very considerable measure from his fidelity to the primitive motives of his psychic existence.

The *value* of Gide's writing, however, is not primarily a matter of its lyrical (personal, irrational) energy. His genius dates from the moment when he began to see his personal history in relation to the culture that surrounded him. Even as a child he was made aware that the strict authority of his mother did not spring solely from her personality, but that she was acting in the name of a church and a social class.

Gide grew up in the atmosphere of minoritarian sensitivity that hangs over Calvinism in Catholic France. Every act and every circumstance of his life were related to Calvinism. His mother constantly held up to him, by precept and example, the Calvinist ideals of austerity, modesty, and obedience. She succeeded so well that Gide was never quite able to differentiate between her personality and the religion that governed her life. He was bound to his mother by the indissoluble ties of infantile love, and at the same time he was bitterly resentful of the restraints she placed upon him. His relations with Calvinism were of the same order. He was a Calvinist in every essential trait of his character, and yet he rebelled all his life long against the restrictions of puritan morality.

Calvinism makes a monster of the flesh, but it inflates and emancipates the mind that can respond to its lofty visions. It imbues the communicant with the sense of singularity and election; it puts God within his reach; it makes the pursuit of virtue the main purpose of his life; it imposes upon him the knowledge of his freedom and demands that he exercise it. In the adolescent Gide every one of these notions found a ready response. When, in preparing for confirmation, he began to read the Scriptures seriously, their effect on him was that of a deliverance comparable to his love for Madeleine Rondeaux. The gospel, he later said, "explained to me, by reinforcing it, the sentiment that I felt for Emmanuèle [that is, Madeleine]; it did not differ from it; it simply deepened it . . . and endowed it with its true situation in my heart" (J-S, 499). He had found in the life and the words of Jesus a divine justification of his own need to exclude the flesh from his love of woman. The fervor that he continued throughout his life to express for the gospel is always referable to this moment in his youth when his erotic impulse found its reason in the religion of his fathers. The conjugation of love and piety is a commonplace but usually transient phenomenon in adolescent psychology. In Gide it persisted, no doubt because his eroticism retained to the end its adolescent character. In the absence of a societal sanction for his Catharist love, he had a pressing need for the sanction of God.

The other expression of Gide's sexuality, the onanistic and homosexual impulse, was severely condemned by the same religion that gave him the consolation of the gospel. It was a condemnation without reserve and of such an explicitness that Gide felt hindered and degraded by it. He very early began to invent a way out of his discomfiture under the law. His first step was a declaration of war on the Epistles of Saint Paul. He called them oppressive and dogmatic in contrast to the liberating words of Christ, and he wondered why Protestantism had not rejected them along with the hierarchies of the Catholic church (*J*, 96). In Saint Paul Gide saw one of the sources of the repressive parental control from which he had suffered as a child. In attacking the legislator of Christianity he was, in a remote way, avenging the injuries of his childhood.

The New Testament gave Gide a substitute ground upon which to separate what he loved from what he hated in the maternal image. It allowed him to introduce into his emotions and his understanding an order that had been impossible before. This displacement deserves in the history of Gide's genius an emphasis equal to that placed on his decision to marry Madeleine Rondeaux.

The dismissal of Saint Paul was not, however, radical enough to ease the burden of guilt. Gide's nature was so deeply divided and his erotic desires so utterly opposed that he could not live with the orthodox notion of evil as a defect attributable—in an otherwise wholly good creation—to human weakness. His feeling of election, his thirst for virtue, his sense of freedom were all undermined by the memory of past transgressions and repeated lapses into impurity. It was inadmissible to such a proud and austere nature as his that his descents into vice could be produced by the same will that impelled him upward to pure adoration and virtue. To avoid this unthinkable conclusion, Gide revived in his mind the Manichean dualism of good and evil. His falls from virtue were provoked by the presence in him of a devil who was so like himself that it was difficult to detect his alien presence. "I had heard tell of the Evil One," Gide wrote in 1916, "but I had not made his acquaintance. He already inhabited me at a time when I did not yet distinguish him. . . . I did not yet understand that evil is a positive, active, enterprising principle" (*J*, 607–8).

Despite the tardiness of his perception, the belief in an evil principle coefficient with the good is clearly present in Gide's imaginative writing from *Les Cahiers d'André Walter* onward. It is in fact the fundamental, and most important, assumption of his metaphysics. Gide never described himself as a Catharist, but that is what he was. His belief in dualism, his conception of love as a pure devotion of the soul, his enthusiasm for the gospel and its vision of a joyful yet poor and nomadic life, and over all the lyricism of his religious outlook are all identifiable with the ethos of the "Church of Love."[10] This religion—which had its center in the region from which his father came—give Gide a position effectively outside of Christianity and permitted him to attack Protestantism and Roman Catholicism without doing violence to his own piety. Again it was his personal genius that had found the way to live with the contingency of his past by transforming the given of his Christian culture into a religion that more perfectly mirrored his psyche.

The Dissenter

Gide rescued his religious impulse from Calvinism, but he left behind as a pledge his moral character. The love of virtue, the struggle for merit, the relentless criticism of the world and of his own compromises with it persisted in him and became a kind of separate power within his being. It was a negative power, a counterforce that acted as a limit and a restraint upon the primary assertions of his ego. Put in rudimentary terms, it was his mother's authority, implanted in him in childhood and become an inalienable fiber of his adult personality. Gide cherished that austere, dissenting, self-denying power within himself, no doubt because he understood that it was his mother's voice still protecting him against the excesses of his primitive impulses. On a "loose page" inserted in his diary after the year 1896, he wrote:

Sometimes, convinced as I was that every action of mine would always turn to the greater glorification of my life, I dreamed, almost spitefully, of giving in to myself, of relaxing my will, of allowing myself respite and leisure. I never could do it, and I understood that with me constraint was more natural than giving in to pleasure is with others, that I was not free to suspend the exercise of willpower, to relax and cease to resist. And I understood by the same token that precisely from that lack of freedom came the beauty of my acts. (*J,* 104–5)

Gide thus found his personal value in the contention within him of two radically incompatible wills, one that of a love-drunk, god-drunk Dionysiac poet, and the other that of a haughty, ascetic puritan. The role of the puritan is reactional, but in no sense petty and tyrannical. It is yet another mark of Gide's genius that his moral resistance espoused the particular forms of what it opposed, and instead of stifling the assertive drives of his ego, it added to them a quality of lofty restraint. In spite of his claim to erotic freedom and his radical separation of love and pleasure, he retained a horror of sexuality and made extraordinary efforts to sublimate its effects. Even though he was essentially a poet of exuberant excesses, he imposed upon his work a rigorous artistic discipline. In voicing his claim to be considered "the best representative of classicism" in his time, he said: "The classical work will be powerful and beautiful only by virtue of its subjugated romanticism" (OC, 11:36).

Lastly, in what was undoubtedly the most important decision of all, he confronted his society as a reformist critic in the style of Luther, Calvin, Rousseau, and Nietzsche, and by accusing its lies and concealments he constructed a defense for his own aberrant and immoral nature. He thus employed one of the most powerful weapons of his culture to justify the naive being—himself—who had been mutilated by that same culture. In a letter to Ramon Fernandez written in 1934, he acknowledged that his entire nonconformist program had its origin in the anomalous sexuality that was the result of his first encounter with the moral order in which he was obliged to live: "I think it entirely correct to say (as you have done so well) that sexual nonconformity is, for my work, the primary key; but I am particularly grateful to you for having indicated how, after this monster of the flesh—the first sphinx in my path and one of the most devouring—my mind, having developed a taste for combat, slipped beyond, was invited to go on to challenge all the other sphinxes of conformism, which it suspected thenceforth of being brothers and cousins to the first" (quoted in Delay, 2:549).

With the emergence of the social critic the structure of Gide's mature personality was complete. He was still, and always would be, a deeply divided being. The demands of his ego had grown monstrous through repression. His social consciousness—which was that same repression assumed inwardly—was equally overgrown. There was a war within him between the irreconcilable forces of the ego, on the one hand, and the moral order, on the other. That war is the essential matter of Gide's work.

But the work, as the formal objectification of the conflict, is something more. It is the product, not of strife, but of alliance among the contending forces of Gide's personality. It reveals to us a great erotic who has submitted his desire to the judgment and control of a puritan moralist, an evangelistic enthusiast who is held back from the leap into mysticism by a skeptical critic, and finally a Dionysiac poet who has subordinated his voice to that of a severe, self-effacing classicist.

Chapter Two
Decadence and Symbolism

Schopenhauer and Mallarmé

Gide began writing in the 1890s in the presence and under the influence of certain poets and storytellers who were called "Decadents" and "Symbolists." Decadence and symbolism are overlapping concepts in the history of European styles and sensibilities. Both have their roots in German romantic idealism, in the poetry of Novalis and Hölderlin and the philosophies of Schopenhauer and Fichte. The pessimism and the irony engendered by the pursuit of the Ideal shaped in the most positive sense the feelings and the expression of two generations of French men of letters who flourished in the 1880s and 1890s. It was the influence of German idealism no doubt that enabled them to discover their affinity with certain earlier writers of their own national tradition: Sade, Chateaubriand, Gautier, Baudelaire, Flaubert.

Mario Praz in his exhaustive description of decadence (*The Romantic Agony,* 1933) says that it was a sensibility whose poles were sadism and Catholicism. At the root of the Decadent's apparent delight in perverse forms of sexuality was the far more real appeal of sterility, of the utter futility of the sensual. What attracted him to Catholicism was the concrete possibility of sin and sacrilege. These are the negative aspects of religion, as sterility is the negative expression of the erotic. The typical demonic themes of decadence were cruelty, perversity, incest, profanation, and suicide. The representative writers of this current were J. K. Huysmans (1848–1907), Count Auguste de Villiers de l'Isle-Adam (1840–89), and Octave Mirbeau (1848–1917). The then little known Count de Lautréamont (1850–70) is recognized today as participating in the same sensibility and style.

At the same time the poet Stéphane Mallarmé (1842–98), upon whose personality and work symbolism reposed altogether, gave a more angelic expression to the same idealism, pessimism, irony, and sterility. In Mallarmé's poetry and fiction (*Igitur*) the aspiration to the Ideal is always disappointed by the persistence of the real and the phenomenal. He gave as complete an expression to the sentiment of sterility and nothingness as any writer of the period.

Another generation of writers born in the 1860s prolonged the decadent sensibility and its typical themes up into the twentieth century. Jules Laforgue (1860–87) represented its angelic face while Henri de Régnier (1864–1936) and Maurice Barrès (1862–1923) gave a refined, intellectual statement of the demonic.

Gide's neurotic personality, with its primary movement toward the sensual and the shameful and its compensating countermovement toward purity and sublimity, disposed him to decadence even before he had encountered the chief works of that tendency. A description of the new Eros such as the following one that Octave Mirbeau wrote in *Le Calvaire* would have been instantly comprehended and espoused by the young Gide: "It was no longer the becurled, pomaded, beribboned Cupid who goes rapturously in the moonlight, a rose in his teeth, to scrape his guitar beneath balconies; it was Eros smeared with blood, drunk with filth, the Eros of onanistic frenzies, accursed Eros who glues his leech-shaped lips to a man and sucks his veins dry, pumps out the marrow of his bones, and denudes his skeleton!"[1]

Gide was a youth well endowed also to understand and appreciate one aspect of Huysmans's character Des Esseintes, whom Barbey D'Aurevilly described as "no longer a being organized in the manner of Obermann, René, Adolphe, those human, passionate, guilty heroes of fiction. He is an unhinged mechanism. Nothing more." (quoted in Praz, 291). (What Gide was probably not prepared to recognize was Barbey's further reasoning that Huysmans had not only given the biography of "a particular solitary and depraved personality," but also "the nosography of a society putrefied by materialism." Gide was too nearly "an unhinged mechanism" himself to be very sensitive to the social causes of Des Esseintes's anomaly—or of his own.)

Gide encountered Schopenhauer quite early in his life, during the year when he was reading philosophy for the second part of the baccalaureate examination. "I penetrated into his *World as Will and Idea* with an unspeakable delight," he wrote, "read it from cover to cover, and reread it with an application of mind from which, during several long months, no appeal from outside was able to distract me" (*J-S*, 518–19). He had thus in a sense gone to the source of the whole movement that surrounded him. When, after the publication of *Les Cahiers d'André Walter,* he gained access to Mallarmé's circle, he had already acquired something of the outlook that characterized that group. Recalling this period in his memoirs, he wrote:

> The movement took shape as a reaction against realism, with a backlash against the Parnassians as well. Supported by Schopenhauer, to whom I did not understand that others could prefer Hegel, I considered as "Contingency" (that is the word we used) everything that was not "absolute," all the prismatic diversity of life. For each of my companions it was about the same; and the error was not in trying to extract some beauty and some truth of a general order from the inextricable thicket that "realism" then presented; but rather, as a matter of bias, in turning our backs on reality. I was saved by greediness. (*J-S*, 535)

He was saved, but not right away and perhaps never altogether. It was the latent Catharist in Gide, the worshiper of purity and immaterial beauty, who was sensitive to what Valéry later discerned in symbolism as "a revolution in the order of values," "a mysticism," "an askesis," "a sort of religion . . . whose essence would have been the poetic emotion."[2]

The part of Gide's work that we are about to consider is, in most important respects, a recapitulation of decadent and symbolist themes, imagery, and outlook. The drama of demonic possession, as well as that of angelic possession, is enacted in *Les Cahiers d'André Walter* and *Le Voyage d'Urien*. *El Hadj* and *Philoctète* are infused with the lofty pessimism of the disappointed idealist. *Le Prométhée mal enchaîné* is an amusing version of the hopeless effort to discover a metaphysical basis for the conduct of life. And *Paludes* exposes, with an ungentle irony, a sterile life in a sterile milieu.

Gide's virtuosity in the realization of the idea is matched by the stylistic means he employs to that end. From the emotional subjectivity of *André Walter* to the sensuous descriptions of *Urien* and the sarcastic humor of *Paludes,* he exhibits a consummate mastery of tone. The form of his sentence is as varied as the sense it aims to convey: ejaculatory in *André Walter,* ample and colorful in *Urien*, languorously prolonged in *El Hadj,* witty and urbane in *Prométhée* and *Paludes;* Gide multiplies his voice without any apparent limit.

But in other ways these first books are very homogeneous. There is in all of them what he called a "geometrical" statement of the idea; each story is a "theorem." There is, moreover, a universal rejection of the concept of character, of a human personality treated as a source of conflicts and determinations and as a locus of drama. Whether borrowed from myth and legend or invented for the occasion, the personae of Gide's stories are as abstract as the ideas they illustrate. They are simply means of expression and have none of that romantic autonomy that will distinguish the characters of his later fiction.

On the whole Gide betrays a rational, demonstrative, perhaps even pedantic, intention in the first period of his work. The critical motive plays a very large role in his strategies, and that fact viewed in conjunction with the deployment of artistic controls makes this body of work one in which the cultural counterforces of his personality outweigh the assertions of instinct and desire. This was mainly a time of exploration and decision in Gide's life. He had no grounds until after 1895 to feel very sure of his own power. The two great decisions that polarized his erotic life were made in 1893 (the initial act of pederasty) and 1895 (his marriage to Madeleine Rondeaux). He was still very much in the formative stage of his intellectual life. In 1894 he wrote to Pierre Louÿs that he was involved in organizing his thought for the future: "I am going through a period in which I feel that all my intellectual value will be determined" (quoted in Delay, 2:388–89). As far as his poetic life was concerned, we must recognize that he was the captive of a literary atmosphere whose radical negativity was alien to the primary expressions of his personality, which were fervor, avidity, daring, and nobility.

Les Cahiers d'André Walter

Gide's literary career begins with Les Cahiers d'André Walter (The Notebooks of André Walter) (1891), an intensely personal, intensely lyrical fiction that the author qualified in his memoirs as the Summa of his youth. From a formal point of view this manner of entry into literature was easy and natural, since the book is written in the style of the intimate journal, with which Gide had gained great familiarity—not as a literary exercise but as a way of externalizing his inner complexity. We have it from the author himself that many pages of the Cahiers came directly, without alteration, from his journal.

The young writer was, even so, much preoccupied with the composition and the tone of his book. His hero's notes for the book that he was intending to write give us some insight into Gide's thought about the work that he did write. They begin: "Two actors: the Angel and the Beast, adversaries—soul and flesh." In order that "the Idea" stand forth from the work, he wrote, it would be necessary to "reduce everything to the ESSENTIAL."

The action determined, rigorous, characters simplified to a single one. And as the drama is intimate, nothing appears on the outside, not a deed, not an image, except perhaps as a symbol: phenomenal life absent,—only the *noumena;*—therefore no more picturesqueness and the decor neutral: anytime, anywhere: outside of time and space.

Only one character, and a nobody at that, or rather his brain, which is only the ordinary site where the drama takes place. . . . The adversaries are not even two rival passions—but just two entities (?): the SOUL and the FLESH;—and their conflict resulting from a single passion: *to act like an angel.* (*OC*, 1:94-95)

In "The White Notebook," which is the first part of the story, André Walter gives voice to his angelic nature. This is the record of his love for Emmanuèle, a love developed in intimacy and encouraged and prolonged by a common culture of books, music, prayers, and ideals. The angelic temper demands that love be pure, and that the flesh, which "serves no end," be refused, in order that their souls find an "immaterial embrace." But love demands concrete expression, and as André says: "The sad thing I have so much suffered from is that the soul has no other signs to reveal its affections than the same caresses that are inspired by shameful desire" (*OC*, 1:66).

It is through the reality of his love for Emmanuèle that André discovers and reflects upon the war within him between the Angel and the Beast. "What is pure and what befouls—we cannot know; the connection of the two essences, so subtle; their causes so mutually entwined;—so much the stirring of the one is felt in the other" (OC, 1:45). He is tormented by the presence of sensuality in the world around him and by the possibility of its irruption in his own life. On one occasion he unintentionally arouses Emmanuèle by playing a Chopin scherzo and accuses himself of villainy. "Could I satisfy her soul," he wonders, "once I had made it thirst?" (*OC*, 1:79). "In order not to disturb her purity," he decides, "I will abstain from every caress . . . even the most chaste, even holding hands . . . for fear that afterwards she might desire more, that I could not give her" (*OC*, 1:81).

It is only by an act of renunciation that André is able to preserve the purity of his love. His mother, on her deathbed, asks him to give up Emmanuèle to another suitor. "Your affection is fraternal," she tells him. In response to her plea, André plots a secret virtue: he will cause Emmanuèle to disapprove of him, to despise him. He will merit her all the more for having made such a sacrifice. He blesses his dying mother for separating their bodies, for their souls are thereby joined in a virtuous abnegation.

"The White Notebook" is centrally, and almost exclusively, preoccupied with the erotic. The influence of literature, music, and religion, the
speculations about the nature of man, are all contributory to the erotic
dilemma. The strategy by André Walter to deal with the problem is that
of the Catharist. He asserts the supremacy of a pure love, and through
resistance to the flesh and renunciation of the beloved object he makes it
triumph. That this is a symbolic solution of Gide's own erotic dilemma
seems abundantly clear; but the most interesting aspect of his symbol-
izing is not in the *truths* that he transposed to the work but in the fictions
that he invented to facilitate its solution. The first is the death of André's
mother. Her disappearance is necessary to liberate him from the frustrating oedipal relationship. (The book was written some six years before the
death of Gide's mother.) Next is the insistent transference of the incest
taboo to Emmanuèle. The intimacy of the two lovers is familial; they call
each other "brother" and "sister." Gide even invents a dead sister for
André with whom Emmanuèle becomes "indistinctly confused" in his
mind. Finally, he invents another suitor for Emmanuèle and has André
renounce her altogether. These motifs can only mean that for the author
of the *Cahiers* every heterosexual love is a recapitulation of the desire for
the mother. It is a love that is too insistent to be denied but too awful to
be indulged.

"The Black Notebook," which is the other face of the *Cahiers,* is the
book of Narcissus. Here André is alone with the erotic impulse. Emmanuèle, first separated from him by marriage, is now dead. André tries to
preserve in himself the purity of their love. He strives for a life of
spontaneity, intuitive knowledge, and faith, but he is haunted by doubts
and dreams. "One sees only *one's own* world, and one sees it alone; it is a
fantasmagoria, a mirage, and the prism that diversifies the light is in us"
(*OC*, 1:103). "We, when we are not merely spectators, become involuntary actors in a play whose meaning we do not possess. We do not know
the second significance of our acts; their importance in the immaterial
escapes us" (*OC*, 1:128). "Not knowing whether the desired goal is
humanly possible—ignorance of everything, of evil and its remedies.
Fighting alone against an unknown enemy!" (*OC*, 1:129). He studies his
features in a mirror, wondering if *he*, rather than the face he sees on the
glass, is not the image, "an unreal phantom."

Music, prayers, and work are of no avail against the insistent demands
of the body. They only exaggerate and exalt sensibility and in so doing
abet the demon: "The evolution is always the same. The mind becomes
exalted; it forgets to be vigilant; the flesh falls. We wake up; then comes

an excessive labor to distract oneself from evil thoughts. The labor wears us out; we say: What's the use? We pray, we look for ecstasy again,—and the evolution begins anew" (*OC*, 1:148).

Two dreams in particular torment André. The one is of a band of naked, brown-skinned children bathing in a river. His first reaction is revulsion: he will not be one of such a vagabond crew. But then comes desire to be among them, to caress their bodies. The other dream is of Emmanuèle. She appears in a stately, embroidered gown. A monkey playfully raises her dress. André tries not to look, but does, and sees nothing but darkness. Emmanuèle grasps the hem of her gown and throws it up over her head, and still there is nothing underneath.

André's desires become depraved; his mind discovers debauches in which the body does not participate. Chastity he reckons to be "a pride in disguise." The Devil is never defeated. Like the ancient Proteus he changes forms and offers "a more specious, more subtle delight. . . . Depraved continence!" he reflects; "as a perversity, that is rather refined!" (*OC*, 1:171). He feels threatened by madness.

The diary closes upon a vision of pure white snow. A note informs us that André Walter died of a cerebral fever.

It is not hard to see in this part of the novel the victory of Narcissus, or the demon of autoerotism. His triumph entails first of all the removal of Emmanuèle. This is accomplished by her death, and then more vividly by the dream in which her sexual nature is revealed as darkness and void. The ecstasies induced by music and prayer help the demon to triumph, and so does the sort of metaphysical speculation (Schopenhauer) that alienates the subject from the reality of his phenomenal being and leaves him only sensuality as the bond between his thinking self and his sentient body. The satisfaction of pederasty is only a possibility and a promise, a tentative desire at most, revealed in the dream of the bathing children. Narcissus is not yet ready to assume the role of Corydon.

Looking at the *Cahiers* three decades after its publication, Gide was not exactly indulgent:

When I open again today my *Cahiers d'André Walter* their jaculatory tone exasperates me. I favored in those days words that allow complete license to the imagination, like *uncertain, infinite, indescribable*. . . . Words of that type, which abound in the German language, gave it in my eyes a particularly poetic character. I understood only much later that the native character of the French language is to tend toward precision. Were it not for the testimony that these *Cahiers* bear on the uneasy mysticism of my youth, there are very few passages of the book that I should want to preserve. However, at the moment when I was writing it, that book seemed to me one of the most important in the world, and the crisis that I was depicting in it, of the most general, most urgent interest; how could I have known, at that time, that it was peculiar to me? My puritan education had made a monster of the flesh; how could I have known, at that time, that my nature was shying away from the most generally accepted solution as much as my puritanism was reproving it. However, the state of chastity, I could not help but be convinced, was insidious and precarious; every other outlet being closed to me, I fell back into the vice of my early childhood and despaired anew each time that I did so. With a great deal of love, music, metaphysics, and poetry, that is the subject of my book. I have said previously that I saw nothing in the future; it was not my first book, it was my *Summa;* it seemed to me my life must end, must conclude, with it. Still, sometimes, leaping out of my hero, while he sank into madness, my soul, at last delivered of him, of that moribund weight it had so long been dragging behind it, glimpsed intoxicating possibilities. (*J-S,* 522)

It is impossible not to recognize and acknowledge that with this little book, so juvenile in some respects, so subtly mature and provocative in others, Gide established, beyond mistaking, certain of the essential features of his future work. The first of these is the central and underlying erotic drama and the delineation of its major roles. Next is the transposition of the Narcissus figure to the literary work: two notebooks, both aspects of the same being, confront and contradict each other. Gide, as Narcissus contemplates his own image in his double, André Walter; and André in turn projects his image in the hypothetical Allain, hero of the story he hopes to complete. (The irony of disclosing in the fiction the process of fictional creation remained a temptation for Gide—a narcissistic compulsion it might even been called. He gave fullest rein to it in *Les Faux-Monnayeurs.*) Finally, there is the theory of the work of art as the transparent symbol of the idea, which was to remain the chief article of Gide's poetics.

Le Traité du Narcisse

Having divested himself of his adolescent style of expression—though not entirely of his adolescent preoccupations—with *André Walter,* Gide began immediately to elaborate his symbolist work, which was to fill the decade of the 1890s. This work is characterized above all by the imposition of intellectual form upon lyrical content and by fidelity to the Symbol as the means of revealing the Idea. In 1891, the year in which *Les*

Cahiers d'André Walter was published, Gide brought out *Le Traité du Narcisse* (Treatise on Narcissus), subtitled "Theory of the Symbol." As potently expressive of his own psyche as Narcissus was, in this brief "treatise" it was not himself that Gide sought in the myth but rather a symbol, first, of human consciousness, and second, of the poet.

Narcissus, trying to see the form of his soul, looks into the river of Time and there discovers the phenomenal world of the present. The revelation of the appearances, however, draws him intuitively to the knowledge of the original forms, or noumena.

After this Platonic overture, Gide transforms the Paradise of the essential forms into the biblical Garden of Eden, where Adam is the sole spectator. But he, like Narcissus, becomes bored and desires to know his own form and his own power. With one gesture he shatters the harmony of Paradise and discovers his androgynous nature. Eve, sprung forth from Adam, seeks to re-create in his embrace the perfect being of the beginning but succeeds only in engendering a sad new race that possesses only the memory of a lost Paradise and is condemned forever to seek to restore it in the world. Thus are born the prophets and the poets. "Paradise must always be made anew; it resides not in some distant Thule. It lies beneath the appearance."[3] It is the Poet who sees Paradise, for he intuits in each thing the archetype of which the appearance offers him the symbol.

Returning to the myth of Narcissus at the end, Gide describes his amorous approach to the image reflected on the surface of the water. But instead of falling in and drowning, as the classical myth relates, Gide's Narcissus, who is the symbol of the Poet, realizes that what he sees before him is simply his own image, and that he is alone. He withdraws to reflect upon what is before his eyes, the appearance of the World.

It is quite evident that Gide intended *Le Traité du Narcisse* to be just what it appears: a statement of the symbolist theory of poetic composition. In that sense it contains nothing very surprising except perhaps the use of biblical myth alongside classical mythology in the development of the idea. The whole thing seems more than a little naive and juvenile today, and it is hard to see how it could have failed to evoke the same reaction in 1891. Such was not the case, however. Gide's friend and contemporary Pierre Louÿs was enthralled by its style and declared that it expressed his credo in art. Francis Jammes, an older friend and a well-established poet, assured Gide of his admiration for the work; and Paul Valéry, to whom Gide had dedicated it, was likewise well pleased with it. Paul Claudel gives us the best idea of what the poets were reacting to in the piece when he wrote, in a letter to Gide, of his pleasure in the style, "wherein the words and sentences are assembled, not by any logical concert, nor by the needs of the harmonic that they conceal, but by a sort of humid attraction, a secret circulation that animates the whole work and seems to make of the whole thing the metamorphosis of a single word" (*RRS*, 1458–59).

Gide himself was not entirely satisfied with his achievement, and that may account for his having appended to it the note explaining his use of the term Symbol, which has for a long time been the best-known and most often quoted part of the treatise:

The Truths dwell behind the forms—Symbols. Every phenomenon is the Symbol of a Truth. Its only duty is to make it manifest. Its only sin, to prefer itself.

We live to manifest. The rules of morals and aesthetics are the same. Any work which does not manifest is useless and by that very fact, bad. Any man who does not manifest is useless and bad. . . .

The artist, the scientist, must not prefer himself to the Truth that he wants to tell. That is his entire moral; neither the word, nor the sentence, to the Idea that they seek to demonstrate. I should say, almost, that that is the whole of aesthetics. . . .

The moral question for the artist is not that the Idea that he manifests be more or less useful to the multitude; the question is that he manifest it well. —For everything must be made manifest, even the most dreadful things: "Woe to the man by whom the temptation comes," but "the temptation must come" [Matthew 18: 7]. The artist and the man who is truly a man, who lives for something, must have beforehand sacrificed himself. His whole life is nothing more than a progress toward that. (*RRS*, 8–9)

One feels, in reading this note, which is introduced rather gratuitously, that the fable of Narcissus was perhaps merely a pretext for its utterance. That of course is not the case. Gide's communications with his fellow poets are more than ample evidence of the primacy of the artistic motive in his mind. His aim was to explain the symbolist aesthetic by disclosing its Platonic idealism and to illustrate it by means of the freshness and the unity of his style. The fable is a prime example of Gide's capacity for self-effacement. He is barely discernible in it. He does not yield to the temptation that the story of Narcissus exerts upon his own psyche. He abstracts from the myth only the general idea of self-consciousness and leaves untouched the matter of absorption in self and fascination with self. This is the matter of passion, not of philosophy.

The note, on the other hand, is passionately urgent and personal. In it

Gide declares the artist subject to a higher imperative than that of his poetic talent. He, as every man "who lives for something," must employ his art to manifest the truth. There is no allusion here to the myth of Narcissus or to the phenomenology of consciousness. The voice is prophetic; the imperative has a religious character that is reinforced by the quotation from the Gospel of Saint Matthew. Moreover, the "temptation" ("scandal" in the French version) hints at things to come in the life of Gide, things of which he was only partly aware in 1890 when the words were written.

No wonder that the note is better known than the "Treatise on Narcissus" itself. This is Gide himself, speaking for himself; not merely for the artist and the symbolist but for the man inspired and illuminated by the gospel. The tension that we observe here of two fundamental motives in Gide's complex personality—the artistic motive, which is controlled and self-effacing, momentarily overcome by the Calvinist voice insisting that artistry is good only when it is employed to reveal the divinely given truth that is in every individual—is a clue to the power of his mature work. In this instance the tension is rather wasted, because the voices that embody it are so disparate. But this is just the beginning of Gide's career: he was only 21.

Le Voyage d'Urien

In *Les Cahiers d'André Walter* Gide revealed his "native" style, the style that he had learned through the exercise of the diary. His narrative was introspective in mode and lyrical in tone, and he refused to employ the effects of décor and picturesqueness. *Le Voyage d'Urien* (Urien's Voyage) (1893) is precisely the opposite. Its style is artificial; its mode is that of the sensual imagination. Objects, colors, and landscapes express the underlying motives and tensions of the author's personality.

In the preface to the second edition (1894) Gide explained at some length, for those who had seen in *Urien* nothing but stylistic virtuosity, the value of the landscapes described in the story. They are nothing less, he said, than the visible equivalents of the emotion that organized and dictated the work, an emotion too abstract to be described in its own terms. "Will you understand me if I say that *what is apparent and visible is equal to the emotion, wholly and in every detail?* There is a sort of aesthetic algebra in this; emotion and the apparent form an equation; one is the equivalent of the other. Whoever says *emotion* will therefore say *landscape*; and whoever says *landscape* will then have to know *emotion*" (*RRS*, 1464).

"There is no emotion," he continued, "however special and new it may appear, that does not have in nature *all its equivalents.* . . . But the central emotion of this book is not a special emotion; it is simply the one that the dream of life aroused in us, from astounded birth to unconvinced death; and my characterless sailors become by turns either the whole of humanity, or are reduced to myself" (*RRS*, 1465).

When the sailors represent men in general, they are the author's means of enunciating a theme of social criticism; when they are reduced to him alone they express the dominant theme of his private life, the erotic choice. The latter theme is certainly the more striking of the two.

The "voyage" is presented from the outset as a symbolical one. The pun in the title (*d'Urien: du Rien*) suggests that "nothingness" is the stuff of which it is made. One of the travelers says as they set out: "Perhaps we are living our dream . . . while we lie sleeping in our bed chambers" (*RRS*, 18). And the narrator, in his verse envoi, says: "Madam, I deceived you: we did not make that voyage . . . it was only mirages . . . only pipedreams. . . . That voyage is only my dream, we never left the chamber of our thoughts" (*RRS*, 66).

In the Prelude, as the "knights" who have abandoned books and study in order to discover life gather for their voyage aboard the *Orion,*[4] they see in the port two ships that prefigure the poles of their own journey: one, from the East, brings beautiful slave girls and bales of crimson dyestuff; the other, from the North, is loaded with ice and snow. One cargo tempts and corrupts their senses; the other offers the repose of ideal purity.

The first leg of their cruise takes them to the "Pathetic Ocean" (that is, to the sea where feelings are aroused). Everywhere they encounter incitements to sexual desire. They are tempted by sirens; they see a child playing with his "hideous penis"; they see dervishes whose mad whirling dance reveals their obscene nakedness under billowing robes. At night, aboard ship, the sailors and cabin boys sleeping on the deck reach amorously for each other. The chaste knights are afraid to lie down. A few of their number succumb to the lure of the island women and return to the ship bearing blood-red fruits. Their companions are afraid to taste them. The voyagers long to bathe in the tropical waters among the saffron-skinned men who dive for sponges, but fear of the things that lurk in the depths restrains them. They bathe only in sheltered pools. In the city of Queen Haïatalnefus, where women long deprived of men besiege them, the sailors and all but 12 of the knights are lost. These fallen ones are soon afflicted with a plague. They die in the midst of frenzied embraces with the island women.

In this "Temptation of Saint Anthony" Gide has staged another battle between the Beast and the Angel, or we might more appropriately say between Narcissus-Corydon and the Cathar. The latter's victory, if it can be called a victory, is at best equivocal. Most of the knights succumb to desire. Those who resist do not prevail solely by their virtuous determination to remain chaste. Fear and revulsion are in fact their primary defenders. Of one of the Cathari it is said "that he did not understand how anyone could join with another to do such indispensable nastiness, and that at such moments he hid even from mirrors" (*RRS*, 27). All of them fear and loathe contact with women, and with whatever suggests or stands for the feminine—especially water. (The water is not only a feminine element but a maternal one. The pure knights are powerfully drawn to it but are just as powerfully restrained from plunging in. This is no doubt an expression of the oedipal ambivalence: desire to possess the mother but horror of defiling her person.)[5]

The second leg of the cruise takes "the Twelve" into the "Sargasso Sea," a colorless landscape of marshes, cypress groves, and stagnant, or back-flowing, waters. The dominant note here is ennui. The virtue of the knights, built of resistance to temptations, begins to disintegrate for lack of opposition. Their need for glorious actions, for occasions to manifest their strength, will never be satisfied in this region.

The erotic theme is continued in Urien's encounter with Ellis, who has come overland to meet him (thus dissociating herself from the sensual). He finds her sitting under an apple tree reading a metaphysical treatise. She has a suitcase stuffed with metaphysical and moral works. These external attributes tend to identify Ellis with Mother Eve. Her name on the other hand (Ellis: Isel: Iseult), and her blondness, make her an ironic refiguration of Tristan's fated lover—ironic because Ellis inspires little passion. Urien becomes increasingly sure that she is not the ideal bride he had supposed, and as they sail out of the marshy region he abandons Ellis. "You are an obstacle to my fusion with God," he tells her, "and I will only be able to love you when you too are fused with God" (*RRS*, 51).

In rejecting Ellis it is not sensuality that Urien is refusing, but marriage with a fiancée who is also a mother. He rejects her in order to pursue a religious ideal of purity.

The last leg of the voyage takes the eight remaining knights to a "Glacial Sea." This landscape of icebergs and snow fields signifies their arrival in a region of purity and abstraction free of sensual temptations. It is the land of the Eskimos, a small, ugly people who make love without tenderness and whose joys are theological. Eric, the "bird-killer," in a symbolic attack upon heterosexuality, drives off the guillemots that are incubating their eggs on the cliffs. The eggs roll down the precipices, break, and stain the sea. (This "pollution" motif introduces ambiguity into the episode.)

In the polar climate the knights suffer from scurvy, brought on by the absence of pleasure. They dream of the pernicious islands they have left behind them and of the ripe fruits they dared not taste.

Urien finds in the snows another Ellis, the true one, who says to him: "Urien! Urien, sad brother! If only you had gone on dreaming of me! Remember our games in other times. Why did you try, in your ennui, to grasp an accidental image of me? You knew that back there it was neither the time nor the place when possession was possible. I am waiting for you beyond time, where the snows are eternal" (*RRS*, 60). She encourages him to look ever ahead toward God, in whom alone all things end. When she has done speaking, Ellis ascends to Heaven in a wedding gown.

At the end of their journey the knights find a man frozen in a block of ice. An inscription declares that he is "despaired of." In his hand he holds a blank paper. The seven Cathari (one more of their number has perished) have no wish to turn back to life. Had they known the end of their voyage, they probably would not have come; so they thank God for having concealed the end from them, for having allowed them to enjoy their effort to reach it, and for having led them to believe it would be splendid in proportion to their sufferings.

The erotic "voyage" terminates in a victory for Catharism, but on the whole, the erotic theme weighs less heavily in this last episode than the critical one. A number of things suggest that the "glacial" region is the ideal realm of the symbolists. The Eskimos, who have fled real experience and found a refuge in abstraction and "theological joys," are Gide's malicious image of the literary circles that he had been frequenting since the publication of *Les Cahiers d'André Walter*. The man encased in ice and holding a blank sheet of paper could only be Mallarmé, and Eric's "swan-killing knife" may even have been aimed at the *cygne d'autrefois*. In a letter to Jean Schlumberger dated 1 March, 1935, Gide said of Mallarmé's influence:

Under the influence of Mallarmé, without realizing it too clearly, and in complete reaction against Naturalism, a number of us would admit nothing that was not *absolute*. We dreamed in those days of works of art outside of time and "contingencies." With respect to social questions, we were not so much ignorant and blind as scornful; a scorn born of a misapprehension. Whatever was only relative (to time, to places, to circumstances) seemed to us unworthy of an artist's attention; in any case we tried to keep at a distance, and carefully excluded from the work of art, from our work, all incidental preoccupations.[6]

Le Voyage d'Urien is also Gide's ironic offering of his "poor generation who desire heroism in an age which does not satisfy their thirst for beauty" and who "asked the novel to replace the great voyages they had not made" and "to satisfy somehow the vague desire for heroism that their imaginations retained and their bodies did not accomplish" (*RRS*, 1465).

The book echoes a far-flung literary tradition. At its publication Paul Valéry mentioned "various odors" that he detected in it, notably those of Flaubert, Barrès, and Maeterlinck (*RRS*, 1463). (Gide, within the work, indicated the influence of Novalis.) Guerard and Brée see a reflection of Poe's story *The Narrative of A. Gordon Pym of Nantucket*. O'Brien detects something of Rimbaud's "Bateau Ivre" in the story, as well as a memory of the *Odyssey* and *The Arabian Nights* and a great deal of Dante's *Divine Comedy*. I might add an insistent echo of Mallarmé's "Brise marine" at the beginning of the "voyage."

All of these "echoes" and "odors" are genuine. *Le Voyage d'Urien* is a compendium of decadent and symbolist literary conventions.[7] Still, the intentions that animate it could not be more Gidean. We see in the work an early example of Gide's skill in combining several strategies in the same narrative. The erotic theme and the critical theme, though they have in fact little common ground, are unfolded side by side and held together by three devices: the archetype of the voyage, the figure of Ellis—who is both the refused bride and the *anima* ideal—and above all the tonal gradation of the work. Beginning with timidity and revulsion from sensual reality, Gide shifts to a tone of boredom and lethargy in the Sargasso Sea, and then to one of near extinction in the abstract regions of the Ideal. This itinerary is appropriate to the development of both of the novel's "ideas." On the one hand, it mimics the sexual rhythm of tumescence, detumescence, and detachment. (In the "Pathetic Ocean" desire is provoked by vision after vision until pollution finally occurs with the orgy of the plague-stricken sailors and knights. The cruise in the "Sargasso Sea" corresponds to the despondency that follows release, and the "Glacial Sea" brings a period of reflection relatively unclouded by sensuality). On the other hand, it is the image of a mind forcing itself away from the contemplation of phenomenal reality toward a reflection on the abstract ideal.

The threefold voyage of the *Orion* is representative of a number of "outlines" that we have discovered in Gide's personality. Germaine Brée has remarked that Gide's thought as a whole tends to fall into three categories: the sensual, the introspective, and the metaphysical. These are also the three centers of his sensibility and of his private mythology. The Narcissus-Corydon locus (the sensual) is symbolized the the "Pathetic Ocean"; the "Glacial Sea" (the metaphysical) is the realm of Tristan and the Evangelist; in between lie the stagnant waters haunted by the guilt-ridden Oedipus.

La Tentative amoureuse

Gide's *Journal* for 1893 reveals one overarching theme: his impatience and vexation with the nullity of his sexual life. In March he writes: "I have lived to the age of twenty-three completely virgin and depraved, so maddened that I was seeking everywhere some bit of flesh to which I might apply my lips." In April he turns to God for deliverance:

And now my prayer (for it is again a prayer): O my God, let this too strict moral code burst, and let me live, oh! completely; and give me the strength to do it, oh! without fear and without always believing that I am going to sin.

I must now make as great an effort to let myself go as ever before I made to resist doing it.

At this point in his life Gide envisaged his emancipation as a heterosexual experience and attributed all his resistance to that adventure to the moral precepts that had been drilled into him from early childhood, and that were now in his first adult years firmly implanted in his flesh and mind. What he clearly had not yet grasped was that his resistance came even more from the taboo that, for him, surrounded the female body.

It was in this frame of mind that Gide wrote, as a wishfulfilling fantasy, *La Tentative amoureuse* ("The Attempt at Love," later subtitled "The Treatise of Vain Desire"). In the foreword he explained, "Our books will not have been the very truthful accounts of ourselves—but rather our plaintive desires, the wish for other lives forever forbidden, for all the impossible actions. Here I write of a dream which was disturbing my thought too much and demanding an existence" (*RRS*, 71).

Despite his disclaimer, Gide's story does reveal what was most truthful about himself, which was his resistance to the sort of love that desire made him imagine. He first relates Luc's hesitation. "Luc wished for love but was afraid of carnal possession as of a battered thing" (*RRS*, 74); but then he pushes his hero to overcome his scruples and to take Rachel, who has offered herself to him. Their love begins near the end of spring in a well-cultivated setting of fields, woods, and streams.

But no sooner has Gide embarked on this tale than he drops his storyteller's voice and addresses with some sarcasm the woman for whom he has invented the story of Luc and Rachel:

Madam, it is to you that I shall tell this story. You know that our unhappy loves have got lost in the wasteland, and you are the one who complained in former times that I had so much trouble smiling. This story is for you: In it I have sought what love bestows; if I have found only ennui, it is my fault; you had untaught me how to be happy. —How brief joy is in this book, and how quickly it is told! How banal a smile is without vice and without melancholy. And what do we care about the love of two other people, the love which made them happy. Luc and Rachel loved each other, so much the worse for them! For the unity of my story, they did really nothing else; of boredom they knew only that of happiness itself. Picking flowers was their monotonous occupation. They did not put desire aside in favor of a more distant goal and little relished the languor of waiting. They were ignorant of the movement which repulses the very thing that one would wish to embrace—as we did, Madam—out of fear of possession and love of pathos. . . . Happy are those who like them are able to love without conscience! (*RRS*, 77)

Gide's mettle is nowhere in his entire work better revealed than in this ironic commentary on the love idyll that he had begun to construct. He does not abandon his story; he tells it to the end, when, with winter coming, the lovers who have long since grown weary of love—first Luc, then Rachel—go their separate ways. The story has its own logic of refusal, and Gide spins it out faithfully. But in truth he had already reduced the whole thing to vanity when it was barely begun.

In his *Journal*, in the late summer of 1893, Gide wrote:

I tried to indicate, in that *Tentative amoureuse*, the influence of the book on the one who is writing it, and in the course of that very writing. For in coming forth from us, it changes us, it modifies the pace of our life. . . . Our acts turn around and act upon us. . . .

So I was sad because a dream of unrealizable joy was tormenting me. I recount it, and by taking that joy away from the dream, I make it mine; my dream is freed of its spell; I am joyful for that.

It is hardly possible to overestimate the value and the importance of this analysis by Gide of his psychic process. He discloses to himself—for we must remember that this diary was the record of his private thoughts, and that he decided only many years later to make it public—as he had done in other reflections, but never so cogently as in this one, why he had to be a poet, one who gave substance and circumstance to desires, and how his poetry worked therapeutically upon his soul. At 23, tormented by desire for love—which he had not yet known in any form—he imagines the satisfaction of his desire in the terms that were conventional in his culture, in the unhindered embraces of a youth and a maiden in the midst of a flowering nature. He records those images in a prose fashioned to enhance and to fulfill them. But in the very doing he convinces himself that the idyll does not satisfy his own temperament, and thus, as he said in his *Journal*, he separated the dream from his joy and retained only the joy.

The genius of Gide's writing and that of the precarious equilibrium that he realized among the forces that constituted his being are visibly the same in *La Tentative amoureuse*: to allow the contention of the opposing forces in his psyche—which here meant to allow the dream of love to seek its satisfaction in the only forms available to it—but at the same time to give full vent to the hesitancy, the resistance, the doubts, and finally the refusal of that dream. The artistic expression of the same opposition is simple but by no means commonplace. It consists in the alternation of two very unlike voices: first, the dreamy, wish-fulfilling voice of the narrative; second, the sarcastic, lapidary voice of the critic who denounces the impossibility of the idyll. At bottom it is the same device as that employed in *Le Traité du Narcisse*, only here in a more balanced expression. The thematic form of the contention of heterosexual love and its refusal, whether idealistic, comical, or perverse, is the very marrow of Gide's work.

Paludes

Paludes (*Marshlands*) (1895) was first designated a "treatise" by its author ("The Treatise on Contingency"). Two decades later Gide gave it the generic label *sotie* (along with *Le Prométhée mal enchaîné* (*Promethens Misbound*) and *Les Caves du Vatican*) (*Lafcadio's Adventures*). In the four-teenth and fifteenth centuries the *sotie* was a piece of merrymaking, a spoof, staged by the clerks of Paris. It offered the spectacle of a world of fools (*sots*) governed by a prince as foolish as any of his subjects. This is no doubt the sort of world that Gide aimed to portray in his *soties*. *Paludes* is a work of broad satire, as far removed in tone and style from *Le Voyage d'Urien* as that book was from *Les Cahiers d'André Walter*. Gide considered it to be one of his most important books. In his *Journal* on 15 July 1922 he wrote: "Throughout my 'career' I have hardly known anything but failures, and I might even say that the dismalness of the failure has been in proportion to the importance of the work and its originality, so that it was to *Paludes, Les Nourritures*, and *Les Caves* that I owed the worst ones." At least one of Gide's contemporaries, however, saw something of the importance of *Paludes*. Paul Claudel, in a letter to Gide on 12 May 1900, said: "It is the most complete document that we possess on that atmosphere of suffocation and stagnation that we breathed from 1885 to 1890."[8]

In the dedication Gide called *Paludes* "this satire on what," and indeed there is more to the subject than Claudel's excellent judgment reveals— although the satirical portrayal of the symbolist milieu may seem to outweigh the rest. *Paludes* was the first book that Gide wrote after the trip to Africa that so radically changed his outlook.

> I brought back, on my return to France, the secret of one restored to life, and I experienced right at first that sort of abominable anguish that Lazarus must have tasted on his escape from the tomb. Nothing of what had formerly occupied me seemed to be important any more. How had I been able to breathe up until then in that stifling atmosphere of *salons* and *cénacles* in which each one's agitation stirred up a smell of death? . . .
>
> Such a state of *estrangement* [in English in the text] (from which I suffered especially in my own family) might very well have led to suicide had there not been the escape I discovered in describing it ironically in *Paludes*. (*JS*, 575–76)

Everything that had constituted Gide's prior life fell within the purview of his satire: the complacent society nourishing itself on its meager accomplishments and negative virtues; the men of letters knowing nothing, and aspiring to know nothing, outside their own *salons* and *cénacles*; and last but not least the young man who, seeing the hollowness of his world, could not break the grip of habit and lethargy.

That young man (in Gide's *Paludes*) is writing a book called *Paludes*, which is the story of Tityre who lives contentedly alone in a marsh and desires nothing more than a closer assimilation to his milieu. (The Tityrus of Virgil's *Bucolics* was happy with his rocky, marshy land and was not curious about the great world. He stayed at home while Menalcas

went to see the city of Rome.) Tityre, satisfied and "recumbent" (as
Virgil described him) is the emblem of the world the narrator sees around
him. He is "the normal man," "the third person," the occupant of "the
neutral ground, that which belongs to everyone" (*RRS*, 116).

The main scene of the social satire is Angèle's literary soirée. In her
tiny, crowded, airless *salon* the same thoughts and phrases pass from
mouth to mouth until they become the common property of all the men
of letters gathered there. These are people who never travel, who seek no
new experience. They are content to repeat without end the same stale
maxims and observations. The writer of *Paludes* attacks their complacency and the "malady of retrospection" that makes them do again and
again what they have already done once; but he is nonetheless one of
them. The psychiatrist Valentin Knox attacks their reasonableness and
preaches the contrary value of sickness, of disequilibrium and idiosyn-
crasy; but he ends up repeating word for word what he has heard the
young writer say in describing his story of Tityre. Angèle, for her part,
knowing that the evening will be hot and breathless, has installed a fan,
but it is far too small for her *salon* to begin with, and she has drawn a
curtain over it to diminish its noise. This hermetic atmosphere of
abstraction and repetition is Gide's sarcastic reflection of the symbolist
gatherings in which a few years earlier he had suffered frustration and
irritation.

Another isolable feature of the social satire is the ridicule directed at
bourgeois virtue and moral scruples. The young author's friend Richard
is a victim of privation and failure, but he is richly satisfied with his
mediocre lot because it allows him to cultivate a character of virtuous
humility. He is Tityre. But Tityre or not, the example of his virtue is not
without power, for he is able to make his writer friend feel restraint
merely through their association and the genuine esteem he professes for
him. The author feels that Richard's abnegation holds him a prisoner of
passivity.

The restraint of which Richard is a model is given a doctrinal expression by the moralist Barnabé, who says (at Angèle's party): "our
role . . . is not to engender great actions more or less by mediation, but
rather to make the responsibility for small actions greater and greater."
The author of *Paludes* replies: "To increase the fear of acting, isn't that
it?—It is not responsibilities that you increase; it is scruples. Thus you
reduce freedom even more. The really responsible act is the free act; our
acts are no longer free; it is not actions that I want to provoke; it is
freedom that I wish to emphasize" (*RRS*, 119).

We see articulated here the theme of moral revolt that was to occupy Gide throughout his career—and we see its cause as clearly as he ever exposed it. The young author judges that the virtue exemplified by Richard and acclaimed by Barnabé is sterile and useless, but he remains subject to its prestige. In this, the satire, aimed ostensibly at a certain class and culture, is turning back on the spokesman himself and exposing him to a greater ridicule. (In his *postface* to the second edition of *Paludes*, 1897, Gide said that his young writer "found equally ridiculous the one governed, the governor, the one who wants to suspend the rules, and the one who cannot break away from them [*RRS*, 1476].)

The protagonist of *Paludes* is, like André Walter and Urien, a Gidean double. Gide was seeking to repudiate through ridicule a certain version of himself. Delay, in his biography of Gide, has evaluated at some length the psychological finesse of Gide's portrait of the psychasthenic, or indecisive, personality in *Paludes*. We know that narcissism, and with it the sense of unreality, indeterminacy, and ambivalence, was the juvenile form of Gide's personality. His double in *Paludes* is a comical version of the neurotic Narcissus. The power of decision is replaced by his agenda in which he projects not only the activities of his day but his surprises, pleasures, and disappointments. The agenda also serves as a moral conscience: he keeps it in double-entry fashion; on one side he writes what is to be done, on the other, what he does in fact; so that on one side, he reads his duty and on the other his moral deficit. At other times, the gap between intention and act affords him the joy of a pseudospontaneity which he calls the "negative unforeseen."

The action of the protagonist is concentrated very largely in the book he is writing. *Paludes* is about "the emotion that my life gave me . . . *ennui*, vanity, monotony" (*RRS*, 95). When his more active and determined friend Hubert suggests that he might do better to write about something else, he replies with irritation: "I'd like nothing better, but understand that in this as in other things I am hemmed in by banks; our paths are forced upon us, our works likewise. I am here because there was no one else here; I choose a subject by elimination, and *Paludes* because I am sure there will be no one so disinherited that he will come and work on my land; that is what I have tried to express by these words: *I am Tityre and solitary*" (RRS, 112).

He feels sufficiently occupied with writing *Paludes*, but he is concerned about the monotony that his fellow men accept as their daily lot. "I want to disturb," he says; "I go to a lot of trouble to that end—and I only disturb myself" (*RRS*, 126). In an effort to lead Angèle out of the blindness and monotony of her life, he proposes that they set forth on a little voyage of discovery. On Saturday morning they take the train to a village a few miles north of Paris and from there set out on foot. But the young adventurer is soon discouraged by a rain shower and decides to turn back (to Angèle's chagrin, be it said). The next day, reflecting on their sad little outing, he declares that it was of a piece with his book. "I leave it here; I find it again there; I find it everywhere; the sight of other people makes me obsessed with it, and our little voyage would not have delivered me from it.—We do not use up our melancholy; by repeating each day our yesterdays we do not exhaust our maladies, we only exhaust ourselves and lose more strength each day.—What prolongations of the past!" (*RRS*, 140).

At the end of this complaint (which goes on to some length) he broaches a subject that has been waiting for some time: "And our relations, dear Angèle, how transitory they are! That is exactly what allows us, you understand, to continue them so long." When she protests, he replies: "I want you to observe the impression of sterility that they give." With that, Angèle says that she will spend the night with him. He refuses, however, saying: "Confess that you don't really want to; besides, you are, I assure you, delicate, and it was while thinking of you that I wrote . . . that sentence: '*she feared sensual pleasure as a thing too strong that might perhaps have killed her*'" (*RRS*, 141). Though he had sometimes slept *at* Angèle's, he had never slept *with* her, "having never done anything with her except harmless little imitations" (*RRS*, 104). The Catharist theme, illustrated by this comical version of Tristan and Iseult, is thus exposed to laughter along with all the rest.

In the final turn of the narrative, the decisive, active Hubert, encouraged by his friend's earlier complaints about the marshland in which they live, decides abruptly to take off for Africa—with another companion. The writer, having finished *Paludes*, is engaged in writing *Polders*. ("Polders" are tracts of marshy land reclaimed from the sea and protected from it by dikes.) The title suggests that this book too will depict a lifeless, shut-in world.

At the very center of *Paludes* stands the contest that Gide staged between his critical genius and his poetic genius. In ridiculing the very urgencies that defined his personality—moral unrest, nomadism, sexual nonconformity—he proved that the "new" man in him could dominate the "old." The critique, once begun, is quite easily and naturally extended to the literary milieu and the morals of the middle class, since they too were characterized by constraint, withdrawal, and lack of enterprise. Without being precisely coincident, these traits are very much in harmony with the indecisive, immobile personality of the narrator.

The decadence of *Paludes* is apparent in its themes of ennui and impotence and in its self-destructive aim. At the same time its poetic irony—the narcissistic obsession, within the story, with the story that is being written—offers an excellent illustration of symbolist style and sensibility. In the *postface* earlier referred to Gide said: "I like too that each book bear within it, but hidden, its own refutation" (*RRS*, 1479). This utterance, in which the ambivalence of Narcissus is so openly expressed, is at once a capsule explanation of *Paludes*, a glimpse into the Gidean personality, and a clue perhaps to the decadent mentality.

El Hadj

El Hadj (subtitled "The Treatise of the False Prophet") was written in the summer of 1896 and published in a volume with *Philoctète* in 1899. It is a modest little gem among the brilliant works of this period of Gide's career, one in which his effort to "style" an emotion in the symbolist manner was especially successful. Of the three main features of the work—the fable, the landscape, and the narrative sentence—the author himself tended to place the greatest emphasis on the second. In a letter to Paul Valéry in July 1896 he wrote: "I have worked and have nearly finished a tale ('in which my tendencies are manifested') on this epigraph: *'Dans l'Orient désert quel devint mon ennui'* ('In the Eastern desert how great my ennui became')" [Racine, *Bérénice*, Act I, scene 4] (*RRS*, 1505). And to Francis Jammes he wrote on 2 August 1896, "I am writing a tale that is about nothing but the desert" (*RRS*, 1505). It is the vision of the endless waste across which the invisible prince leads his followers that is principally charged with translating "the feeling that the dream of life gave us." The fact that it was a real landscape, one that Gide had seen at close hand on his second journey to North Africa, and not an imagined one as in *Le Voyage d'Urien*, has no effect whatever on its role in the story. The desert is not a reality but a symbol. It lends to this allegory, in which there are only three roles, El Hadj, the prince, and the people, a continuous significance and a continuous tone of melancholy and despair.

The pessimism of *El Hadj* resembles that of Schopenhauer. It has wholly accepted itself, has even transcended itself toward a virtue without hope. This sense is made explicit in the despairing mission of El

Hadj. It is also implicit in the languorous sentence that Gide invented for the tale. Jammes likened it to "muffled drums beating in the desert," and Valéry remarked, with humor but no less pertinently: "You chloroform the words before putting them in place." Louis Martin-Chauffier observed that the lengthening of the sentence was effected by "a sort of reprise, of perpetual rebound at the moment when the sentence seemed to end" (*RRS*, 1510). It is evident that for some of Gide's most sensitive and knowing readers his syntax and vocabulary were more important even than the landscape in creating the emotion that he intended.

The fable itself is susceptible to several interpretations. To begin with the most general, *El Hadj* is an allegory of the genesis of the prophetic (Abrahamic) religions. (The desert locale contributes mightily to this reading, since the three prophetic religions were born in the desert.) The prophet-to-be, El Hadj, is at first a simple storyteller and singer engaged by a company of pilgrims who are following their prince on a journey to the north. It is the uneasiness of his companions about where they are going ("We all seemed to be following him, who did not appear to be leading" [*RRS*, 346]) that makes El Hadj take the first step toward leadership. He promises to talk to the prince, even though he has no idea how to reach him. He sings in the night outside the prince's tent, pouring out the doubts and the devotion that they all feel. Captivated by the passionate urgency of his own song, he falls in love with the invisible prince. When the latter at length admits him to his tent, it is to tell him that he does not know where the journey will end. "And so, from virtue to virtue we shall press on, El Hadj, unto death, always hopeful, and we shall sustain ourselves to the end with the mirage of some uncertain felicity" (*RRS*, 351).

Thereafter it is the servant's love that keeps the master's hopes alive. El Hadj sings of the splendors and joys that the prince desires to find, and in singing of them promises them—not only to his beloved but to the pilgrims as well. When the prince dies without having seen the northern sea, El Hadj realizes that he must keep up the lies that love inspired him to tell, if the people, who are now his charge, are to be kept from despair. Without revealing the prince's death or the failure of their pilgrimage, he patiently and resourcefully leads his flock back to the gardens of their own southern city, governing them now through fear more than love.

Finally rid of the burden of his life, El Hadj declares: "For we know now that there are prophets, hiding from the people they lead during the day the uneasiness, alas, and the bewilderment of their souls, simulating their former fervor in order to conceal that it is dead—who weep when night comes and they are all alone—when their only light comes from the unnumbered stars and the too-distant Idea perhaps—in which they have, however, ceased to believe" (*RRS*, 345). "But I know now that if there are prophets it is because they have lost their God. For if He were not silent, of what use would their words be?" (*RRS*, 363).

Even though he has brought the people back home and is free, the role of prophet still sits heavily upon him, keeping him from being what he was before. In the palace a younger brother of the prince is growing up. "Is he waiting for my voice to guide him? And will I begin again with him, with a new people, a new story, that I will recognize step after step . . . ?" (*RRS*, 363). With this apparent allusion to the historical succession of the prophetic religions—Mosaic, Messianic, Mohammedan—the story ends.

The disenchanted tone of the allegory reflects very accurately the decadent religious sensibility, which was quite another thing from Gide's evangelical fervor. The joyless resignation of the prophet who finds himself the guardian of an empty cult is as characteristic of the end phase of romanticism as the angry pride of Vigny's Moses was of its heroic beginnings.

Equally conventional is the stereotype of the poet's career, which *El Hadj* may also be thought to reflect. The poet, inspired with an enchanted vision, sings to the crowd, who immediately acclaim him their savior and leader. Thereafter he exercises a public charge and must repeat, without inspiration, the promises that his people demand to hear. The myth so stated recalls an imperishable romantic theme illustrated by Vigny, Musset, Leconte de Lisle, Baudelaire, and Mallarmé.

In the last analysis, however, *El Hadj* is best interpreted in the manner of the previous works that we have considered, as the symbolic version of an event or situation in Gide's own life. This approach does not in any sense invalidate those we have just explored. Gide in fact labored and plotted to achieve manifold significations in his stories.

A Gidean interpretation has the immediate and distinct value of allowing us to put the accent where it falls in the story, on the homoerotic motif. By the summer of 1896 when he was writing *El Hadj* Gide had been married for some months and had revisited on his wedding journey the North African locales where his great emancipation of 1893 had taken place. Furthermore, he wrote the story while he was still in the midst of *Les Nourritures terrestres* (*Fruits of the Earth*), which was to be the lyrical celebration of his emancipation. *El Hadj* may be regarded as an antidote to the exuberant optimism of *Les Nourritures*. It is a story not of liberation but of sublimation. The poet, in becoming a prophet, has had to renounce desire and gratification in favor of an austere, self-denying love. While the prince lived—that is, while the homoerotic relation was possible and admissible—love, poetry, faith, and devotion went together, sustaining and creating each other. When the prince died, so did love and poetry, and in their place came theology, morals, and the prophet's sense of responsibility for an unloving and unloved people.

El Hadj is not a statement of the Catharist theme of purity in love. The story expresses none of the fervor that characterizes that ideal in Gide's work. It is rather the lament of Corydon when he finds himself obliged to sacrifice love and joy to a duty that seems endless and unrewarding. Marriage had satisfied the Oedipus-Tristan character in Gide but had forced the pederast to sublimate his desire. It is this sacrifice that accounts for the plaintive melancholy of the narrative and its outlook of irreversible pessimism. The aesthetic sublimation of the sentiment is accomplished by directing attention away from the author himself and toward conventional interpretations of the allegory.

Le Prométhée mal enchaîné

Le Prométhée mal enchaîné (*Prometheus Misbound*) (1899), which Gide classified in 1914 as a *sotie*, is the most complex construction of his decadent-symbolist period. First, there is complexity in the narrative: three anecdotes, or histories (Coclès and Damoclès, Prométhée, and Tityre), complement and complicate each other. Second, there is complexity of tone: this work is just about the liveliest, most humorous, and most deeply satirical that Gide wrote, but its humor reposes on a base of seriousness that is by turns lofty, pathetic, and oracular. Finally, there is complexity of meaning. This does not mean that the tale is obscure or equivocal, but rather that it has several meanings—each incident or episode tends to have its own—and that they frankly conflict with one another.

In its apparatus (the ensemble of means employed to make the story) *Le Prométhée mal enchaîné* resembles the other works of this first period. Its internal agents, with the exception of the waiter, are legendary figures. Gide achieves a comical effect by mingling figures from different legendaries: Prometheus and Zeus from the Greek; Cocles and Damocles from a later Latin legendary; Tityrus and Moeliboeus from Virgil. Angèle we might say is from the Gidean legendary, since she has already appeared in *Paludes* and in the *Lettres à Angèle* (1898–1900). These agents are not, properly speaking, characters; they lack the autonomy and individuality suggested by that term. They are symbolical figures whose names suggest certain exemplary attitudes and actions, and who serve in Gide's story to express the several aspects of the Idea.

Another comical incongruity is achieved by introducing these legendary figures into the modern world and by relating their attributes to modernity: Zeus is a powerful banker and Prométhée, the fire-giver, is imprisoned for manufacturing contraband matches. The meeting of Coclès, Damoclès, and Prométhée is arranged by a waiter in a restaurant on the Grands Boulevards. Paris, with its wit and fatuousness, provides the stage upon which these exemplary figures act out their histories.

The subject of *Le Prométhée mal enchaîné* may be stated in one word: morals. And since the subject is dealt with in an irreverent manner, we may say that it is a satire on morals—on the morals of being, or self-perfection. The first part of the story is entitled "A Chronicle of Private Morality," and the first sentence says: "I shall not speak of public morality because there is none" (*RRS*, 304). This statement, so perfectly expressive of the anarchism of the middle class, is Gide's clue to the satire. It points beyond the immediate question of morals to those who raise the question, that "court of fools" who appeared in *Paludes* and who will turn up again in *Les Caves du Vatican*.

The desire for self-perfection through understanding, commitment and action is depicted in three modes: as low comedy by Coclès and Damoclès, as heroic myth by Prométhée, and as pastoral romance by Tityre. The waiter introduces the subject by his reflection on "gratuitous action." Is man the only being capable of an unconditioned action; or is he, on the contrary, the being whose acts are all conditioned by his consciousness?

Damoclès and Coclès existed in solitude and anonymity. They had nothing and were nothing. The former was happy in his condition; the latter wanted something to structure and motivate his existence. The intervention of contingency, or fatality, in their lives is represented by the gift from Zeus—"the spirit of initiative," as he calls himself, the false giver who really only lends, the banker who does not contradict when people call him God. His anonymous present of 500 francs to Damoclès makes that man forever obligated to an unknown benefactor. He is a debtor who does not know how to discharge his debt, a being, in other words, who does not know how to assume his individuality. He lives thereafter in anxiety (this is his bond with the legendary Damoclès who was condemned to sit eternally beneath a sword suspended by a thread) and finds an escape from his torment only in death.

To Coclès Zeus gives a resounding slap, but this abusive indignity (compounded when Prométhée's eagle blinds him in one eye) furnishes him with the pretext he has been seeking. Having suffered unjustly, he becomes the champion of all those who have suffered injustice. As a recipient of charity and a dispenser of benefits, he fills his life with philanthropy and shows that the assumption of suffering and degradation can be a triumphant choice.

Damoclès and Coclès illustrate quite clearly the problematical quality of human liberty. Fate imposes upon Damoclès a fact that cannot be satisfactorily inserted into his project of selfhood. The fact is a benefit; but that makes no difference; it will not accord with his desire for anonymity. The result is a life of utter frustration. To Coclès fate is kinder. It offers him an injury that helps him to be what he had already chosen to be: a good man. There results for him a deep sense of righteousness and a full life.

It needs to be emphasized, for the further sense of the story, that success and failure are here determined by the project of selfhood, by that "private morality" of self-perfection that was mentioned at the beginning. An ethical aspect of the situation should also be noted. Zeus first established a relation between Damoclès and Coclès by relating their "gifts," and the waiter, by presenting them to each other, makes them discover this relationship. Damoclès is to some degree indebted to Coclès for having written his name on the envelope that contained the 500 francs—even though it was a matter of chance that Coclès selected his name. He tries to discharge his debt by buying Coclès a glass eye. But Coclès feels that his injury somehow resulted from Damoclès's good fortune, and he repeatedly makes this feeling known to Damoclès. Therefore the two men are divided by the fate that might perhaps have united them had they been less involved in their own personal projects. That is, if they had given more attention to the action of Zeus and less to its effect on their private aims, they might have seen the gratuitousness, the incongruousness, and the injustice of what had happened to them.

For the hero, Prométhée, the eagle is the equivalent of the "gifts" of Coclès and Damoclès. Since he is a mythical hero, his story is told in two versions. In the first, the eagle is the symbolic expression of his freedom, of his possibility of being, which begins as a paltry conscience and becomes a great soaring determination. In prison Prométhée feeds the eagle on his liver. (He adopts the maxim of John the Baptist: "He must increase but I must decrease."—John 3:30.) As Prométhée grows weaker, the eagle grows stronger, until one day it can bear him upward and out of his prison. In this parable it is the choice of self, of one's own possibility, which rids the mind of scruples and bends it toward its desire.

In the second version, Prométhée says that his "eagle" was his devotion to men. He revealed to them the possibility of betterment and implanted in them the will to self-perfection. And now, speaking before an audience in Paris, he urges his listeners to cherish their "eagles." "The history of man is the history of eagles," he says (*RRS*, 324). We do not know where our eagle comes from, or why it comes, or who gives it, or where it leads, or why it is ours; but "in any case the eagle devours us, vice or virtue, duty or passion" (*RRS*, 327). If the eagle is not fed with love he remains a wretched, colorless thing; "it is then that he will be called a conscience, unworthy of the torments that he causes" (*RRS*, 327).

Prométhée is half hero, half god. As a hero, he undergoes the revelation of his freedom, which is his possibility of being himself, a unique personality constructed of self-dictated decisions. As a god, he reveals this freedom to men and urges them to cherish it.

Damoclès is deeply affected by Prométhée's sermon, which drives him more rapidly toward recognition of the impasse of his own existence. When Damoclès dies shortly thereafter, Prométhée kills his eagle, and by way of a funeral oration for Damoclès he tells the story of Tityre, who also received a gift, a seed that grew into a great oak. The oak in turn became the center of a human community governed by Tityre. At first his devotion to the community brought him nothing but satisfaction; then one day he observed that his cares were wearing him away. "If they increase, I decrease" (*RRS*, 337). At the urging of Angèle he quit his community and his "oak" and came with her to Paris. There Angèle abandoned him for the naked piper Moelibée; and Tityre found himself once again alone in his swamp.

The fable of Tityre parallels more or less the story of Prométhée, but one might be tempted to say with Coclès: "I don't get the connection" (*RRS*, 340).

Prométhée killed his eagle not because he felt burdened by it but because he saw, in the death of Damoclès, the absurdity of abandoning oneself to one's eagle. "Since the death of Damoclès," he says, "I have found the secret of laughter" (*RRS*, 339–40). Killing the eagle was a vengeful act, perhaps, or an ethical act committed on behalf of Damoclès, whom Prométhée had driven more deeply into his dilemma by speaking of the need to love one's eagle. At the least, killing the eagle betokens rejection of the morals of self-perfection in favor of a more flexible, more open morals; a practical ethics, say, in which men would stand together against the the fate that distributes so unequally their "gifts" and would seek a more equitable and generally useful disposition of these.

Of course, this is only what seems to be implied by Prométhée's action. Tityre's story does not quite suggest the same conclusion: it simply ends upon an irony that might lead to a philosophy of the *praxis*.

Le Prométhée mal enchaîné is motivated primarily by the critical spirit, which is antireligious in the sense that it opposes the godly behavior of both Zeus and Prometheus (whom Gide many years later assimilated to God the Creator and Christ the Savior). The keen wit, which is everywhere in the tale, and the satire on morals and the human condition represent nothing but the play of the critical intellect. There is very little to suggest the presence of the other motives that figure so large in Gide's works of this period. The erotic is evoked in only two details. Prométhée, in describing what he was before he became aware of his eagle, recalls playing joyfully in the lascivious embrace of his mother, Asia. This detail has no essential significance in the story; it may therefore refer obliquely to the origin of Gide's erotic complex. The incident of Angèle quitting Tityre to follow Moelibée to Rome brings up fleetingly the dissolution of heterosexual relations. (It hints still more archly at a leaning toward Catholicism of which Gide some years later accused his wife.)

Narcissistic motifs, pointing to the self-conscious poet, are absent. There is no Gidean double in *Le Prométhée mal enchaîné*. Even in the artistic structure of the story, the ambivalent narcissism of so many of Gide's stories is lacking. The sense of *Le Prométhée* may not be altogether clear, but the story is not genuinely ambiguous or hesitant. An abstract symbolism has simply left its interpretation rather open. Gide's epilogue, written "to try to make the reader believe that if this book is what it is, it is not the fault of the author" (*RRS*, 341), implies that he was aware that wit had at times assumed priority over ideas.

Philoctète

Philoctète (*Philoctetes*) (1899), or "The Treatise of the Three Moralities," is composed in dramatic form and has been presented on the stage. It nonetheless shares with certain of the narrative works of this period a legendary source and with all of them a parabolic type of statement. Like the narrative works, it is essentially characterless: it presents symbolical, or representative, figures rather than characters. The action of the play is on the whole more ideological than psychological, more confrontation than conflict; but in its final development there is an assertion of the Gidean personality that endows the otherwise austere and abstract piece with warmth and feeling.

Certainly the stereotyped figures of Ulysses and Philoctetes arouse no feeling of "Gidean" urgency at the beginning of the work. Gide's Ulysse voices a public morality based on obedience to the gods and the ordinances of the city. He offers as the supreme example of virtue Agamemnon's sacrifice of his daughter Iphigenia in the interests of the state. Philoctète proclaims a moral doctrine of self-fulfillment. Alone on his icy island he no longer feels despair or hope. Since he has ceased speaking to other men, his own utterance has become beautiful to his ear. In the deathly stillness around him there is no process, no becoming; there is only being, plenitude, and truth. He has ceased to be a Greek and to interest himself in the fortunes of Greece. There is a principle higher than the gods, he says: oneself. Philoctète has, in a word, found virtue in solipsism. But Ulysse asks: "What is the good of a solitary virtue?"

The youth Néoptolème is torn between the two moralities, acknowledging the authority of both, but seeking still some greater example of virtue. In his conduct he aims to keep faith with Philoctète as well as with Ulysse and Greece.

It is Néoptolème who forces Philoctète to discover another good and another virtue—and it is in this development that the specifically Gidean poetry appears in the play. Philoctète is troubled by the presence of Néoptolème and by the boy's hunger for virtue. He becomes tongue-tied before him. He allows him to hold the bow of Hercules (that Ulysse must bring back to ensure victory to the Greeks in the Trojan War), and when he sees him draw it, he secretly decides to give it up to him. Love shows him the way to a new ethic of sacrifice and self-effacement. By voluntarily taking the sleeping potion with which Néoptolème was supposed to overpower him, he aims to force Ulysse to admire him. But he refuses to have his act construed as a devotion to Greece or to his former countrymen: "Of all devotions, that to others is the maddest, because one becomes superior to them" (*OC*, 3:57). He abandons the pursuit of virtue: "What we undertake beyond our strength, Néoptolème, that is what we call virtue, Virtue . . . I no longer believe in it, Néoptolème" (*OC*, 3:58).

Ulysse is indeed struck with admiration—but not so much that he will delay their departure for Troy. The victory of the Hellenes is still uppermost in his thoughts. When Ulysse and Néoptolème have gone

Philoctète contemplates his solitude and is happy. Flowers bloom in the snow around him and birds descend to feed him.

The interplay of motives in *Philoctète* is more complex than we may realize at the first reading. The theme that has appeared paramount to many readers is the conflict between individual right and public morality or interest. It is this opposition that led Louis Martin-Chauffier to sense in the play "a distant echo of the Dreyfus Affair" (*OC*, 3:viii) and Yvette Louria to see it as a symbolical account of the unhappy career of Oscar Wilde.[9] Gide would have had no reason to be discontented with these interpretations of his play. They stand as tributes to the openness of his discourse and the generality of his symbols.

Looking at the same feature—the conflict of Ulysse and Philoctète—from a slightly different perspective, we can say that the two legendary figures represent two clearly defined attitudes of the bourgeoisie: chauvinism and anarchistic individualism. To show these moral outlooks in contention is more than a little false because they are normally found together in the middle-class mind. When the interests of the class coincide with those of the entire nation, chauvinism is the likely response. Individualism asserts itself when the interests of the nation are felt to be at odds with those of the class. The way in which Gide resolves the conflict between Ulysse and Philoctète indicates that he was not unaware of their fundamental complicity. Their opposition is not only resolved but overcome—I might risk saying rebuked—by the "third morality" that emerges in response to the demand of Néoptolème. At the same time neither chauvinism nor individualism is defeated. Ulysse gets the bow of Hercules and returns to the war. Philocete, having proven his virtue, is left to enjoy his solitude. The contention is resolved in favor of both of them.

The strategy of the play, however, is not completely revealed in the foregoing interpretations. Both fail to take account of the "third morality," which is the combined powers of love and the gospel operating to overcome bourgeois morality in both of its manifestations. It is in this resolution that we see the Gidean "signature" on the play.

Gide was conscious of offending the social order to which he belonged by the nature of his erotic needs and by the choices he had made to satisfy them. His Catharist marriage and his love of boys were equally subversive, judged by the norms of his class. Philoctète's stinking wound and his enforced exile are the emblems of Gide's estrangement from the erotic norm. Ulysse, with his devotion to the gods and the nation, represents the morality that Gide acknowledged and feared, that he respected and at the same time rejected. Philoctète's austere and solitary virtue is the response to guilt of the puritan who seeks to redeem his past action by displaying such restraint and fortitude that his judge is bound to acknowledge his virtue.

But for Gide redemption was not enough; he thirsted for justification. The "third morality," the way of love, is the symbolical justification that he invents in *Philoctète*. The unconcealed motif of pederasty is the principal clue to this interpretation. His capitulation to the charm of Néoptolème delivers Philoctète from the icy virtue of self-denial and permits him to discover another conduct based on surrender, humility, and self-effacement. Religion, inspired by love, triumphs over puritan virtue; for it is clear that in responding however little to desire, Philoctète has sacrificed his pride and strength and has thereby acted out Christ's precept of giving up one's life in order truly to live. By making the choice of Corydon he sacrifices heroism to abjection and becomes a saint. (The birds and flowers that surround him in the last act make this transformation eloquently clear.)

In order to achieve justification by holiness Gide had of course to transform certain aspects of his own situation. Philoctète's surrender, unlike his own, is made in the spiritual body rather than in the fleshly one. He surrenders at the same time to love and to the renunciation of love. Thus Gide combines in the one act of Philoctète the two acts of his own erotic history, pederasty and Catharism.

Chapter Three
Romantic Resurgence

Goethe and Nietzsche

Even as Gide continued to write books in the impersonal, allegorical style of the symbolists and to explore the decadent themes of impotence, sterility, and withdrawal from life, a revolt was brewing in him against those forms. They had served to express, authentically and appropriately, the personality of his neurotic youth, but from 1893 onward Gide was wholly involved, body and soul, in overcoming the residual effects of his malady. In the first paragraph of his preface to the 1927 edition of *Les Nourritures terrestres*, he wrote: *"Les Nourritures terrestres* is the book of a sick man, or at least of a convalescent of someone who has got well, after having been sick. There is in its very lyricism the excessiveness of someone who is embracing life as a thing he had almost lost" (*RRS*, 249). We must not assume that "sickness" and "health" are mere metaphors here. Gide was attempting to describe quite literally the evolution of his personality during the period 1893–96, when so many things happened to alter the content and direction of his life and his work.

Getting well meant giving expression to his fundamental being, to those feelings and wishes that had for so long been frustrated and repressed. The crucial event in the process was the journey to North Africa in 1893–94 and the discovery of sexual pleasure with another male, an Arab boy. A second trip to the same locales in 1895 confirmed beyond any doubt Gide's inclination to pederasty. Two other events of critical importance, followed in that same year: first, the death of his mother; then, after a mourning period of a few months, his marriage to Madeleine Rondeaux. It seemed that, in this development, Gide's deep erotic attachment to the maternal figure had undergone a *natural* transformation. Even more than his initiation into sexual pleasure with another person, this apparent resolution of the Oedipus complex fostered in him the assurance of health and maturity. (The extent to which he was deluding himself will become evident as we scrutinize the strategies of his stories and plays. Far from being resolved, the Oedipus complex continued to haunt him and to demand symbolic dissolutions.)

The recovery of health was not, however, purely a matter of alterations in the scheme of Gide's intimate relations. There was a parallel development in his intellectual interests and literary tastes. As we observed earlier, Gide's decadent-symbolist style was an outgrowth of his enthusiastic study of Schopenhauer and Fichte, Novalis and Hölderlin, and of the more immediate prestige and influence of Mallarmé and his circle, on the one hand, and of Maurice Barrès, on the other. About 1892, Gide began to detach himself from these guides and to reorient his thoughts on a more vital and exuberant literature.

His greatest inspiration—it followed him to the end of his life—came from Goethe, whose name appears repeatedly in Gide's *Journal* from 1892 onward. In the first entry he simply notes: "Read some of Goethe's poetry; the *Prometheus*" (*J*, 30). In 1895, however, he was saying: "Nothing will have brought more calm to my life than the contemplation of that great figure" (*J*, 57).

Describing many years later (1928) the revelation that Goethe had been to him, Gide wrote: "Confronting the Christian ideal and that sublime inquietude which, destroying the balance of the human being, puts down the flesh and its joys and makes the contemplative soul leap up to high heaven, I discovered a completely human, completely earthly ideal, made of health, equilibrium, wise adaptation, smiling harmony, and activity. All the gods of Olympus came back to dwell in my heart." It was not the serenity of an unperturbed nature that he sensed in Goethe, however, but that of an inner turbulence mastered and brought to order: "There is also in him," Gide went on to say, "something demoniacal, untamed, Promethean, which makes him kin to the Satan of Milton and Blake" (*OC*, 15: 515–16).

Goethe was the intellectual and artistic symbol of that health that Gide felt he was gaining by acknowledging the truth of his nature and attempting to satisfy its demands. The stimulus of some other writers was less important than that of Goethe, but not inconsiderable even so. For a while at least, Rimbaud's "vital turbulence" was tonic. In a letter written in 1911, Gide said: "*Les Illuminations* were my viaticum, my nearly exclusive nourishment during the most important months of convalescence of my life" (quoted in Davet, 41–42).

In 1894 Gide was reading Strindberg and Ibsen, about whom he said, in a letter to his mother: "That Northern literature is terrifying; it is as brutal as their ancient gods; the history of Protestantism continues on in it; when Luther proclaimed free inquiry, the powers in the shadows must have laughed. The history of Protestantism is a chapter in the history of freethinking. How admirable to have shown (as it did) that freethinking can be religious" (quoted in Delay, 2:365).

Gide's discovery of Nietzsche, in 1895–96, was a major event of his intellectual life. It was not, as it had been with Goethe, a revelation that suddenly opened new vistas before his eyes and authorized him, as it were, to be what he desired to be. With Nietzsche it was rather a matter of recognition, of seeing his own halting thoughts expressed triumphantly, without reservation or hesitancy. In the twelfth of his "Letters à Angèle," published in 1898, Gide wrote a summary estimate of the work of Nietzsche, in which he said:

We all owe Nietzsche a full-blown debt of gratitude: without him generations might perhaps have been used up in insinuating timidly what he affirms with boldness, mastery, madness. Speaking more personally, we ourselves ran the risk of letting our entire work become encumbered with shapeless sketches of thoughts—thoughts which now are said. It is *starting from that* that one must create, and that the work of art is possible. . . .

I have said that we were expecting Nietzsche long before we knew him: that is because Nietzcheism began long before Nietzsche. Nietzcheism is at once a manifestation of superabundant life, which had already been expressed in the work of the greatest artists, and a tendency also, which, depending on the epoch, had been baptized "Jansenism" or "Protestantism," and which will now be called Nietzcheism, because Nietzsche has dared to formulate to the last detail everything latent that was murmuring in it. (*OC*, 3: 236–37)

Goethe and Nietzsche, Rimbaud, Ibsen, and Strindberg: these are some of the writers in whom Gide found authorization for the style of life and the artistic ventures on which he embarked after 1895. The book that heralded his "rebirth" was *Les Nourritures terrestres*, conceived in 1893–94, written for the most part in 1895–96, and published in 1897. It had nothing of the manifesto about it, but it was nonetheless a declaration of independence. A discerning, though hostile, critic, Henri Massis, later saw it primarily as a reaction "against the person, the ideas, and the prestige of Barrès."[1] Gide, in the 1927 preface, said that he wrote the book "at a moment when literature smelled furiously artificial and musty" (*RRS*, 249).

The stories and plays that Gide wrote between 1896 and 1918 all depart from this declaration of independence and from his assurance of having overcome a sickness. He did not abandon everything that he had acquired as a young symbolist. The ironic detachment of the artist who loves the work of art more than the expression of his own personality and who shuns rhetoric in the interest of achieving harmony and limpidity in his work continues to be a primary trait of Gide's writing. But his themes and characters, and his attitude toward them, are best described as romantic. Every work of this period expresses vitalism, individualism, and excessiveness. These forces are held in check, but only barely, by his "Protestantism"; that is to say, by the will to virtue, to self-effacement, and to self-criticism.

The feeling of health and mastery that Gide had at the start of this phase of his work—and which persisted, in spite of some notable lapses into despondency and depression, until 1918—is manifested in the strenuous opposition in stories and plays between imperious, violent characters on the one hand and the unyielding blame and incomprehension of their milieu on the other. This is what health meant to Gide: giving expression to *all* the forces of his nature and pitting them against one another in symbolic conflicts.

Les Nourritures terrestres

Les Nourritures terrestres (*Fruits of the Earth*) (1897) is commonly regarded as the one book that comes nearest to being a complete and typical expression of Gide's sensibility and "doctrine." This view has much to recommend it, for *Les Nourritures* is the book in which Gide announced the themes and the tone of just about everything he would write up to his fiftieth year. The estimate seems more than a little paradoxical, however, when we consider that it took nearly 20 years to exhaust the first printing of 1,650 copies. In the first 10 years, according to the author, the book sold only 500 copies (*RRS*, 249). The public's tardiness in recognizing the value of *Les Nourritures* is a fair measure of the book's revolutionary character—and for that matter, of most of what Gide wrote between his symbolist beginnings and the end of the First World War. He was writing for an audience that hardly existed before the calamitous effects of the war had been felt. Much of his public was in fact unborn when *Les Nourritures* appeared. Gide had enjoyed a small but sensitive and sympathetic group of readers—mainly fellow writers—from the publication of *Les Cahiers d'André Walter* onward, but *Les Nourritures terrestres* evoked little else than incomprehension among them. (Paul Valéry was a notable exception.)

The truth is that *Les Nourritures terrestres* was first of all a calculated

rebellion against the morals of withdrawal and the artificial poetics that
symbolism had installed as the literary fashion. Writing in the twenties,
Gide said of this period: "When my *Nourritures* appeared, we were in the
very midst of Symbolism; it seemed to me that art was running great
risks in thus separating itself from naturalness and from life. But my
book was much too natural not to appear factitious to those who no
longer liked anything but artificiality; and precisely because it escaped
from literature they saw in it at first only the quintessence of literature"
(*OC*, 13:440).

Les *Nourritures terrestres* is the first unequivocal manifestation of that
spontaneity which was to be a kind of lifelong ideal of Gide. Spontaneity
meant a great many specific things to him, but in the final analysis they
are all reducible to the decision, or sometimes simply the wish, to relax
the cultural controls that made him feel false and constrained and give
free rein to instinct and desire. Gide's psychic structure was such that
these two aspects of himself were very clearly developed as adversary
forces and were of very nearly equal strength. In the first period of his
work we were able to discern clear traces of his erotic complexity, of his
poetic impulse to self-disclosure, and to a lesser degree, of his piety. But
on the whole, the group of works we examined revealed the preponderant
power of the artistic and critical controls. The former was manifested in
the theoretical frame upon which each book was mounted and in the
studied and calculated use of language and image. The critical eye was
directed toward a world of ideas and manners, but also toward the poet
himself; so that Le *Voyage d'Urien, Paludes, El Hadj, Le Prométhée mal
enchaîne*, and *Philoctète* were books of self-criticism as much as anything
else.

Les *Nourritures terrestres* is a corrective to that self-criticism and to the
intensely self-conscious artistry of the works of the first period. It is an
assertion of the erotic, poetic, and religious impulses against the restraints developed and fostered by environmental and doctrinal culture.
It does not sweep those controls completely away, but it does subdue
them. It is a declaration of independence whose force persists to the end
of Gide's career, one that remains effective even after the cultural
repressions have been fully reinstated in the pattern of his work. There is,
from Les *Nourritures terrestres* to the end of this period of his work, a certain
excessiveness, a kind of daring overshooting that is as characteristic of
Gide as it is of Dostoyevski, Nietzsche, Kierkegaard, or Rimbaud. His
being, one would say, having once found its real voice would no longer
bear suppression.

The relaxation of formal control is what first meets the eye in *Les Nourritures terrestres*. It is not *composed*, as *Les Cahiers d'André Walter* was. Rather, it simply grows from one outburst of thought and feeling to the next. Gide said that it was a book that "had to be left alone to write itself" (*RRS*, 1486). Its expression is spontaneous, exuberant, and artless. These are the qualities that have suggested the term "dithyrambic" that is often used to describe its lyricism. A number of set pieces in verse style (rounds and ballads) are included, but in the main it is a book made of aphorisms, exhortations, eulogies, anecdotes, and catalogues. A number of models have been suggested for it: Whitman's *Leaves of Grass*, Rimbaud's *Illuminations*, Nietzsche's *Zarathustra*, Virgil's *Bucolics,* and the lyrics of the Persian poet Hafiz (Gide put an epigraph from the Koran and one from Hafiz at the front of the volume). None of these suggestions is inappropriate, but the truth is that *Les Nourritures* is so very personal and so uninhibited in its expression that the question of its possible models does not assume a very large importance.

One rather important observation needs to be made about the style. The poet of *Les Nourritures* renounced the use of metaphor. "When I began to write my *Nourritures*," he said many years later, "I understood that the very subject of my book *was* to banish from it every metaphor" (*J,* 718). What he was rejecting in the metaphor was a *studied* (and therefore not spontaneous) effect that would signify that the poet had put a mental object between himself and reality. The modes of experiencing that Gide wanted to illustrate in *Les Nourritures* were *intuition* and *encounter*, both of which tend to be betrayed by a rhetoric of analogy.

In *Les Cahiers d'André Walter*, the lyrical work that opened the first period of Gide's career as an imaginative writer, the poet structured the image of himself as a division: in one book he revealed his angelic possession; in the other, his demonic possession. In *Les Nourritures terrestres* the angelic and the demonic are unified and harmonized rather than opposed. The longings of the body and the aspirations of the spirit have the same object: the concrete, immediate reality that is God. There is throughout the book a perfect mingling of profane themes, like *pleasure, consumption*, and *adventure*, with the evangelical themes of *fervor, divestment,* and *nomadism.*

Considered as a doctrine, the instruction of *Les Nourritures terrestres* contains these essential elements:

1. Life—existence in the present instant in the midst of a concrete world of things—is the unique source of knowledge and wisdom. Our access to authentic knowledge of that reality is gained through *sensation.*

"Any knowledge which has not been preceded by a sensation is useless to me" (*RRS*, 164).

2. Desire for pleasure is the energy that impels us to know reality. The poet had to discover his hunger for reality by divesting himself of the insulation of culture. "That unlearning was slow and difficult; it was more useful to me than all the teachings imposed by men and truly the beginning of an education" (*RRS*, 154).

3. Desire discloses the multiplicity of things in the world, and things reveal the liberty of choice. "Every choice is frightening when you think about it: frightening, a freedom no longer guided by a duty" (*RRS*, 155).

4. Liberty of choice discloses to each man his singularity as a domain of possibilities. His discovery of reality can only be his own; no predecessor can make a real world for him. "There are strange possibilities in every man. The present would be pregnant with all the future if the past did not already project upon it a history. But alas, a single past proposes a single future" (*RRS*, 158). The poet tells his pupil at the end: "Don't cling to anything in yourself but what you feel exists nowhere but in yourself, and make of yourself, whether impatiently or patiently, the most irreplaceable of beings" (*RRS*, 248).

5. Desire discloses the possibility of plenitude and of totality in the present instant. "Understand that at every instant of the day you can possess God in his totality. . . . Nathanaël, you possessed God and were not aware of it. Possessing God is seeing him. . . . Don't differentiate God from your happiness, and place all of your happiness in the instant. . . . The tiniest instant of life is stronger than death, and negates it" (*RRS*, 162).

The first tenets of the doctrine are therefore: the primacy of pleasure, the liberty of choice, the singularity of human destinies, and the possibility of wholeness and of union with all things. They constitute a kind of pantheistic, anarchistic hedonism. But they are not Gide's complete message—indeed, it would be strange to see him project so uncomplicated an image of his personality. There is a transcendent version of the philosophy of pleasure that is offered in concurrence with the first version, and in it we see the lineaments of an evangelical life that may be called ascetic, as long as we understand that it is based not upon self-denial but upon the search for a still greater joy.

1. In the light of his freedom and of the fearful nature of choice, the poet discovers that desire is greater and more delicious than possession. Possession can be deferred in favor of a posture of openness and expectation. "What we wish for, Nathanaël, is not so much possession as love"

(*RRS*, 165). Thus desire becomes fervor and takes on a religious character. "Nathanael, I will teach you fervor," the poet says (*RRS*, 156, 157).

2. In order to be truly open to reality and ready to accept what the instant offers, one must be naked. Divestment is then the first condition of wholeness. "Every being is capable of nudity; every emotion of plenitude" (*RRS*, 157). The poet had to shuck off his learning before he could discover life. He tells his pupil: "Nathanaël, you must burn all the books within you" (*RRS*, 163).

Deprivation can become a more intoxicating pleasure than indulgence: "Nathanaël, I will tell you about drunkenness. . . . Nathanaël, often the simplest repast was drunkenness for me, so drunk was I already from desires. And what I sought on the highways was not so much an inn as my hunger" (*RRS*, 208). And Ménalque recounts: "My happiness came from the fact that each spring reaveled to me a thirst, and that in the waterless desert, where thirst is unquenchable, I still preferred the burning of my fever beneath the exaltation of the sun" (*RRS*, 185).

3. The second requisite of a full life is mobility. In order to desire the world and to know it, one must encounter all things. Encounter demands ceaseless movement, a constant leavetaking. "Nathanaël, don't stay around what resembles you; don't ever *stay*, Nathanaël. As soon as a place has come to resemble you, or you have become like the environment, it is no longer profitable to you" (*RRS*, 172). And Ménalque says of his vagabond youth: "I lived in the perpetual, delicious expectation of whatever future might come" (*RRS*, 185).

4. The free individual is the source of value in the concrete universe, but it is only through transcending himself—through forgetting himself—that he can fully know and value the reality that is at once the world and God. In his opening address to his pupil, the poet says: "May my book teach you to be more interested in yourself than in it—then in everything else more than in yourself" (*RRS*, 154).

By deferring the immediate gratification of desire, Gide is able to construct a religious ethic of which the *end* is still the obligatory state of joy, but whose *ways* are fervent expectation, voluntary renunciation of possessions, the nomadic life of perpetual encounter, and most important of all, forgetfulness of self. ("And whoever loses his life will save it.")

Les Nourritures terrestres is openly sensual and erotic. The poet addresses his book to Nathanaël ("Gift of God") to whom he would "give a joy that no other had yet given him." His attitude before his pupil is that of the classical pederast who is not only a lover but a teacher. He would have his pupil love him but not imitate him. "Nathanaël, throw away my book now," he says in his envoi. "Emancipate yourself from it. Leave me" (*RRS*, 248). The love that he offers to Nathanaël he has himself experienced with Ménalque, that "hater of families" and "suborner of youth." Throughout the book the names of Virgil's shepherds are a constant reminder that this is a world in which homoeroticism is not proscribed. The desert, the vagabond life, and the chance encounter have, as we know, a homoerotic significance in Gide's private repertory of motifs. Though specific references to sexual desire and pleasure are few, they are amply evoked by other forms of bodily appetite and feeling. Hunger, thirst, and desire for sensation have a common focus of erotic suggestion.

The restraints of codified morality are totally refused. "Act without *judging* whether the action is good or bad. Love without worrying about whether it is good or evil," the poet says (*RRS,* 156). And also: "Nathanaël, I no longer believe in sin" (*RRS,* 171). This does not mean, as we have seen, that restraint is lacking. It is only the negative controls of social regulation and moral scruple that the poet rejects. Desire, because it transcends its object, can be a restraint upon possession and enjoyment. In this form desire is called fervor and love, and its objects, in their totality, are God. In this manner Gide draws love and piety from a common source and offers them as the natural limits of human experience and as limitations upon each other. If the erotic and the religious are contained together in the energy of desire, it is the *obligation to joy* that brings them into being and joins them, as it were, at the other pole of realization. "Refuse not the joy that each instant offers you" is an exhortation heard again and again throughout the book.

The motifs of rebirth, of convalescence after sickness, of palingenesis, which are stated by both the poet and his teacher Ménalque, are in essence evangelical. I might venture the suggestion that Gide conceived his book under the inspiration of the imperative "Except a man be born again. . . ."

Les Nourritures terrestres is not just a doctrine, or a program, however. It owes its power as much to rhetoric and poetry as it does to the strategy of uniting eroticism and evangelism against conventional morality. The urgent invitation to emancipate desire becomes very heady as it is stated over and over again. The songs of the open road, of the desert and its fruits—pomegranate, fig, and date—(Books 3 and 4), of the gardens of Blida (Books 3 and 7), of oases and caravans (Book 7), of wells and fountains, sleep and beds, cities and cafés (Book 6); the songs of the farm (Book 5) and of leavetaking that is like a foretaste of death (Book 5): these are the truly compelling forces of the poem. They are at bottom nothing but the unabashed and unadorned projections of Gide's erotic wish raised to the power of a system for realizing vital plenitude and happiness.

It is not at all difficult to sense the impact of *Les Nourritures* in the work of a great many talented writers who reached manhood during and after the First World War: Aragon, Montherlant, Saint-Exupéry, Malraux, Sartre, Camus. Their thirst for authenticity, for action and adventure, and for passionate comradeship with other men are put in settings often very different from those employed by Gide, but their desires were provoked and authorized by this book with which Gide's maturity begins.

Saül

Saül was written in 1896–97 while Gide was working on *Les Nourritures terrestres*. The play was to have been staged by Antoine at the Théâtre Libre, but a financial loss suffered by the theater made it impossible to realize that intention. Gide published the work in a very small edition in 1903 and finally saw it performed at the Théâtre du Vieux Colombier in 1922.

Like *El Hadj*, which was written at about the same time, *Saül* was conceived as an "antidote" to the optimistic hedonism of *Les Nourritures*. From one point of view the play may seem to belong to the first period of Gide's work, since its theme—the dissolution of authority and power under the impact of sensuality—is a typically decadent one.[2] It might even be taken as a companion piece to *El Hadj*: the prophet's authority grew as truth was supplanted by falsehood and illusion; Saül's authority declines as the truth of his nature displaces the prestige of kingship. The two works are ironical and pessimistic to about the same degree.

However, *Saül* differs markedly from the books of Gide's decadent-symbolist period in the fact that the *idea* does not stand paramount in it. Rather it is the *character* of Saül that is step by step disclosed, and it is done with such a passionate directness that we are bound to sense a radical shift in Gide's conception of the work of art. *Saül* is an ancient legend retold, just as *Philoctète* was, but here the legend does not have the air of being borrowed to illustrate an abstract thought. On the contrary, the legend is everything; its abstract (in this case, psychological) significance derives altogether from what appears on the stage. Nowhere else has Gide evoked more vividly the complexity and the fatality of a personality. Saül is dominated by erotic and religious drives. The only controls upon him are the shame and disgrace that befall him at the

hands of his subjects, who bear the burden of the moral culture. He is
therefore an exemplary vindication of Gide's strongest personal motives
and a privileged expression of the Gidean *poesis*.

The inspiration for the drama of Saül was said by Gide to have been a
curious entomological discovery: he had found a chrysalis that showed
the perfect outline of the moth-to-be; seeing it apparently lifeless he
opened the envelope and found on the inside the cocoons of some
parasitic animal that had completely devoured the pupa. "Thus, I
thought, my Saül would say: 'I am totally suppressed'" (*J-S*, 233).

The idea of the play is expressed somewhat differently in a passage of
Les Nourritures terrestres (one to which Delay has accorded a considerable
value in his psychobiography). Hylas is speaking:

And each one of my senses has had its desires. When I tried to return within
myself, I found my men servants and my handmaidens at my table; there wasn't
the tiniest place for me to sit down. The seat of honor was occupied by Thirst;
others thirsts vied with him for the best seat. The whole table was quarrelsome,
but they were in league against me. When I tried to approach the table they,
already drunk, rose up in a body against me; they drove me out of my house.
(*RRS*, 200)

This extraordinary allegory, in which the desires of the body are
represented as servants displacing their master in his own house, foreshadows those scenes in the play in which Saül's demons make sport of
him.

As for the possible model of the play, Justin O'Brien has noted certain
resemblances to Shakespeare's *King Lear* and *Macbeth* and has cited a
letter of Gide to Marcel Drouin (written toward the end of the year 1895
from Rome, where Gide and Madeleine were on their wedding journey)
in which he said: "I shall write a poem in which I shall compare my
desires to the daughters of King Lear, for I feel like the dispossessed king
for having listened to the passions that delight me."[3]

Gide's play is conceived in the tragic mode. It shows the downfall of a
king who loses the favor of his Lord and is made a prey of evil spirits. The
fatality that strikes Saül down is both outside him and in him: it is both
metaphysical and moral. The withdrawal of God's favor and the appoint-
ment of a successor are the direct causes of his ruin, but at the same time
his sensual nature, which cannot refuse any solicitation, makes him
incapable of exercising authority.

Saül's dissolution is revealed in the very first scene where we see him, far gone in wine, surrounded by his demons; but his fall is spelled out in some half dozen moves, beginning with the appearance of David.

The play derives a good measure of eloquence and beauty from its mythical infrastructure. We are, from the start, in the presence of a figure who is at once a celebrant of the cult of Dionysus and a king of epic proportions. The biblical legend of Saul is commonly explained in terms of the cultural history of Israel, but there are at least three elements of the story that demand some other sort of justification: the surpassing beauty of David, the love of David and Jonathan, and the mysterious curse that the Lord inflicted on Saul. Gide, always sensitive to the unelucidated significance of the ancient myths, founded his play on these very elements. Their sense, for him, lies in homoeroticism. They lend him access, as it were, to the legend and make Saul a possible expression of his private and personal drama.

Gide gave full rein to the fundamental assertions of his nature in *Saül*. The erotic is of course the overriding one, and it is largely responsible for the eloquence of the work. Saül's love for David (for Daoud, that is, since this variant form of his name is the "sign" of his erotic person in the play) is devastating. He kills the queen in a fit of jealousy over him—and thereby destroys the rival heterosexual relation early in the game. When he overhears David's declaration of love to Jonathan and sees them embrace, he bursts in, saying: "And what about Saül?"[4] He shaves his beard in order to be more visible to the handsome youth. But his desire is fruitless, for David has given himself wholly to Jonathan. Saül, in his decline, dreams of shepherds embracing in the desert; he plays amorously with his cupbearer Saki; and his demons gain access to him by appearing as errant waifs whom he cannot resist caressing.

Saül's religiousness is entwined with his eroticism. He never forgets his special relation to the Lord, and he tries devoutly to regain the power of prayer. But in him the erotic is inimical to the religious. The biblical legend dictated Saül's decline and fall, but it no doubt served Gide's personal needs as well to see one basic need of his nature threaten another. The exercise of depicting Saül was cathartic for him on two counts: it gratified his impulse to self-division and chastised his sexual appetite.

The development of Saül's self-awareness—of his moral character, in other words—is the countertheme to the erotic. He is tormented from the outset by the memory of his innocence, of the time when he was a simple shepherd hunting his father's she-asses in the desert. He is aware that God has abandoned him, and that there is a "secret" in his nature that even he cannot grasp. ("Horror! Horror!—They want to know my secret, and I don't know it myself" [*Th*, 205].) He is at times shocked by his own looseness as he drinks and sports with his demons ("Ah! My robe is all stained!" . . . "God of David, succor me!" [*Th*, 64, 65].) He is careless of his kingship and puts the symbols of his majesty on Jonathan, who thereupon puts them on David. He consults the witch of Endor, who tells him: "Close your door! . . . Everything charming is hostile to you!" (*Th* 100). But he cannot desist.

When, at the end, Jonathan begs Saül to get rid of the boy (demon) he is hiding under his cloak, the king is unable to comply. He says to his son: "You are too young to understand me; I feel that I am becoming very astonishing!—My value is in my complication!" (*Th*, 143). And then: "With what shall a man console himself for his degradation, if not with what caused it?" (*Th*, 144). In these utterances he acknowledges his incapacity to recover himself and resist the evil of his nature. "I encourage everything, against myself" (*Th*, 145), he says. And just before his death, in prayer he asks: "Will I find any remedy for my desire, other than its satisfaction?" (*Th*, 149).

Looking at the character of Saül from the outside, we realize that his weakness spelled his nation's incapacity to defend itself, and that the accession of David to the throne meant the return of strength and the reestablishment of moral order. At the same time there is a moral decline within Saül that parallels his displacement as the ruler of Israel. It was to this that I referred earlier in speaking of the dual aspect of the tragedy. There is little if any pathos aroused by what happens. Gide has rather concentrated, as the Greek tragic poets did, upon the justice of Saül's fate; for if he has lost a glory that was promised him, he has been perversely compensated by the rich complexity of his nature.

Saül is not a Gidean double. The era of the double ended with *Paludes*. He is an expression of what was most assertive in Gide: his erotic-religious nature. At the same time he is what Gide could never be, a genuinely tragic character. Gide was able to put himself in the drama only in the lesser motifs that surround Saül—the desert, where a wandering Gide met his particular destiny; the little brown boy whom he once took to his bosom; the name "Daoud" that was told to him by Athman, whom he loved.

Le Roi Candaule

The drama *Le Roi Candaule* (*King Candaules*) was written soon after *Saül* and more or less contemporaneously with *Philoctète*. It was published in the review *L'Ermitage* at the end of 1899 and was staged by Lugné-Poe in 1901. Like *Saül*, the play has a "decadent" subject and a "romantic" hero. Candaule's action in inviting another man to look upon his queen's naked beauty is morbidly perverse. But his motive for the strange deed is immoderately noble and generous. He is not content to be alone in the possession of wealth and beauty. His nature is such that he must share to enjoy.

Herodotus, whose *Clio* is the primary source of the legend, interpreted the story of Candaules as a piece of folk history marking a change of dynasty in ancient Lydia. La Fontaine repeated the story in his *Contes et Nouvelles* ("Le Roi Candaule, et le Maître en Droit") but only to illustrate a latter-day *conte galant*. Théophile Gautier gave a rather lengthy version of it in his *Nouvelles*, in which he emphasized the fierce vengeance that Nyssia demanded for Candaule's offense. His theme is the typically decadent one of the Deadly Female who destroys (castrates) her consort.

Gide, in the preface to the first edition (1901), states that he was in some measure inspired to write the play by an article challenging the governing classes to educate the people to appreciate art and beauty. The questions the author did not deal with, says Gide, are whether the people will be allowed to touch the possessions of the privileged class and what will result from their contact with them. His *Candaule* was a response to those questions. Of the legend he says further on in the preface: "Yet it is perhaps not impossible to see in it also the defeat, the suicide almost, of an aristocracy which is going to be disarmed, and then prevented from defending itself, by its own excessively noble qualities" (*Th*, 158).

What this amounts to is the outline of a tragical action. The king is destroyed by the disproportion between his own generosity and openness and the acquisitive instincts of his subjects. The play develops on the ethical level; that is, in terms of relations among men. The king makes generous offers that are misinterpreted by his courtiers, by the fisherman Gygès, and finally by Nyssia, who is mortally offended by his action in sharing her with Gygès. And yet there is a quality in the play, a fatality let us say, that surpasses the ethical: it is simply impossible that Candaule and his subjects could ever have understood each other.

Gygès, at the very beginning of the play, announces his character when he says: "Let him who holds happiness hide himself! Or let him hide his happiness from others" (*Th*, 169). He possesses few things in order to possess those few better, and when he learns that his wife has lain with one of the king's courtiers, he slays her, saying: "It is better for me to have little, but to have it alone" (*Th*, 201). The queen holds the same view of the happiness of possession. She says to Candaule: "There are certain joys that one kills before being capable of sharing them" (*Th*, 184).

Candaule suffers at being alone in the enjoyment of his wealth and in the knowledge of Nyssia's beauty. His happiness, he says, draws its power and violence from others; it exists only in the knowledge that others have of it (*Th*, 195). Every possession, for him, has to be assayed and proven (*Th*, 196). There are two forms of happiness: for the poor man, desiring and working for what he desires is happiness; for the rich man, happiness lies in risking his possession (*Th*, 196–97).

Candaule is shocked and offended when he discovers Gygès' poverty existing so close to his own riches, and he is struck with the simple fisherman's ferocious nobility when he kills his wife, the most precious of his possessions. Candaule befriends him and makes him wealthy, saying to him: "What does it matter that one gives and the other receives, where two enjoy the same wealth together" (*Th*, 209). Seeing Gygès lonely for his wife, and knowing that he will be able to appreciate the queen's beauty, Candaule conceives the gesture that will demonstrate to his friend a conduct nobler than jealous possessiveness. With the aid of the magic ring that renders its wearer invisible, he will allow him to see, and then to embrace, Nyssia. His courage nearly fails him when Nyssia extracts a promise from him never again to make her appear unveiled, but he recovers his resolve, saying to himself: "Who would ever do this thing, if not you?" (*Th*, 221).

From that moment on, the fatal machinery is set in motion, and Candaule can no longer dictate the course of events in his world. Gygès and Nyssia discover their moral kinship, and together they destroy the king. This bloody end marks the triumph of a certain privative ethics, characterized by severity, rectitude, and constraint, over a gentler, vaguely evangelical ethics of generosity, risk and openness. Candaule bears some resemblance to Saül in that he also is too open and too hospitable to maintain his power and prestige among people of another stamp.

This interpretation of the drama is all right, as far as it goes, but we all sense that something more has to be said. Gide showed his awareness of the aesthetic problem of his play when he noted on a "loose leaf" (probably in 1911), under the heading "New preface for *Candaule*": "Difficulty of having an idea accepted as a *motive*" (*OC*, 6:372). But this is at best an oblique approach to the matter. The trouble is that

Candaule's action, which is not lacking in dramatic consequences, seems to be motivated by a wish far more fundamental to his nature than the one alleged—by a wish, in short, that is related *essentially* to his action.

The "subterranean" power of Gide's play—and of the legend itself—lies in the erotic signification of the king's gesture. Gide once referred to this aspect of Candaule, but in a curiously detached way. He wrote in his journal that he was struck, in reading Rousseau's *Confessions*, by the writer's expression of friendship for the rival with whom he was sharing Madame d'Houdetot's favors. Gide detected a similar sentiment in Prince Myshkin of Dostoevsky's *Idiot* and in his own Candaule. He closes his reflection by saying simply that the expression of such a feeling is of "the highest importance" (*J*, 188–89). But what is important about it?

Looking at *Candaule* as an expression of the Gidean *poesis*, we are necessarily encouraged to regard the erotic theme as paramount. Ignoring the idea of generosity, what appears in Candaule's gesture is his depreciation, and dissolution, of a heterosexual relation in favor of a consuming friendship for another man. Candaule is moved by an irresistible desire to make Gygès happy: he finds him at first a homeless derelict; he gives him wealth and ease and makes him his bosom companion; and at last he gives him his wife to prove his devotion. This latent strategy of the play is revealed more clearly in the action than in the argument that supports the action.

It is also an important part of Gide's strategy to have Candaule's design destroyed by a countermorality which, by implication at least, upholds the bourgeois values of possession, exclusivity, and privacy. This is a device of self-punishment, a rather sophisticated one, in fact, in which the author condemns his erotic nature on moral grounds but allows it to triumph on the aesthetic level.

One satisfaction that the legend did not offer Gide's taste, in the person of Gygès, was youth. Perhaps it was in compensation for this lack that he borrowed from Plato the idea of the magic ring that makes the wearer invisible. He could not well make Gygès a boy, but he was able by this device to hide him from view and make him a secret treasure. "I conceal happiness," read the inscription on the ring.

Le Retour de l'Enfant prodigue

Gide wrote *Le Retour de l'Enfant prodigue* (*Return of the Prodigal*) very rapidly and with little effort in February and March 1907 and published it shortly thereafter. A note in his Journal on 16 March 1907, reads:

"Finished *L'Enfant prodigue* a few days ago. The idea of the poem's composition having hit me suddenly in Berlin, I set to work on it immediately; for the first time execution followed conception without interval. I was afraid that if I brooded on it longer the subject would increase and grow deformed."

One of the reasons for his hurry with the work was an urgent need to communicate to Paul Claudel his position in a dialogue that they had been engaged in for some years. Gide explained this urgency in a letter to Christian Beck on 2 July 1907:

Perhaps you do not know that Claudel, after having found in Jammes a stray easy to bring back to the Lord, wanted to take me on in turn. That is called "converting," I believe. He probably did not deceive himself into thinking that with my Protestant heredity and upbringing he had an easy task; anyway, he persisted, encouraged to the point of excess by the very lively admiration I showed for his work and by the immense credit that it gave his words, in my ears. Both in letters and conversation we went very far. At this point, Jammes let me understand that an article by him, a dithyrambic "study," would celebrate my conversion. I saw that there was risk of a serious misunderstanding, and being determined not to owe Jammes's praise to an (involuntary but acknowledged) compromise of conscience I wrote him a long letter of explanation, which produced on his part a sudden coolness. He felt that "I was getting away." Even so, understanding in the marrow of my bones the stake that Claudel and he had in the step they wanted to see me take, and why I wasn't taking it—and how, if I had done so, it could only have been in the manner in which my Prodigal Son returned Home, and in order to help his little brother to get away—I wrote this little "topical" work into which I put all my heart, but also all my reason.[5]

In spite of the specificity of its origin and the ease and rapidity with which it was written, *Le Retour de l'Enfant prodigue* has become a "representative" Gidean work. And this is not due alone to its being of a convenient "anthology" size. Much of Gide's personal myth and much of his style have found their way into the story.

The first thing to note about *L'Enfant prodigue* is that it is a throwback to the type of fiction favored by Gide in the symbolist period of his career. It is an allegory based upon the parable of Jesus that is recounted in Luke 15. There, it was a question of a father who had two sons, one who squandered his fortune in a foreign place and one who remained by his father. Gide adds the figures of the Mother and the Youngest Brother, and he endeavors to give to each person of the story, and to the story as a whole, meanings quite different from the one that Jesus intended in his parable.

The interpretation of the allegory volunteered by Gide in his letter to Christian Beck is that it symbolizes his relations with Claudel and Catholicism. According to such a reading, Gide would be depicting what he would expect to find in Catholicism: his Father's (God's) love would be unchanged; he would enjoy the solace of his Mother's tender presence (the Mystical Body); but he would have to suffer his Eldest Brother's blame and discipline (the dogmas and the priesthood). Under these circumstances the Prodigal Son (Gide) would be drawn back to the Catholic church only out of weakness and defeat. He would know that his flight from dogmatic authority was right, but he would not have the strength to live without spiritual provision and governance. The Youngest Brother, whom he helps to run away, would represent Gide's renewed determination to maintain his liberty of conscience outside the church. As a response to Claudel's efforts to convert him this would seem to be an unequivocal refusal.

At the same time *L'Enfant prodigue* very readily yields meanings of larger proportions. This is not unexpected since it accords with Gide's customary artistic effort to expand his personal problems to the point where they become general issues. The work may be read as a history of the prophetic religions: the Eldest Brother would then stand for the Mosaic tradition, and the Prodigal Son would represent the new faith propagated by John the Baptist and Jesus the Messiah. After a flight from the House, Christianity returns to the Law under the influence of the Apostle Paul. The Youngest Brother would be Islam, the third prophetic religion to emerge within the Semitic world and the one that has remained entirely independent of its predecessors.

The allegory may just as well be a history of Christianity seen from the Gidean angle. The dissenters leave the Catholic church to live in liberty of conscience, taking with them their share of the patrimony, presumably the Scriptures but not the Tradition. But they fail in their venture and end up founding a church that differs little, in the essential, from Catholicism. The Youngest Brother would be Gide's expression of his own evangelical position outside of Catholicism *and* Protestantism and of his feeling that such a departure was both possible and necessary. We begin to find Gide's critique of Protestantism in his journals for the 1890s; the subject continued to be one of importance to him even after he had ceased to be much concerned about religion in his own life. His quarrel with the Pauline influence on the Protestant mind was to furnish him the intellectual and critical theme that he juxtaposed to the erotic theme in *La Symphonie pastorale* (1919).

These three readings—the response to Claudel, the history of the prophetic religions, and the history of modern Christianity—are about equally complete and equally acceptable. Certainly, this range of possible interpretations has been one of the reasons for the interest—and in some quarters, for the hostility—aroused by the story. There remains, however, something more to be said about *L'Enfant prodigue.* Leaving allegory aside, I detect in it a good measure of what I have been calling the Gidean *poesis.* It is particularly significant that it appears here mainly in the features that Gide added to the parable. What do the Prodigal Son's conflicting affections for his Mother and his Youngest Brother suggest if not Gide's erotic division? The oedipal relation—the tender, protective, stable, secure order—is what the Prodigal Son has returned to. His adventure in the desert (the desert!) has exhausted him. He has had to serve "other masters" who abused him. Still, when it comes to choosing between devotion to the Mother and complicity with his Youngest Brother, it is to the latter that he yields. The little brother is the Narcissus image of Gide's psyche, the self as an adolescent, the phantasmal figure in whom he invested so much of his erotic interest.

In the call of the desert, the taste of wild fruits, the desire to break out of the confines of a familiar culture and wander freely in the universe of uncultured nature, we discover one of the most lyrical expressions of that "nomadism" that Gide conceived as the unique way to love, joy, and authentic being. The fact that he states his most insistent dreams and desires within the context of a theological allegory that is in turn founded upon a parable of Jesus should not strike us as incongruous. In the Gidean sensibility the voices of Eros and Jesus made a profound harmony. We cannot really be insensitive to this undercurrent of erotic dreaming in the story. It would be no exaggeration to say that the inexplicit appeal of the work lies precisely in the fervor of a half-concealed desire. In *L'Enfant prodigue* Gide has stated in the symbolist mode of understatement and emblematic representation effectively the same wish, and the same obstacles to its fulfillment, that are expressed by means of romantic character and action in *Saül* and *La Symphonie pastorale.*

L'Immoraliste

L'Immoraliste (The Immoralist) (1902) is the first representative of that most remarkable category of Gide's work, the psychological novel. Gide did not invent the genre, but he did revive it in a period when prose fiction was more or less divided between the pseudosociological chronicles of the Naturalists and the delicately perverse romances of the Decadents. Gide's models, we may reasonably presume, were *La Princesse de Clèves, Manon Lescaut, René, Adolphe,* and *Dominique.* But there was something in this type of fiction that was more important for him than any model, and that was the kind of action that the narrative represented. In "Un Esprit non prévenu" (An unbiased mind) Gide made a distinction between two sorts of novels, "or at least two ways of depicting life":

The one, exterior and commonly called "objective," which visualizes first of all the other person's gesture, the event, then explains and interprets it.

The other, which seizes first of all emotions and thoughts, then creates the events and characters most fitted to bring these out and runs the risk of being powerless to depict anything that the author has not first felt himself. His inner riches, his complexity, the antagonism of his too diverse possibilities, will allow the greatest diversity in his creations. But everything comes out of him. He is the only guarantee of the truth he reveals, the only judge. The hell and the heaven of his characters is in him. It is not himself that he depicts, but what he depicts he could have become if he had not become precisely himself.[6]

What the psychological novel offered Gide was a means of dramatizing his inner turbulence in terms appropriate to it. The *action* of these books is in the conflict between desire and inspiration on the one hand and the restrictive force of pain and obligation on the other hand. Physical encounters and displacements are to be interpreted as symbolic inventions employed to reflect and enrich the psychological action. This does not make them any less important: indeed, one of the outstanding qualities of Gide's psychological novels is to be found in the suggestive power of these secondary effects of scene and situation. (Such effects, we must remember, were the *primary* value of his symbolist tales.)

The central strategy of *L'Immoraliste* is one that we have already seen in Gide's work: the dissolution of a heterosexual relationship and its replacement by a homosexual one. The difference here is that the strategy is neither concealed nor abbreviated; it is the subject of the story from beginning to end, and the course of its development is punctuated with peripeties and discoveries. Gide found the way to involve all the motives and countermotives of his personality in this one plot. The result is a story that is at once direct and clear in its depiction of the growth of a desire and complex and ambiguous in its thought about the demands of that desire.

The attack upon heterosexuality (which for Gide was always an attempt to be rid of the frustrating oedipal relationship) begins on the first page of Michel's story when he says of his bride Marceline: "I had married her without love, mainly to please my father, who, dying, was worried at leaving me alone" (*RRS*, 372). The illness that strikes him on their wedding journey to North Africa is not an accident but rather a defense against the undesired relationship.

Michel begins his recovery by refusing Marceline's attentions. He avoids her and seeks health in the company of a band of Arab boys. When he sees one of these steal Marceline's sewing scissors he is delighted to be a silent accomplice in the theft. He does not understand his joy, but its reason is not to our eyes impenetrable: the scissors are an emblem of feminine power, an instrument of castration. When the child takes them he disarms Marceline and displaces her as an object of erotic interest.

Michel not only recovers from his illness, he becomes a new man whose strength and vitality are based upon his acknowledgment of the claims of his fundamental being—what he calls, in biblical language, "the old man." As a sign of rebirth he shaves his beard. (So did Saül, and so did Gide.) At this point there occurs a reversal in the process of homoeroticism. In southern Italy, on the way home, he finally accomplishes his conjugal duty to Marceline—but it is of the utmost importance to note that this act takes place after he has wrestled with and thrashed a drunken coachman.

At home on his Norman farm Michel puts his new strength to work practicing in all things what he calls "a science of the perfect utilization of self through an intelligent restraint" (*RRS*, 411). He is relieved of his marital obligations by Marceline's pregnancy, and he enters into a warm virile relationship with the 17-year-old son of his farm manager. Together they plan to carry out certain projects in agricultural economy. Michel's latent homosexuality finds a sort of symbolic expression and a partial satisfaction when, one day, he paddles around barefoot in a pond helping Charles catch the eels that have been exposed by draining the pond.

The next major episode of the novel is the turning point in Michel's history. He meets Ménalque, a godlike figure who manifests and professes a doctrine of risk, expenditure, and egoism. Ménalque is a notorious homosexual. (His name, of course, recalls *Les Nourritures terrestres*, and still more pertinently Virgil's *Bucolics*.) In token of his authority over Michel he brings the scissors that Moktir stole from Marceline. In a single conversation he undermines the prudent plan of Michel's life and teaches him to despise his possessions and his expectations. On the night of their meeting Marceline suffers a miscarriage and becomes very ill.

The accident marks the end of her ascendancy in Michel's life. Ménalque plays no other role in the story than this one of being the means through which Michel discovers a little more of his hidden and repressed nature. He is a kind of demonic intercessor who could better be called a force, or an idea, than a character.

When Michel and Marceline return to the farm, Michel no longer has any thought for productive economy. He poaches game on his own lands with the disreputable young son of his farm manager. This relationship has the same homoerotic character as the one with Charles, but the setting of Michel's encounters with Alcide endows them with an illicit and clandestine value. Finally, restlessness overcomes him and, abandoning the farm, Michel drags the ailing Marceline away on a journey that leads them step by step back to Africa.

Michel's conduct this time is the reverse of what it was coming north out of Africa. He is no longer prudently building his health and strength but recklessly expending and risking both by drinking with the riffraff of Naples and Sicily, and sleeping in their company on tavern floors. On one occasion he frankly embraces and kisses his carriage driver. Back in Africa, he seeks out his former companions and, freeing them from want and subservience, he indulges their appetite for pleasure, as well as his own. Marceline, weakened by his demonic pursuit of satisfaction, dies; Michel consoles himself with the little boy Ali. It is in this manner that the heterosexual marriage is definitively destroyed and the homosexual encounter put in its place.

The essential action of the story is this protracted conversion from the normal, socially sponsored sexual relationship that is inimical to Michel's nature to the forbidden relationship that satisfies his native desires. The knowledge of who and what he is, and of what he must do to become who he is, comes in the form of impulses rather than decisions. The powers of clear vision and determination are stifled in him by his moral and intellectual culture, which has proscribed the solution that he is unconsciously striving to find.

It is in the conflict between the hero and his culture that Gide develops his accompaniment to the main action. This secondary conflict seems at times to override the major one because its terms are clearer and franker. Being more verbal than imagistic, and conscious rather than unconscious, it tends to seize tonal control of the narrative.

At the very beginning of the novel Michel is referred to as "the very learned Puritan," and as he begins to tell his story he mentions "the grave Huguenot teaching" given him by his mother. This is his moral capital:

a stock of austere, inflexible precepts. To his father he owes a similarly dogmatic training in classical philology, which has taught him to regard Athens and Rome as the two foci of human history.

Michel's bondage to his culture is symbolized by his marriage to Marceline, who represents the Christian ideal at its most excellent. Her virtues of devotion, abnegation, restraint, and pity are all expressions of the triumph of human weakness. To complete the image of submission Gide makes her a Catholic.

In going to North Africa, Michel crosses the frontier of his culture, and when he loses its protection and guidance he falls ill. His recovery is owed entirely to the assertion of a primitive power within him that is independent of traditional and collective values. This "authentic being" is discovered only when the veneer of acquired knowledge peels off. "There was more here than a convalescence; there was an augmentation, a recrudescence of life, the inflow of a richer, warmer blood which was to touch my thoughts, touch them one by one, penetrate everything, stir, color the most remote, delicate, and secret fibers of my being" (RRS, 399).

Michel's first task is to create physical strength, but concurrently he must reshape his moral and intellectual being to conform to that strength. The first stage in his moral revolution culminates in that "perfect utilization of self through an intelligent restraint" that he formulates in the midst of work on the farm and the preparation of the course that he will give at the Collège de France. This course entails a complete revision of his historical studies. He is no longer interested in the "abstract and neutral knowledge of the past." Philology is now a means of approaching the human personality of an earlier time. He is drawn more and more to the rough, uncultured Goths and especially to the rebellious and debauched young King Athalaric (A.D. 516–534). The thesis that he subsequently proposes is that culture, born of life, ends by stifling life and preventing the contact of mind with nature.

Michel's critical thought has in fact preceded and opened the way to a new conduct. His prudent, economical way of living is in conflict with this new conception of man. When he meets Ménalque after his first lecture his thought is: "The life, the least gesture of Ménalque, was it not a thousand times more eloquent than my course?" (RRS, 429). This new man enunciates a doctrine of radical individualism, sensualism,[7] and consumption that makes the ground give way under Michel's feet, as he puts it. From that moment forward, his thought and conduct are directed toward a new end: to discover what man is yet capable of. "And each day there grew in me the obscure feeling of untouched riches, covered over, hidden, smothered by cultures, decencies, moralities" (*RRS*, 457).

When Marceline says to him: "I understand your doctrine—for it is a doctrine now. It is fine, perhaps . . . but it suppresses the weak," Michel replies: "That is what is needed" (*RRS*, 459–60).

Up to this point, Michel's "immoralism"—his rejection of conventional Christian, middle-class morality and his effort to found a vital and authentic ethic on the acknowledgment and pursuit of desire and possibility—bears a close resemblance to the Nietzschean "revaluation of all values." Gide was familiar with Nietzsche's work and had written about it in 1898 in his "Letters à Angèle" (12). In later years he attempted to minimize the influence of Nietzsche on the book,[8] and in a sense he may have been justified in doing so. Ménalque could be called a genuine Nietzschean hero: his life is a risky pursuit of his own unrealized possibilities; he refuses the restraint of principles and retrospective judgments; and still he sublimates his more aggressive instincts, finding in ascetic self-denial a pleasure superior to that of indulgence and satisfaction. Michel is another matter. He is very unsure about the grounds of his revolt. With Marceline very near death, he reflects: "Ah, perhaps there would still be time. . . . Shall I not stop?—I have sought, I have found what makes my value: a sort of stubborn commitment to the worst" (*RRS*, 467). And to the friends who have answered his call for aid after his wife's death he says: "It seems to me sometimes that my real life has not yet begun. Drag me away from here now and give me reasons for existing. I no longer know how to find them. I have freed myself, possibly, but what difference does it make? I am suffering from this unutilized freedom. Believe me, it is not that I am overcome by my crime, if you choose to call it that—but I must prove to myself, that I have not overstepped my rights" (*RRS*, 471).

This speech, and indeed the whole development of the moral counter-current in the novel, imply that Michel's erotic impulse has not been able to conquer altogether his moral resistance. The erotic has achieved its end but at the cost of painful division within the hero's soul. He feels that he was right to follow his own desire and Ménalque's teaching, but the puritan in him is still alive, and he has not been proven wrong. It is on this ambiguous note that Gide ends his story.

The erotic conflict provides the basic energy of the novel. That is the problem that has to be solved. Unlike Gide, Michel is unable to create and play two lovers' roles. One has to be sacrificed to the other. But there is ambiguity in this, for Michel never fully recognizes that he is a

homosexual, and that his conduct is inspired by *distaste* for the heterosexual relationship he has passively accepted and by *desire* for love with a
boy. Instead of seeing his problem for what it is, he does something
extravagant: he poses it in terms of the entire moral and intellectual order
of his world. He effects a transference that makes his personal dilemma
appear, in the first place, to be directly related to the revolution in
Western moral thought that is represented principally by Friedrich
Nietzsche, and in the second place he assimilates it to the revolution in
historical thinking that established philosophical anthropology as a rival
to antiquarian historiography (another development in which Nietzsche
played a primary role).

It is this elevation and expansion of his personal anomaly that makes
Michel a hero. He attacks the very heart of the ideology of his society, and
he offers himself as an example of the new thought that he is advancing.
But his heroic rebellion, by its very vigor and honesty, turns Michel into
a satanic figure, for it leads him to destroy a gentle and unprotesting
victim who is sacrificed as a representative of her culture. The immola-
tion of Marceline casts a deep shadow over Michel's entire venture,
obscuring its value and making it profoundly questionable.

The result is, as we have seen, a downcast hero, one who has asserted
his notion of the truth and had it strike back at him in its consequences.
However, there is no inscrutable fate working against him, nor any
vengeful god. His difficulty is located entirely in the human condition,
and more specifically in the fact of human freedom. The problem is one
of conflicting rights among persons, and Michel's action in attempting
to resolve it becomes an episode in a continuing drama within Western
civilization. He illustrates with great force and clarity the manner in
which the conflict may appear to a particular man in a set of particular
historical circumstances.

Gide's artistry is abundantly displayed in *L'Immoraliste*, and nowhere
more impressively than in the narrative style. The story that he invents is
a romantic one in all essential respects—in its glorification of self, of
desire, and of will; in the excesses of action and thought that it depicts;
and in the ironies that it sustains from start to finish, the irony of Michel
and the irony of freedom. But the narrative is the work of a symbolist who
foregoes all rhetorical effects in order to make his language a purely
descriptive instrument. The voice that recounts is that of Michel, not
that of Gide. The haughty tone, so often stiff and artificial, is precisely
that of a scholarly puritan who is trying to set forth his turbulent inner
experience without knowing quite what it is all about. This austere,

insensitive voice is Gide's primary means in making the character of Michel. It is an unceasing evidence of what he is, a man whose action and thought are governed by impulses that he either fails to comprehend or misrepresents to himself.

The symbolical representation of ideas in the story is extraordinarily rich, and so too are the symbols that reveal the constant presence of the erotic motive. The composition of the narrative mirrors both the Gidean personality division and the antithetical character and action of Michel. Half the story is allotted to the productive, or angelic, phase of Michel's reform and half to the consumptive, or demonic, phase. The encounter with the mythical, archangelic Ménalque stands at the midpoint. The effect of this perfect division can hardly be overestimated. It gives the book an air of equilibrium and resolution that is at odds with the ambiguous sense of the story. Perhaps it is to this aspect of his work that Gide was alluding when, after declaring in his preface that he had intended to pose a problem and not to judge it or solve it, he added: "I use the word 'problem' here with reluctance. To tell the truth, in art there are no problems—of which the work of art is not a sufficient solution" (*RRS*, 367).

However important a work *L'Immoraliste* may appear to be today, at its publication it found few readers, and among those few some greeted it with hostile indignation. Gide felt that this reaction was wholly unjustified since he had not sought to make Michel's excesses seem anything but ignoble. The indignation, however, was probably provoked by something deeper than Michel's *conduct*. What he *does* is easy enough to judge and condemn. What he *is* would have been harder for Gide's indignant readers to get at. Michel's arrogance, anarchism, and insensitivity are essentially class attributes, and the readers of the novel were mostly of Michel's class. Their outcry was provoked really by Gide's association of their guilty being, which they had felt was adequately hidden, with guilty deeds that could not be concealed.

La Porte étroite

If Gide offended the sensibilities of his class with *L'Immoraliste*, he made ample recompense for the injury with a second psychological novel, *La Porte étroite* (*Strait Is the Gate*) (1909). In its emphasis on dignity, purity, self-sacrifice, and pious renunciation, this book offered to middle-class readers a very flattering portrait of their ideals. This again was not Gide's primary, or even his secondary, purpose, but it was nonetheless a fact, and it had a lot to do with the book's popularity. Its obvious Protestant (or as Claudel said, Jansenist) orientation was no real impediment to its reception by a public who were never tired of seeing their Christian character revealed.

However, he had earlier insisted that *La Porte étroite* was conceived as a twin and necessary sequel to *L'Immoraliste.* In the outline of a preface (that never appeared) the following statement appears:

> Those who were captivated by my *Immoraliste* cannot forgive me for *La Porte étroite.* However, I cannot separate these two books in my mind; I bore them together; they complement and sustain each other; it is in the excess of the one that I found a sort of permission for the excess of the other. If the author had been able to produce them simultaneously, as they were conceived, he would doubtless have escaped a rather serious misunderstanding: whereas he was occupied only with his art . . . a certain public, arrested by the choice of subjects, saw in it the indication of an evolution, of a return to earlier preoccupations, of a palinode. (*OC*, 6:361)

The "misunderstanding" provoked by *La Porte étroite* is much the same as the one that arose with *L'Immoraliste.* The clue to both is perhaps to be found in the term "excess." Guerard, in his commentary on *L'Immoraliste*, began by remarking that previous criticism had systematically ignored the sexual complex that is at its center.[9] The same thing has been true of *La Porte étroite*, with only a little more justification. The reason why Gide conceived the two books together and felt bound to insist on their complementarity is that they represent the two solutions of his own erotic complex. *L'Immoraliste* revealed the strategy of Corydon; *La Porte étroite* contains that of Tristan.

La Porte étroite presents a considerably more limited action than *L'Immoraliste.* Reduced to the essential, it comprises the reiterated attempts of Jérôme to win Alissa's consent to marriage and her hesitations, deferments, and refusals of his proposal. Everything takes place within the intimate confines of a family group.

The strategic problem that Gide assumed in the novel is more difficult in some ways than that of *L'Immoraliste*, if for no other reason than that Catharism was very little understood by the world to which he addressed himself (less understood probably than homosexuality), and it could not therefore be anything but an ambiguous motive. His problem was to depict a heterosexual love that was at once passionate and pure, like his own love for Madeleine Gide. He intensified the personal character of the story by borrowing liberally from his own life. Alissa and Jérôme are first cousins; she is rather older than he, and she resembles Jérôme's dead mother.

The first step in Gide's strategy is to place a severe ban on the sensual expression of love. To this end he begins his story by recounting, through Jérôme's lips, the shocking behavior of Alissa's Creole mother. One day when Jérôme was still a growing boy she tried to seduce him. Another day, entering the house unexpectedly, he saw her with her lover. On that day he learned that Alissa knew about her mother's conduct and was trying to conceal it from her father. It was in this circumstance that Jérôme made his first gesture of love toward Alissa, and that she accepted his devotion. Their love is thus founded on the refusal of the sensual.

Immediately following this incident Jérôme's account reveals another restraint put upon sexual love. He and Alissa hear together a sermon made upon the text, "Strive to enter by the narrow door"; and in the vision that it calls up in Jérôme's mind he sees himself and Alissa, clad in white, walking hand in hand toward a distant goal. After the service, he flees from Alissa, "thinking to merit her more by going away from her immediately" (*RRS*, 506). He adds that this austere discipline is easy for him: "It was as natural for me to restrain myself as for others to give in, and that rigor to which I was subjected, far from disheartening me, was gratifying. I sought from the future not so much happiness as the infinite effort to attain it and already mixed up in my thoughts happiness and virtue" (*RRS*, 506). The desire that he feels for Alissa is not to *possess* her but to *deserve* her.

What this amounts to is that Gide is bringing the full weight of Jérôme's Calvinist upbringing to bear upon the suppression of sexual desire and at the same time leading him to regard Alissa as the reward of his virtuous continence. He tells Juliette, Alissa's sister: "But I never talk to her about that! Never; that is why we are not yet engaged; there is never any question of marriage between us; or of what we will do afterwards. Oh, Juliette! Life with her seems so beautiful to me that I don't dare . . . do you understand? . . . that I don't dare speak of it to her" (*RRS*, 519).

We would not go far wrong in calling this the stereotype of puritan eroticism. Jérôme's ready acceptance of discipline and his delight in renunciation are essential to the accomplishment of the novel's design. During his long separation from Alissa he says: "In truth I bore joyfully the rather severe discipline to which we were subjected. I stiffened my back against it all and in the letters I wrote to Alissa complained only about our separation. And we even found in the length of that separation a trial worthy of our courage" (*RRS*, 550).

In the final stage of Alissa's campaign of refusal when she urges him to believe that they are not made for a simple, earthly happiness, he is not convinced by her reasoning, but he still must rise to her challenge. "Against the snare of virtue," he says, "I was defenseless. Any sort of heroism, by dazzling me, attracted me—for I did not separate it from love" (*RRS*, 565). It is only later that he realizes that Alissa has led him to a dizzy height from which she can more easily escape him altogether.

Gide represented in Jérôme the best and the worst of that indestructible particle of Calvinist morality that remained in his own nature. Jérôme's character exhibits very convincingly the puritan's love of disciplined effort for its own sake and his willingness to give up present joy for a future reward, which, however, carries no guarantee. (Gide called it "that sort of superior infatuation, of heady scorn for all rewards."[10] The very thought of a reward for virtue was, in his view, an offense to the puritan's sensibilities.) But he also demonstrates how such a penchant toward abstract virtue undermines the sense of reality and makes the subject the dupe of his own goal. In *La Porte étroite* there is no rebellion against a traditional morality. Puritanism is Tristan's primary ally.

The major effect in the plot, however, is the character of Alissa. She is by no means so easy to outline as Jérôme. To begin with, the central motive of her personality is not moral but religious. It is an assertive, enterprising trait. Gide exposes her religiousness and the determinations that spring from it in such a way as to reveal their radical ambivalence.

The discovery of her mother's looseness has to be considered an effective inhibition upon Alissa's erotic life, but Gide did not allow it to assume an obvious role. Once the fact is related there are few references made to it, and Alissa's reluctance to marry is apparently motivated by other desires. But in this matter Gide played a very sly game, for the trauma is there, and we have no reason whatever to discount its force. Furthermore, Alissa's unconscious resistance is revealed to her in a dream which she recounts to Jérôme: "I had a sad dream. I was alive and you were dead. . . . It was frightful; it was so impossible that I finally managed to make it that you were only absent. We were separated and I felt that there was no way to join you; I was trying to find a way, and I made such an effort to succeed that it woke me up" (*RRS*, 516).

The rest of the story is, in a sense, nothing more than a lengthy reenactment of this dream. Alissa's character and conduct develop altogether as functions of her deep-seated reluctance to marry. First she puts

Jérôme off by her concern for his future: a marriage entered into too early may hinder his professional career. She discovers a less equivocal form of self-sacrifice when she learns that her younger sister Juliette is in love with Jérôme. Alissa declares her intention to withdraw in Juliette's favor; but Juliette outplays her at the game of renunciation and accepts the proposal of a middle-aged suitor.

Juliette's refusal of her sacrifice is a severe defeat for Alissa. She must therefore invent a different plan of retreat. Gide very delicately foreshadows her change of style when she mistakenly identifies some verses of Racine as being by Corneille. This error suggests that she has already shifted her campaign from the tactic of heroic devotion and self-sacrifice to one of mystical renunciation of the world.

During the period of their separation Alissa's letters to Jérôme are often surprisingly affectionate, but in their infrequent meetings she is strained and distant. After one such encounter she writes him: "In despair I came back in to write you . . . that I didn't want to write to you any more . . . a letter of farewell . . . because I finally felt too keenly that our correspondence was just a great mirage, that each of us was writing, alas, only to himself, and that. . . . Jérôme! Jérôme! Oh, that we remained always apart!" (*RRS*, 559).

This curious intuition of narcissism points again to the unconscious basis of Alissa's withdrawal. At this point she is exhibiting a desire to yield to affection, but her desire is countered by a resistance for which she has no name.

At her next meeting with Jérôme she has found its name. She tells him that no matter how happy she feels in his presence she knows that they were not born for happiness. "What can be preferable to happiness?" Jérôme asks. "Holiness," she replies (*RRS*, 563–64). When Jérôme protests that everything good in him originates in his love for her, Alissa writes him: "But, my dear, holiness is not a choice: it is an OBLIGATION. . . . If you are the man I think you are, you won't be able to back away from it either" (*RRS*, 565).

From that moment forward Alissa sets out to degrade the image of herself that Jérôme has loved. She gives up the music and the poetry that had once been their closest bond and reads only books of the most dismally pious sort. It was Pascal, she says, who set her on the right path. She neglects her person and presses Jérôme, when they at length meet, to admit that he loves her less.

Three years later Jérôme sees Alissa for the last time before her death. She is terribly faded, but at the same time more sentimental than she has been with him since their childhood. But when he embraces her she cries: "Have pity on us, my dear! Oh, don't spoil our love" (*RRS*, 577). Then she assures him that God has reserved them for something better.

The exercise of mortification has finally accomplished what virtuous restraint and self-effacement could not do. Alissa has evaded the sexual pact and yet preserved her love for Jérôme. To make quite sure that her erotic passion is not lost from sight Gide appends to Jérôme's narrative a journal in which Alissa recapitulates the whole drama. Her version is brief but intensely passionate. It throws a light upon her character that we have nowhere seen in the preceding pages, not even in her letters. At times she has desired Jérôme: "Poor Jérôme! If he just knew that sometimes he had only to make one gesture, and that sometimes I am expecting that gesture" (*RRS*, 586). But then she was horrified by the resemblance she felt between herself and her mother. After that she was afraid of standing between Jérôme and God. And following that there is confusion: "The reasons that make me run from him? I no longer believe in them. . . . And yet I go on running from him, sadly, and without understanding why I do it" (*RRS*, 587). She confirms on many a page the suspicion we have had that her ascetic withdrawal was calculated not to bring her closer to God but to alienate Jérôme. It is only at the very end that the religious character of her renunciation seems to take hold of her. But even so she is filled with doubt about whether she really had to renounce Jérôme in order to find blessedness.

The "Journal of Alissa" is Gide's most prestigious effect in *La Porte étroite*. It depends of course for its clarity on the wonderfully low-keyed narrative of Jérôme, but if we are in the end genuinely convinced that the novel depicts a conflict between a mystical vocation and secular happiness, it is the journal's air of confusion and doubt and its tone of passionate entreaty that make the point. *La Porte étroite* was, and is, generally thought to be a "religious" work. Even Gide referred to it in later years as "the critique of a certain mystic tendency" (*OC*, 13:439), and shortly after its publication he wrote to Paul Claudel: "You recognize that a religious and pure emotion prompts my book; the second acknowledgment, which I consider equally important, is that the very drama of the book exists only by virtue of its unorthodoxy. . . . Protestantism is a school of heroism whose error I think my book depicts rather well" (Claudel-Gide, 103–4).

These statements can only mean that Gide had so well convinced his early readers that they in turn convinced him by their praise. I have already suggested that they were eager to see their class represented as virtuous, modest, and self-sacrificing; and they were probably not inclined to look for the *reason* of all this, especially when it was concealed with a little subtlety. The truth is that Gide accomplished in *La Porte étroite* a transposition of interest that is in every respect comparable to what he did in *L'Immoraliste*. In the earlier book one solution of his personal sexual complex turned into something resembling a Nietzschean critique of bourgeois morals. In *La Porte étroite* the complementary solution of his complex becomes a religious vocation—after having first been an ascetic moral attitude. This sort of transference has a little the air of a tour de force, but we must remember that it is fully authenticated by Gide's personal psychology, and that there is abundant evidence to indicate that displacements of a similar character are frequent in milieus where sexual problems are repressed and discourses on moral and spiritual values are the daily fare. *La Porte étroite* depicts a more common transposition than the one in *L'Immoraliste*, which is no doubt the reason for its unflagging popularity. By presenting Pascal as the model of Alissa's conversion Gide made the shift easy to recognize.

Viewed in depth, however, the central problem of the novel is the one that Gide confronted in his own life: how to resolve the oedipal complex in such a way as to retain its form and yet rid it of repression and guilt. Gide's private solution of the problem involved a deception, as we know. In his book there is a kind of deception too, but it is a noble one that can be explained aloud. Neither Jérôme nor Alissa stands unequivocally for Gide in this symbolic drama. They simply share between them the best motives that he could allege for chastity in marriage. Jérôme embodies the virtues of puritanism: the willingness to devote himself to a love without reward and to regard abstention from pleasure as good in itself. Alissa's nature is more fervent, more religious. She does not abstain from the joy of love: she renounces it in favor of something better. Her love includes Jérôme but reaches far beyond him toward another goal. Both characters represent motives of Gide's personality, but at the same time both are expressed in the negative mode of dissolution and self-loss.

This Catharist drama remains, nonetheless, heavily ironic. The conduct of the lovers is what it should be according to the doctrine of purity—but no such doctrine exists for Jérôme and Alissa! They have motives strong enough to keep desire in abeyance, but those motives are unclear. Therefore they must deceive and disappoint each other and sustain doubt and uncertainty in their own minds. it is in this total complex that we see the Gidean *poesis*: their love affair is a symbol of the personality of the neurotic Narcissus analyzed and dramatized in such a way as to reveal its radical ambivalence and ambiguity.

One other feature of the novel's internal design deserves special mention: the fortune of Juliette. She is made of much the same stuff as Alissa and Jérôme. In refusing Alissa's sacrifice and in responding with a sacrifice of her own she proves her character. Paradoxically, however, renouncing Jérôme leads her out of the puritan world of self-denial and into one that is still pagan enough to accept pleasure and joy without reserve or remorse. The sight of Juliette's happiness causes Alissa to doubt very seriously the value of her own decision to seek a satisfaction beyond the immediate and the worldly.

But the picture of Juliette's happiness is more than a device to stir up uncertainty in Alissa. It is a distinct dimension in the novel. Juliette represents the way out of the morass of sexual repression, narcissistic uncertainty, and puritanical restraint which breeds dissatisfaction with this world and aspiration toward another one. In the Gidean psychology it is not essentially marriage that constitutes the way out. That is merely the appropriate image for this novel. Rather it is the act of yielding to one's own senses and to the desires of others. At best this is to be interpreted not as hedonism but as an act of faith in reality, a refusal of puritanical pride and "useless heroism."

The motif of mobility, of crossing the cultural frontier, emblemized the erotic and intellectual rebellion in *L'Immoraliste*. In *La Porte étroite* it is, on the contrary, a symbol of fixity and of being enclosed that concentrates the action of the story into a single image. The walled garden of the Bucolin house at Fongueusemare is the scene of several crucial dialogues, and this fact alone indicates is central importance in the novel. Aside from this specific use, it is a symbol of the maternal body. (A closed garden is likely to have this value in any imaginative context.) As such, it directs our thought to the Oedipus complex which is the underlying motive of the story. Secondarily, the garden may be considered a metaphor of the Calvinist community. Within it's walls, the "family," which has separated itself from the universe of men, readily falls victim of its own delusions and errors.

The major effect of Gide's artistry, however, is the narrative itself. Everything depends on statement and tone of voice in *La Porte étroite*, for there is scarcely any other kind of action. In 1905, four years before the book's publication, Gide was already struggling with the narrative style. "I spend hours on a group of sentences that I will turn completely around the next day. The scene in Geneviève's [!] room particularly, when he finds her on her knees, caused me extreme difficulty. But I admire now everything that I succeeded in *not saying in it*, in HOLDING BACK" (*J*, 170). The haunting power of *La Porte étroite* is explained very largely by this entry—especially by the last sentence.

Isabelle

Gide wrote *Isabelle* between April and November of 1910. His primary motivation and point of departure are most probably stated in a passage of his *Journal* dated 7 November 1909, where he confided his need to cleanse his mind of the sublime language of *La Porte étroite*. The exalted expression that he had given to his Catharist soul in that novel demanded an antidote. This is by now a familiar movement in Gide's psyche. It is the motor that drove his work and directed its evolution. After every one of the passionate works that fill this middle period of his creative life he felt compelled to compensate for the excesses he had committed in the service of its central idea by writing a new book in a different tone dedicated to an idea that refuted or at least diminished the force of the former work. He wrote *Saül*, he said, as an "antidote" and "counterpoise" to *Les Nourritures terrestres*, and *La Porte étroite* sprang from a need to assert his angelic nature against the demonic frenzy of *L'Immoraliste*.

If this need to restore harmony and equilibrium among the powers of his personality gave the initial impetus to the composition of *Isabelle*, something happened, or something did not happen, before the book was finished that greatly reduced its capacity to satisfy that requirement and robbed it of much of its aesthetic luster. In other words, *Isabelle* is by no means so powerful a work as its predecessors, *L'Immoraliste* and *La Porte étroite*, or its successors in the same genre, *La Symphonie pastorale* and *L'Ecole des femmes*. The reason for the book's weakness is twofold. First, Gide's desire to write a counterstatement to *La Porte étroite* had become focused on his set of dialogues on homosexuality, entitled *Corydon*, which, according to an entry in his *Journal* dated 12 July 1910, he felt to be "indispensable" and urgent. This feeling no doubt robbed *Isabelle* of that passionate personal commitment that was always the source of greatness in his work. Several years later, in 1914, he confided to Charles Du Bos: "There is only one of my books which was made, so to speak, from the outside. That is *Isabelle*. I had seen the story of the book, and I wrote it rather as an exercise to gain skill. That is perceptible in it."[11] He could hardly have said more explicitly that the story did not derive from his inward debates.

The other factor that contributed to the weakness of *Isabelle* is more immediately visible in the writing of the story, in its style and subject matter. The characters and the basic details of the narrative were historically true and had been known to Gide since his childhood. Four elderly people, two sisters and their husbands, occupied the country estate contiguous to that of his grandparents in Normandy. They had living with them the grandson of one of the couples. This couple's daughter lived elsewhere and paid only fleeting visits to her parents and her child. The drama that Gide intended to exploit in their life was also historically accurate: the estate was gradually reduced to ruin by the profligacy of its owners. What was it that attracted Gide to this family history? Was it the theme of moral decadence, which is so immediately apparent? If it was that, he certainly made no attempt to develop it in his story. In the last chapter he recounts with some pathos the sale first of the magnificent trees, then of the house and its furnishings, but without clearly assigning blame for the event, treating it rather as the effect of a general misfortune that afflicts the family who had owned and occupied the domain.

The reason for Gide's hesitancy to pursue the theme of moral decline may very well lie in the fact that a few years earlier in *L'Immoraliste* he had depicted the devastation of a Norman estate as a phase in Michel's conquest of freedom and power through his ruthless rejection of the bonds that his class had placed upon him: his intellectual formation, his property, his wife, his child. Considering how important that book had been in Gide's personal growth, it would not be surprising if he refused to write a story that might have cast doubt on its validity.

The events and the tone of *Isabelle* suggest, in the early chapters certainly, that Gide had no very clear or compelling idea in mind as he began to write; that he was, as he said to Charles Du Bos, merely trying to improve his narrative skills. There is even an air of imitation in the initial situation that he exposes. A young scholar—who is also an aspiring novelist—is invited to a remote country estate to examine some documents belonging to a retired historian who lives there with his wife, his wife's sister, and her husband, their crippled and retarded grandson, a priest who is the child's tutor, a housekeeper, and a couple of servants. The Gothic atmosphere surrounding this strange company and their domain is vaguely reminiscent of the beginning of Edgar Allan Poe's "Fall of the House of Usher" and even more insistently of some of the tales of Henri de Régnier, one of the major symbolists whom Gide had known and admired since his youth. (Gide revealed in a letter to Paul Valéry that the ruined domain in which he set *Isabelle* made him feel the presence of Régnier's stories [*RRS*, 1160].)

An erotic theme is introduced into the scene of stasis and decrepitude when the child, Casimir, shows Gerard a miniature portrait of his absent mother, Isabelle. Gerard is instantly captivated by her exquisite beauty. His fortuitous discovery of a letter that she had left for her lover in their secret mailbox leads to his learning their plan to elope, the murder of her young lover by the household gardener, the birth of her illegitimate child, and finally her departure from her parents' home.

At this point, after six chapters, Gide abruptly dropped the Gothic character of his romance and set about liquidating the erotic current that had animated it almost from its beginning. In a final chapter he reverted to what must have been his original design, the theme of moral decadence; and he turned then the full force of his contempt upon Isabelle, who is revealed as responsible for her lover's death and guilty of abandoning her child in order to pursue a career of sexual promiscuity and of recklessly despoiling her family estate. It is Gerard in the end who saves one small farm within the property to assure a refuge for Isabelle's senile and paralyzed mother, for the boy Casimir, and for the two old servants who care for them.

Isabelle stands distinctly apart from all the rest of Gide's work in being the only element in it that lacks a coherent plan. That is not to say that the story is without a motive. The driving force that led him to start the tale and to see it through is revealed in its end. It has its source in the ambivalence that was the crucible of all his imaginative work. *Isabelle* is an incident, a partial manifestation, of that lifelong war in Gide between his dependence on his mother and his veneration of her and her surrogate, on the one hand, and on the other, his refusal of that galling bondage and the assertion of his personal liberty. *Isabelle*, as he wrote in his diary, was born of the need to clear his mind of the purity and elevation of *La Porte étroite*—which had been written under the impulsion of his need to reaffirm his Catharist vocation against the doctrine of sexual freedom that he had illustrated in *L'Immoraliste*. In *La Porte étroite* he had embodied his passionate desire for purity in love in the female figure of Alissa. Having done it, and done it with such power that even he must have been a little in awe of his own success, a reaction of rancor took hold of him, a need to sully his sublime creation—who was, of course, himself, but the self who was in thrall to the feminine. Thus was the role of Isabelle defined in his mind. But the image of her degradation had already been seriously compromised by Gerard's romantic vision of her person. The artistic problem that Gide had made for himself arose from the fact that he wished also, as he wrote a good many years later, to create an irony in *Isabelle*, "the critique of a certain form of the romantic imagination" (*OC*, 13:439–40). Gerard's consciousness is, of course, the medium in which this irony is articulated; and it is to some extent successfully done, in spite of the excessive rapidity with which Gerard's eyes are opened to the truth of Isabelle at the end. But the two designs are fundamentally imcompatible. They belong to two different stories, the one having its focus in Gerard's mind and the other in Isabelle's conduct. Whatever serves the one must necessarily distract from the other.

Failures, in literature as in anything else, can be instructive. This one, however, is mostly silent. Why did Gide's usually impeccable aesthetic sense fail him in this work? His greatness as a literary artist was concentrated in his ability to discover the tone and the images that were adequate to the idea that he wished to articulate. In *Isabelle* the idea languishes unseen until the very last pages while the author works in a picturesque genre that did not contribute to his primary purpose. By then it was to late to repair the damage—and Gide was aware of that fact. In his *Journal* on 14 November 1910 he wrote: "Finished my novel day before yesterday evening—with too much facility, which makes me fear that I have not put in the last pages everything that I was *charged* with putting there." This is the best critical judgment that can be made of *Isabelle*.

Les Caves du Vatican

Gide set great store by *Les Caves du Vatican* (*Lafcadio's Adventures*) (1914). Like *Paludes, Les Nourritures terrestres*, and *Saül*, it encountered hostility, incomprehension, and depreciatory comment upon its publication; and even when *Les Nourritures* had finally found a receptive public after World War I, *Les Caves* was still waiting for its fortunes to turn. Gide's conviction, expressed in the early twenties, was that it "could wait" (*OC*, 13:443).

But even as he wrote those words the book was being read by a young public upon whom its impact would be immeasurable. It became one of the bases of the great postwar rebellion against the norms of the middle class which erupted first in dada and surrealism, then later in the adventurous lives and books of Montherlant, Saint-Exupéry, Céline,

Malraux, and others. The figure of Lafcadio had assumed before 1930 the proportions of a legend. The dissatisfaction and restlessness of a new generation were exemplified in his attitudes and actions. He is the Julien Sorel and the Raskolnikov of his time, and like them he is a profoundly romantic creation.

Still, *Les Caves* is the book that is least "at home" in the romantic period of Gide's work. On the one hand, its rollicking humor and keen satire are vivid reminders of the satirical works of the decadent period Gide underscored the resemblance of the novel to *Paludes* and *Le Prométhée mal enchaîné* by designating all three as *soties* upon the publication of *Les Caves* in 1914. (He reported to Charles Du Bos that he had begun to plot *Les Caves* in 1893 when he was working on *Paludes* [Du Bos, 162–63].) On the other hand, the panoramic view of the bourgeois universe and the biting criticism of its values project *Les Caves* into the current of critical realism in Gide's fiction and relate it to *Les Faux-Monnayeurs*, which appeared 11 years later.

Les Caves is in fact the central work of Gide's literary life, the "crossroads" of his several styles. It is a hilarious farce, an entrancing adventure story, and an acute novel of manners. It does not readily lend itself to commentary. Its humor and its seriousness are so adroitly combined and controlled that any analysis is likely to disrupt their union and exalt the one to the disadvantage of the other. The great poetic themes of the Gidean personality—erotic fantasy, religious fervor, moral unrest—are all represented in the novel, but they are completely under the governance of the critical intellect. It is in fact the feat of *Paludes* that Gide repeats in *Les Caves*, only on a much larger scale. The subject of his satire is, in the last analysis, himself—his activities, his tastes, the very structure of his life—but the whole business is very artfully concealed behind a remarkable cast of burlesque figures.

Three quadragenarians (Gide was 44 when *Les Caves* appeared) and one gilded youth share the outstanding traits of the public and the private Gide. Julius de Baraglioul is a novelist who is toying with the theme of immoralism. Anthime Armand-Dubois, an amateur scientist, is proving experimentally the thesis that all motivations are ultimately physiological. (Something of this sort appears in *Corydon*, Gide's essay on homosexuality.) Amédée Fleurissoire practices Catharism in his marriage. In addition, each of them acts out some significant aspect of Gide's life. Fleurissoire makes a great journey to the South, and there is introduced to the mystery of sexual pleasure. Armand-Dubois's conversion from scientific atheism to Christian belief and practice is a simplified image of the movement that went on without cease in Gide's soul. Julius de Baraglioul is smarting under the disappointment of an unsuccessful book, and in reaction is plotting a new book that will upset the very values that the first advanced. All of Gide's latent rebelliousness, his thirst for freedom, and his claim to moral autonomy are poured into the romantic figure of Lafcadio Wluiki, who represents the instinctive, impulsive adolescent that Gide concealed within himself most of the time.

In addition to offering comical glimpses of the Gidean person, these four "fools" are also typical expressions of the middle-class character. (Julius's title, like most European titles, is purely vestigial.) Their occupations—writer, scientist, small manufacturer—make a nicely rounded picture of the petty bourgeoisie. What is most bourgeois about them, however, is their devotion to authorities that repose on dogma and mystery: Catholicism above all, but in the case of Anthime, science and freemasonry too.

Lafcadio appears to be the antithesis of these right-thinking bourgeois. He acknowledges no authority but his own impulses. Nevertheless, he represents something quite as fundamental to the bourgeoisie as the orthodoxy of his half-brother Julius and his victim, Fleurissoire. He embodies the latent anarchism of his class, its arrogant self-interest, and its lack of ethical sensitivity (as opposed to its moral righteousness). He murders a man without a qualm because he feels no human kinship with him. ("What have I in common with that dirty scarecrow?"—*RRS*, 825.) This episode is a symbolical approximation of the middle-class attitude toward whomever it cannot identify as being one of its own kind.

Gide is entirely negative in his social criticism. He does not depict the opposition between working class and bourgeoisie; he simply exposes the character of the latter class in its reverence for hierarchy and its deficient ethical sense. The thought of class conflict seems to have been present in his mind, however, since he placed his story in the period immediately following the issuance of Pope Leo XIII's encyclical, "Rerum Novarum" (1891). This document, though not precisely republican in its sentiments, urged a reconciliation between capitalist (gold-capital) and worker (labor-capital) through the practice of Christian charity. The success of the hoax that Protos and his confederates are working on a gullible proprietor-investor class is due very considerably to the radical position expressed in the papal encyclical. The victims of the confidence game cannot conceive that the highest authority of *their* world could betray them by pleading the interests of men from another world. He must be an impostor.

If we stop at this point to consider what Gide has done in *Les Caves* we shall see that, through a familiar operation of his genius, he has directed our interest away from and beyond the satirical exposé of his own life and person and toward a scalding criticism of his class. This undertaking implies the existence of a critic who is able to observe and estimate the foibles of the "fools" who are portrayed in the novel; and this critic is, of course, André Gide. Gide is therefore both the archetypal "fool" of the novel and the satirist who reveals the court of fools to us. In this duality we see an example of narcissism converted to the creation of poetry and art. The adjective "Protean" that has often been employed to describe the variability of Gide's motives from one book to another is most appropriately applied to *Les Caves*. Not only are all of the major characters "forms" of Gide, but the critic himself is represented in the story by the demonic manipulator who sets the whole affair in motion and whose name is almost Proteus.

Protos introduces into the stable and orderly world of the "crustaceans" an antiauthority that breeds consternation on every side. The hoax about the pope's abduction is the basis of a criminal confidence racket to extract money from the faithful; but it produces effects out of all proportion to this modest aim. With the true pope presumed a prisoner and a false one in his place, there is no voice to tell men what is true for all of them. Each man has to become his own authority; in other words, he has to assume his freedom and act according to his own sense of right and obligation. The results of this extraordinary "vacation" are stunning. During the brief pontificate of the false pope, Armand-Dubois is converted from absolute atheism to absolute belief. He becomes as submissive to ecclesiastical authority as he had been to the propositions that governed his scientific research. Julius de Baraglioul, the defender of order and authority, falls under the spell of Lafcadio and plots a novel of anarchy and violence. Amédée Fleurissoire, a timid provincial, is so distressed by the fate of the Holy Father that he leaves home alone and makes his way to Rome to join the perilous "Crusade for the Deliverance of the Pope." He endures ordeals, loses his purity, becomes involved in intrigue, and is finally destroyed by Lafcadio's moral experimentation.

What happens, in essence, is that each of the three men reveals that he is capable of being the very contrary of what he has considered to be his unalterable person. The truth implied in their metamorphoses is that they are free to choose and to create their own beings, that individual persons and human societies are nothing but arbitrary creations in which the artifices, or illusions, of tradition, hierarchy, and consistency mask the underlying fact of freedom. No one of them seems capable of evaluating his adventure in just this way, however. When they learn that they have been living under an exceptional "suspension of the rules," both Julius de Baraglioul and Anthime Armand-Dubois revert to their former types. No doubt Fleurissoire, had he lived to learn that he was the victim of a hoax, would have done the same.

Protos, the master confidence man, discloses his understanding of the delusion and the compulsion upon which civilized life is based when, in his disguise as Defouqueblize, professor of criminal law, he treats Lafcadio to an extemporaneous discourse on the theme "People in society must live counterfeit lives for their own good." Our friends and relatives, he says, "oppose to our uncivil sincerity an image of us for which we are only half responsible, which resembles us very little, the limits of which, however, it is indecent to exceed." "Do you know what it takes to turn a gentleman into a rogue?" he asks. "A removal from his normal surroundings, a moment of forgetfulness are enough. Yes, sir, a lapse of memory and sincerity begins to appear! the cessation of a continuity; a simple interruption of the current" (RRS, 853–54). These observations have something to do with Protos's action, of course, but they are mainly pertinent to Gide's critique of his society.

Lafcadio, listening to Protos, realizes that he has been caught in the trap with the "crustaceans." His only advantage over them is that he knows more or less what has happened to him. It is not that he did not possess the sense of his own freedom, but rather that he exaggerated and idealized it beyond measure. Lafcadio embodies the desire for absolute freedom and total anarchy that haunts the dreams of the bourgeoisie. He extends the habit of excluding others from his schemes to the point of solipsism. His origins and upbringing have been such that he has no nationality and no father; therefore he is subservient to no overlord. His formation has made him fluent in several languages, quick-witted in arithmetic and games, and scornful of literature. He has had no moral instruction. He punishes himself, but only for allowing others to see who he is, what he knows, and how he feels. He acts spontaneously, according to the desire, need, or whim of the moment; but he does not linger to see the sequel of his actions. He is, in short, the image of a perfect human freedom, aimless, careless, and unaccountable. He is the invisible self of the correct, right-thinking bourgeoisie. When he theorizes that he can destroy a stranger without being discovered, simply because no pressing need drives him to the act, and because he will go on his way and not look back, he is enunciating the very principle upon which the exploiting class acts in its relations with the exploited.

Lafcadio, however, is not only this caricature of middle-class anarchism. He also embodies the Gidean ideal of sincerity, which is to say, of authentic being and spontaneous behavior. In addition, he is the image of Gide's erotic wishes. His figure and the sense of his adventure are therefore complex and ambiguous.

Gide exposes Lafcadio's ethical vacancy to the critique of consequences. The young hero discovers that the victim of his casual murder is by no means the stranger and the nonentity he had assumed him to be. Fleurissoire turns out to be the brother-in-law of Julius de Baraglioul, Lafcadio's recently found half-brother, with whom he would like to create a relationship of mutual affection and regard. The murdered man was also a useful tool to Protos, Lafcadio's former schoolmate; and he had become the lover of Lafcadio's former mistress, Carola Venitequa. Lafcadio finds himself therefore bound up in an inescapable web of relations with his victim. He is forced to recognize that the man had a place and a function in the world, that he had a certain human value. As a result of his crime, Lafcadio loses the esteem of his half-brother and is threatened with having to obey the demands of the archcriminal Protos or face legal judgment and imprisonment. He escapes those threats only by chance.

What Gide repudiates in Lafcadio is his class-determined outlook: his arrogant pretension to impunity and his insensitivity to human value outside the sphere of his private interests. What he preserves are his independence from dogmatic authorities, his taste for decision and action, and his spontaneity. In other words, he saved what he loved in his young hero and chastised what he hated. He administered a lesson designed to reveal to him a certain inescapable truth about the human condition and thus made him freer than he was before. In his primitive form Lafcadio was a caricature of human freedom. He experienced only his own freedom within the present instant, and he thought that it was absolute. After his crime he is in a position to see freedom from the perspectives of humanity and history, with some knowledge, that is, of the interdependence of human destinies. His adventure leads from innocence (the terrible innocence of the unbaptized) and anarchy to the possibility of an ethical existence.

The theme of Lafcadio's initiation to error and remorse is not so humorous as that of the liberation of the "crustaceans." It is even rather somber and terrible at moments. The one is the critique of the "counterfeit" life, the refusal of freedom and sincerity; the other is the critique of anarchism and solipsism, the refusal of ethics. Together they form a commentary on the epigraph that Gide (to illustrate Book 5 of his novel) borrowed from Joseph Conrad's *Lord Jim*: "the question is not how to get cured [from being ourselves], but how to live."

The critical motive is overriding in *Les Caves.* It commands and holds in subjection all the primary assertions of Gide's ego. The poetic impulse to reveal himself in the disguise of fictional characters and situations is tightly controlled by the satiric-burlesque genius. He exposes his erotic tastes and relations to an unstinting ridicule. Amédée Fleurissoire offers a comical travesty of the Catharist marriage. All three "crustaceans" betray an unconscious inclination to homosexuality, Armand-Dubois in his attachment to the urchin Beppo, Fleurissoire in his devotion to his friend and associate Blafaphas (which leads him to renounce sexual congress with his wife), de Baraglioul in his fascination with Lafcadio. This taste is laughable in them because it is timid and unaware of itself, and because it is incongruous with their sedate matrimonial circumstances.

We should note, however, that Gide does not expose all of his erotic interests to ridicule. There is still the figure of Lafcadio who captivates more or less every male he encounters—his mother's lovers, Protos, Julius, the priest of Coviliaglio—and who is perfectly aware of the fact and not at all resistant to it. Gide invested in Lafcadio the better part of his pedophilia and in so doing defended it against the bite of his own ridicule.

Religious fervor also falls under the empire of comedy and satire. A conversion so radical, so complete, and so abrupt as that of Armand-Dubois has scarcely been seen since the seventeenth century. Gide puts no doubt upon its sincerity; he is content to expose its incongruity and the physical discomforts and loss of status that it imposes on the convert and his loyal wife. Anthime's humble piety forms a comical contrast with Véronique's disillusionment and the indignation of Julius when he discovers how low the Catholic church has allowed them to sink. Amédée Fleurissoire (when he sets out to deliver the pope) displays the aggressive fervor that faith does sometimes inspire, but his pitiful unfitness for the role and the fact that the "crusade" is a fraud are enough to make his conduct absurd, in spite of its sincerity.

In the matter of religion, Gide did not entirely expose himself, however. The conversion and the crusade are both Catholic events, and there hangs over the entire novel the implicit suggestion that the "crustaceans" have been taken in not so much by Protos's swindle as by the papacy itself. (One translation of the novel's title is "The Vatican's Suckers," *cave* being criminal argot for "sucker.") Gide kept his own sort of fervent piety out of range of this criticism.

Gide's genius as an inventor and composer of fiction is brilliantly revealed in *Les Caves*. His aim to criticize the institutions and beliefs of his class is improved and enlightened by his extraordinary sense of the comical. In one burlesque characterization after another, in a succession of ludicrous anecdotes, we see him transform his own person and its history into something they never were and never could be—except under the special dispensation of the comic genius. The greatest inventions in the novel are certainly the character of Lafcadio and the hoax of the pope's abduction. Lafcadio, as we have suggested, combines an erotic fantasy with a caricature of human freedom. He is of necessity a highly stylized character. But the abominable crime that he commits and certain incidental embellishments that Gide added to his person like his "Italianism" and his contempt for literature, give him a concentrated symbolical value that substantially exceeds the demands of his role in the novel. Like the heroes of myth and legend, he is capable of more and represents more than he actually does in the story.

Gide may not have plotted and designed everything that the figure of Lafcadio has come to mean, but he certainly calculated to the last detail the value of the "Vatican swindle." This marvelous invention, which is the central piece of both the intrigue and the critique, is the truest measure of his fertile imagination and satirical wit. This is his response to a public of readers like the titled lady who lavished exasperating praise on *La Porte étroite*, which she said she had read "nearly ten years ago"—five years after its publication. "She takes me aside in a corner," Gide wrote, "and at each compliment she makes me, I want to stick out my tongue at her, or scream *Merde!*" He ends the anecdote with the comment: "It was high time that I wrote *Les Caves*" (*J*, 446).

La Symphonie pastorale

La Symphonie pastorale (*The Pastoral Symphony*) (1919) was written in the afterglow of two very important events in Gide's life. The first and more remote was the period of intense religious emotion and reflection that he went through in 1916 during the most depressing days of the First World War. The fruit of this experience was the journal entitled "Numquid et tu . . . ?"[12] in which he celebrated the superhuman wisdom of Christ's gospel with its message of love and mandatory joy and rejected the moral teachings of Paul on the grounds that they were antievangelical. The preacher's teaching in *La Symphonie pastorale* is almost word for word what we find in "Numquid et tu . . . ?"

The other experience, still in force during the composition of the novel was Gide's erotic attachment to Marc Allégret.[13] His affection for this youth (whom he legally adopted) extended over a good many years, but in the period that concerns us here, their relationship conformed very closely to the ideal of classical pederasty. Gide's journals for 1917 and 1918 contain many entries devoted to "M." In one series of these, in August 1917, Gide recorded his impressions of an idyllic vagabond holiday spent with Marc in Switzerland. The joy of those days was so intense that Gide was moved (by what: modesty or the instinct of dissimulation?) to recount it in the third person and to give himself and Marc fictitious names (Fabrice and Michel).

Gide's love affair with the adolescent Marc Allégret gave a profound satisfaction to *one* of the pressing demands of his erotic nature. Unfortunately, it also destroyed the confidence of Madeleine Gide; and with that went the security of the Catharist marriage, which was equally necessary to Gide. In his persistent and passionate attachment to Marc, Madeleine apparently saw at last the falsity of her position and the extent of the deception that Gide had worked upon her. (She had long ago and more than once been witness to sudden and intemperate accesses of pedophilia on Gide's part, but he had succeeded in convincing her that these were short-lived eruptions of a compulsive mania, and that they were unrelated to love.) It was in 1918, while Gide was spending another holiday with Marc in England, that Madeleine Gide burned all the letters that Gide had written her from their childhood onward and which contained the record of his devotion to her. This incident provoked a rupture in their relations that never quite healed. It also produced an alteration of the most radical character in Gide's outlook. With this event, which was nothing less than the breakdown of the ethical structure of his marriage and the end of his Tristan romance, the romantic exuberance that had guided and shaped his work since 1895 effectively dried up.

That is the background of *La Symphonie pastorale*. We might very well claim for this novel the prestige of being the most artfully transformed version of the Gidean erotic myth, for very little in it is immediately identifiable with the persons and circumstances it represents. The principle character and narrator, the one in whom the psychological action takes place, is an unctuous, self-deceiving Calvinist minister. It is to this unlikely figure that Gide gives the role of lover. His love for the blind girl whom he rescued from oblivion is forbidden on every account. She is an innocent child, afflicted and totally ignorant of the world. He is a man of mature years, married, a father, and charged with the moral guidance of his community. For a long while he refuses to acknowledge that his affection for Gertrude has any sexual basis. The desire that he feels is so completely inadmissible that it defies identification. He deludes himself, therefore, into believing that he is only Gertrude's foster-father and teacher. And this is not untrue, for his love is expressed first of all in the great effort through which he awakens her intelligence and feelings and reveals the natural world to her dormant senses. His desire to inculcate in her his own unorthodox evangelical outlook is also an expression of love.

In the minister's love for the blind girl we can see a highly condensed statement of Gide's ambiguous eroticism. On the one hand, the love of a man for a girl child is a fantasy usually associated with the Oedipus complex. It gives satisfaction to the psyche by presenting a forbidden love (like that for the mother) in an idealized, and even possible, form. On the other hand, in the minister's devotion to his *pupil* we see a relationship much like that of classical pederasty. (Gertrude's close-cropped head at the beginning of the story and her forthright and aggressive manner later on suggest that Gide might have visualized her as a boy.)

The minister is entangled in a marriage that is a vexing obstacle to his happiness. His wife, no longer young, is surrounded by a brood of children who resemble her far more than they do him. Her joyless severity is a constant restraint upon her husband's spontaneous generosity. In this maternal figure Gide represented all the frustration and dissatisfaction of his mother fixation. The contrast between Gertrude, the ideal lover, whether girl or boy, and Amélie, who inspires disgust and hatred, depicts with penetrating exactness the ambivalence of the Oedipus personality toward the object of his love.

As long as the minister is able to maintain the illusion that his love for Gertrude is not sexual, it liberates him from his bondage to Amélie. But Gertrude, with the frankness of innocent youth, persistently attacks his illusion. She forces him to recognize her beauty. Then she declares her love for him and obliges him to make a similar declaration. Finally she makes him distinguish between the charitable instinct that led him to assume charge of her in the beginning and the erotic passion that has developed from their intimacy.

The minister is at last driven by those who are playing the secondary

roles in his erotic drama to face the irreconcilable conflict between his
two lives. It is then that he reveals, beneath his self-deception and
duplicity, a genuinely romantic character. Confronted with the issue in
all its clarity, he chooses love, and with it the risk of disgrace, over a
marriage that has lost its savor. He removes Gertrude to surroundings
more propitious to their romance. He opposes the efforts of his son
Jacques and Dr. Martins to restore her sight, because she will then see the
evil of their situation.

But the minister is defeated and the strategy of love is undone.
Gertrude in gaining her sight goes over to the enemy and acts to preserve
the minister's marriage by repudiating their love and committing suicide. The decision is thus taken away from the romantic protagonist, and
the conflict is resolved over his head and against his will.

La Symphonie pastorale is Gide's symbolic version of the end of his
Tristan romance with Madeleine and his discovery that marriage with
her was at bottom a reenactment of the hated union with his mother. It
carries with it the implication that he had seen the impossibility of fully
realizing the ideal of pederasty without disrupting his marriage, the need
for which was in spite of everything more deeply lodged in his being than
the desire for Corydon's romances.

The central action of *La Symphonie pastorale* is the resolution of the
erotic conflict in which we have no trouble recognizing the familiar
stereotype of Gide's sexuality. It is unlikely, however, that anyone would
describe the novel in just these terms. Gide called his book "the critique
of a form of lying to oneself" (*OC*, 13:439), but that explanation fails to
account for a number of things that emphatically stand forth in the total
image created by the narrative.

The fact is that in this book Gide succeeded most strikingly in
generalizing and intellectualizing the personal emotional problem that
forms its core. His protagonist is a Calvinist preacher; his setting, an
isolated village in the Swiss Jura. With these two concrete facts he evokes
the drama of the Protestant community existing autonomously within
the borders of the Catholic universe. The atmosphere is immediately one
of solitude, austerity, and unbending rigor. And all of this comes to life
in the story—but not through the actions of the protagonist. This is
Gide's surprise. It is a great stroke of romantic imagination comparable
to that which created the characters of Michel in *L'Immoraliste* and Alissa
in *La Porte étroite*. The minister is so responsive to the imperatives of love
and joy that he finds in the words of Christ that he makes them the
foundation of his living and his teaching, and he rejects all the negative,

moralistic doctrines that more generally define the Christian life. His rule is not the will to be virtuous but the spontaneous impulse to love. In the fervor of his spirit and in the radical interpretation of the gospel by which he justifies his temperament we see an exact replica of the Gidean spirit and thought as they appear in "Numquid et tu . . . ?" and other religious reflections.

However, Gide places his fictional character in an ambiguous light that is absent from his own reflections. The minister is inspired and sincere in his submission to the gospel. His best impulses and most courageous resolves are found in prayer. But his tone of voice is irritatingly unctuous, and he is manifestly insensitive to the feelings and needs of his family. The sentiment of divine sanction that his prayers bring him is an instrument of power that he employs in a thoughtless and overbearing manner. When he cites the parables of the Lost Sheep and the Prodigal Son to justify his conduct in bringing the blind child home and in devoting himself to her to the exclusion of his own children, the minister is at the same time following the teachings of Jesus and using Holy Scripture as a weapon against Amélie's simple, human protests.

In the minister's desire for Gertrude there is of course the primary erotic impulse that he tries not to see, but there is also his desperate wish for a disciple to share his unorthodox vision of the Christian life. He says in his narrative that he had tried to win each of his own children in turn, only to see them all turn to their mother for moral authority. She offered them, not an open and joyful vision of life, but an array of cautions and prohibitions to defend them against its evils. The minister's evangelical zeal is involved in his erotic passion to such a degree that it is in all seriousness impossible to evaluate them separately. The ambiguity created by this interlocking of motives is perhaps Gide's major achievement in the novel. The minister is dishonest about his erotic interest in Gertrude, but given what he is, it is quite possible that the evangelizing motive had in fact displaced the erotic one in the forefront of his thought and feelings. At the end, when Gertrude is dead and his mission is wholly defeated by her defection, the minister tries to pray, but he is unable to do so. His fervor is gone. God has withdrawn from the world.

Just as Gide had spent many years trying to play two incompatible erotic roles, his protagonist in *La Symphonie pastorale* is trying to play two irreconcilable roles within the Christian faith, one as a minister of the Reformed church and the other as the prophet of the true evangel. Gide further complicates the picture by introducing Catholicism as the great adversary of the minister's evangelism. His intention in this was plainly to suggest—as he had already done elsewhere—that the Reformed church was no longer a dissenting body, that it had reverted for all practical purposes to the dogmatic institutions of Saint Paul and the whole tradition of regulators and guardians associated with the Roman Catholic church. In his journal for 1910, when he was already thinking about the novel that was to be *La Symphonie pastorale*, he wrote:

If being a Protestant is being a Christian without being a Catholic, then I am a Protestant. But I cannot recognize any other orthodoxy but the Roman orthodoxy, and if Protestantism, Calvinist or Lutheran, tried to impose its own upon me, it is toward the Roman that I should immediately turn, as toward the only one. "Protestant orthodoxy," these words have no meaning for me. I recognize no *authority;* and if I did recognize one, it would be that of the Roman Church.

But my Christianity springs only from Christ. Between Him and me I consider Calvin and St. Paul to be two equally baneful screens. Oh, if only Protestantism had been able to reject St. Paul at the start! But it is precisely to St. Paul, and not to Christ, that Calvin is akin. (*J*, 300)

The minister has never ceased being a dissenter. He is protesting against the restraints of the new orthodoxy and seeking still the way to live truly under the gospel. Seen from this angle he is a hero, one who is determined to manifest the truth at whatever cost. But it is a heroism heavily overlaid with irony, for at this point the erotic drama casts its shadow over the religious-moral issue. Whatever the value of the minister's evangelizing mission, his love for Gertrude falls under the ban of the established morality and is judged to be an offense, by all who are touched by it, including finally Gertrude herself. The sign of his defeat in the religious contest is the conversion of Jacques and Gertrude to Catholicism. This gesture involves a critique that reaches beyond the character of the minister to embrace a certain possibility that is inherent in Protestantism. The Protestant cell exists as an isolated and atypical particle in the universal body. With no hierarchical authority and no guide but the individual conscience, it is an anarchy that fosters exceptional insights and behavior. It is a school of heroism but also one of error. Gide elaborated on this notion in a letter to M. H. Fayer: "Through him [that is, the minister], rather than trying to express my own thought, I have depicted the pitfall to which my own doctrine might lead, when that ethic is not rigorously checked by a critical spirit constantly on the alert and little inclined to self-indulgence. The indispensable critical spirit is completely lacking in the pastor."[14] *La Symphonie pastorale* and *La Porte étroite* both contain this rational criticism of Protestantism, but it was probably not so much for its value as criticism that Gide injected it into his novels as for the ironic perspective that it afforded him.

La Symphonie pastorale is a fine example of Gide's skill in the structuring of an ideological conflict to shadow and conceal the erotic drama. It is on this score comparable to *L'Immoraliste* and superior to *La Porte étroite*. At the same time there is a rich deployment of symbols that direct us to the source of the Gidean *poesis*—to Narcissus and to the gospel. At the center of this symbolism stands the figure of Gertrude. Her role as a symbol is fully as important as her role as an agent in the drama. Her blindness has two meanings, one rooted in theology and the other in the mythology of the Gidean psyche. Theologically, it is innocence that is suggested by blindness. Gide develops this notion at some length. The minister discovers a blind child who literally knows nothing, neither good nor evil. He determines to make known to her only the good of this world and to conceal all the bad. In this fervor and his love he develops a blindness to reality that is more than equal to Gertrude's. To make the picture of innocence complete, the world itself puts on a snowy mantle of purity. But as the pessimistic Dr. Martins had foreseen, Gertrude gains some knowledge of evil through her other senses, and finally, when she recovers her sight, she sees it plainly in herself and all around her. The earth's false innocence melts away, too, and with it goes the minister's illusion.

The moral metaphor of blindness is authorized by the words of Christ that appear in John 9:41: "If you were blind, you would have no guilt." The minister, finding the condition of blindness in Gertrude, tries to realize its promise, not only in her but in himself and in the world. It becomes the foundation of his mission. If the promise does not prove true it is principally because men are perverse and obdurate to the divine word.

In terms of Gide's private mythology, blindness connotes self-absorption and alienation from the surrounding reality. It is a mirror for looking inward. Gertrude is a Narcissus figure. Her association with water is stated at the beginning of the story when the minister, on his way to discover her, passes by a little lake he had not seen since his youth; again when "the scene beside the brook" in the *Pastoral Symphony* awakens in her the sense of beauty; and at the end when she meets her death as a result of leaning too close to the surface of a stream and falling in. All of these motifs conspire to make us see in the blind child the ideal lover of the youthful Gide's autoerotic fantasies.

In later years Gide expressed little regard for *La Symphonie pastorale*. In

1922 he wrote in his *Journal*: "The one of all my books which . . . brought me the richest, warmest, and quickest praise is the one . . . that remains outside of my work, that *interests* me the least (I am taking this word in its most subtle sense), and that, on the whole, I should most willingly see disappear" (*J*, 737). This was his way of disavowing the book's popularity, a popularity that he knew was based on a misunderstanding of his motives. There is no mistaking the triumph of morality and maternal rule in the story, and it is hard to miss the implied criticism of Protestantism; but to take these as evidence of a reversal in his thought was an error grave enough to render the book poisonous in its author's eyes. The triumph he depicts was a bitter one, and Gide did whatever was aesthetically within his power to debase it. He ends the story with the pathetic death of Gertrude and with a final glimpse of a completely disheartened hero.

La Symphonie pastorale does nevertheless mark a triumph of the world over the poet, and of mortality over the demands of his primitive nature. Still romantic in its conceptions of character, the story depicts the defeat of the romantic temperament. That was another reason for Gide to feel estranged from it. He was not one to take pleasure in the contemplation of his own downfall, even though he had felt at a certain moment the need to represent it.

Chapter Four
Social Realism

Lost Illusions

The third and final period of Gide's work, which extends from his fiftieth year to the end of his life, is marked by a change in outlook and style as significant as the one that occurred in his late 20s. His passionate concern with the dramas of the individual personality, with its excessive desires and imperious will, gives way before an equally absorbing preoccupation with society—or better said, with social reality. The conflicts of individual rights within the social unit, the triumphant power of societal norms over the insights and wishes of individuals, the hypocrisies of official ideology in the light of practical conduct: these are the subjects that Gide dealt with in his later years.

Society is, of course, not a new interest in Gide's work. *Paludes* (1895) and *Les Caves du Vatican* (1914) were essentially social satires. What is new is his acknowledgment, as it were, of the real and effective limitations placed upon the individual by his class and its ideology. The imperious romantic personality represented by Michel, Alissa, Lafcadio, and the preacher of *La Symphonie pastorale* is supplanted by a more subdued, more socialized type. This is particularly evident in the characters of *Les Faux-Monnayeurs* and of *L'École des femmes* and its sequels. But even in the mythical figures of Oedipe and Thésée, the last representatives of the Gidean psyche and its history, there is a kind of willing submission to the interest and the authority of the community that is never apparent in the romantic characters.

The inauguration of the romantic period in Gide's fiction followed close on the heels of his marriage to Madeleine Rondeaux in 1895. This romantic ethos collapsed soon after the disruptive event that destroyed Gide's confidence in his wife's love and esteem. When Madeleine Gide burned the letters that were the concrete record of his lifelong devotion to her, the letters that in his eyes contained the best of him and established the truth and the value of his Catharist romance, Gide saw himself bereft of the illusion upon which his life and his work had reposed for 23 years. In 1939, more than two decades after the event, he described its effect on him in these terms:

The despair into which I believed I was sinking came primarily no doubt from the feeling of bankruptcy; I compared myself to Oedipus when he discovers suddenly the lie on which his happiness is built; I suddenly became conscious of the distress in which my personal happiness kept her whom, in spite of everything, I loved more than myself; but also, less admissibly, I suffered from knowing that that part of me which seemed to me the most deserving of survival had been reduced to nothingness by her. That correspondence, kept up since our childhood, belonged undoubtedly to both of us at once, seemed to me to come as much from her as from me; it was the fruit of my love for her . . . and for a week I wept without cease, without being able to exhaust the bitterness of *our* grief. . . .

Afterwards, I never really recovered my taste for life; or at any rate only much later when I learned that I had regained her esteem; but even then I did not get back into the stream of life, and I lived thenceforth with that undefinable feeling of moving about in the midst of appearances—amidst those appearances that are called reality. (*J-S*, 1147–48).

After receiving this blow to his vitals, a blow that drove him back to a state of uncertainty not unlike that in which he had lived during his neurotic childhood, Gide never recovered the imperious mastery of his middle years, when one book after another revealed the triumph of artistic purpose over the tangled complex of desires and constraints inherited from his early life. The work of his later years is progressively less concerned with the dramatization of this inner turbulence. The tendency toward resolution is exhibited first of all in his effort to give a factual, historical account of himself in *Si le Grain ne meurt* and to examine more or less objectively and scientifically the question of homosexuality in *Corydon*. Both of these projects had been started years before (a part of *Corydon* was published privately and anonymously in 1911), but it was after the break with Madeleine that they were brought to completion and put before the public.

The air of social and political unrest that reigned over the whole of Europe in the postwar years must certainly be reckoned as a secondary cause of Gide's shift from private to public interests. On his return in 1927 from an extensive tour of French Equatorial Africa, Gide published his travel notebooks under the titles *Voyage au Congo* and *Retour du Tchad*. Among other things his report contained a documented account of the inhuman treatment of African laborers by the companies that held exploiting concessions in the colonies. This indictment had obviously political overtones which tended to make Gide the ally of the anticolonialist, anticapitalist left.

It was during the twenties too that Gide interested himself in the social causes of crime and in the judgment and treatment of criminals. Several journalistic works that appeared around 1930 testify to the extent of his investigations and speculations in this area. His interest in social problems was in fact such that it inspired the following entry in his journal for 1932:

I am experiencing anew, just as in the time of my youth, that *state of devotion* in which feelings, thoughts—in which the whole being is oriented and subordinated. Moreover, is not my conviction of today comparable to the *faith?* I have over a very long period of time dissuaded myself from any *credo* that free inquiry could reduce instantly to ruin. But it is precisely out of that inquiry that my *credo* of today was born. There is nothing "mystical" in it (in the sense in which that word is commonly used), so that this state cannot seek recourse, nor can this fervor find release, in prayer. It is simply that my being yearns toward a hope, toward a goal. All my thoughts, even involuntarily, come back to that. In the abominable distress of the world today, the plan of the new Russia appears to me now as salvation. There is nothing that does not convince me of it! (*J*, 1126)

This page of his journal, along with others that expressed the same sentiment, appeared in the *Nouvelle Revue Française* in 1932. Gide's position seemed clear. He was thereafter assumed to be a revolutionary writer. After some initial hesitations he began to take part in anti-Fascist activities after Hitler's accession to the chancellory. He was eagerly sought after to speak and preside at anti-Fascist and antiwar rallies. In 1934 he accompanied André Malraux to Berlin to present to the German government a petition seeking the liberation of Dimitrov and his associates, who had been acquitted of responsibility for the Reichstag fire but not released from custody.

Gide's political action reached a sort of climax with his visit to Russia in the summer of 1936. The publication of his notes on this trip (*Retour de l'U.R.S.S.*), however, provoked a rupture in his relations with the French Communist party. Socialism had been for him an ideal, an evangel. He was by no means prepared to see it become a concrete, historical reality embodying error and imperfection. He expressed his disillusionment with some of the things he saw in Russia and was forthwith judged to be a social traitor by doctrinaire Communists.

Throughout the period of social and political involvement Gide never ceased to differentiate between his public activity and his artistic work. Even though his devotion to socialism had brought with it a return of exaltation, he was conscious that his public preoccupations ran counter to his private genius. In 1936, after reading a study that Claude Naville had devoted to him[1] and in which he had been blamed for the absence of social concerns in his earlier work, Gide wrote in his journal: "For my part, I judge, on the contrary, that when social preoccupations began to encumber my head and my heart, I no longer wrote anything of value." (*J*, 1255).

Another factor that tended to depersonalize Gide's work in his later years was what he called the "withdrawal of the creative demon," by which he meant the relaxation of internal tensions and the disappearance of strictly personal problems. In 1932 he wrote in his journal:

If social questions today occupy my thought, it is also because the creative demon is withdrawing. Those questions occupy the ground only because the other has already yielded it. Why try to overrate myself and refuse to observe (what I see in Tolstoy): an undeniable diminution . . . ?

Has my poetic power declined with my Christian feelings, as Em. said to me this morning? I do not think so, but rather with my perplexity. Each of my books has been, up until now, the cultivation of an uncertainty. (*J*, 1139)

The work of these last three decades of Gide's life is undeniably weaker, less certain of itself, than that of his youth and his maturity. The clarity and grace of his expression are still there, and the power of his imagination is undiminished. What we see disappearing are the desperate private urgencies that informed his earlier fables and drove them to hazardous conclusions. It was only when he felt the problems of the world prolongations of his own that Gide was able to turn them into unequivocal accusations and protests.

Les Faux-Monnayeurs

The last period of Gide's work is dominated by the book with which it begins. He worked on *Les Faux-Monnayeurs* (*The Counterfeiters*) (1926) from 1919 to 1925. It was the summary work of his mature years, just as *André Walter* had been that of his adolescence. This great novel—the only one of his books to which he finally accorded the title of "novel"—is in some respects his greatest achievement in prose fiction. In other respects, it marks very clearly his decline as a poet.

No work of Gide embodies a more complex motivational structure than *Les Faux-Monnayeurs*. In all of his books prior to this one we have seen one force, one desire, providing the impulse, the energy, and the goal of the imagined action. This book began, like a good many others before it, under the impulsion of an erotic-poetic wish. In the long course of its composition, however, the original energy flagged and was replaced by a critical intention that demanded expressive means quite different from those of the initial motive. Conditions and feelings created to speak for the one are relayed en route to the other, with the result that the story demands a conversion of our expectations that is not readily, or happily, accomplished. We are driven to see *Les Faux-Monnayeurs* as a two-headed work. It offers on the one hand a fluid image of the psychology of literary creation, and on the other a comprehensive picture of the manners and morals of the petty bourgeoisie either just before or just after the war of 1914–18. (Gide's thought was embarrassed by the intrusion of that great historical event. His book bears no trace of it.)

The image of the artist striving to comprehend a kaleidoscopic reality and to turn it into a novel has commanded more critical interest than the more ample portrayal of a social milieu. This interest is attributable beyond a doubt to the richer poetic content of the first theme. We must not, however, allow that lure to lead us away from the plain fact that the poetic motive, and its expression, are overborne by the critical purpose of the novel, and that they finally become part of the general critical design. An examination of Gide's initial impulse to write the book and of the record of its evolution, as these are stated in his various journals, is instructive on this point.

When Gide began to think about *Les Faux-Monnayeurs* he was still deeply shaken by the collapse of the romantic illusion that he had built up around his marriage. The novel was to be his principal defense against the destructive effects of that event. Through thinking it and writing it he sought to put his world to rights again. In a journal entry in January 1925 (one of those that he withheld from publication until long after Madeleine Gide's death) he wrote:

I have never stopped loving her, even at the time when I seemed, and she had a right to think that I was, farthest from her; loving her more than myself, more than life, but I have ceased to be able to tell her so. . . .

My entire work is pitched toward her. . . .

Up to *Les Faux-Monnayeurs* (the first book that I wrote while trying not to think about her) I wrote everything to convince her, to draw her in my direction.

It was all one long plea; no work has been more intimately motivated than mine—and whoever does not see that has little insight into it. (*J-S*, 1157)

A few years later, in recalling the pleasure and happiness that he had enjoyed in the company of Marc Allégret on their long journey through Central Africa, Gide wrote in his journal: "It was for him, to win his attention, his esteem, that I wrote *Les Faux-Monnayeurs*, just as all my preceding books were written under the influence of Em., or in the vain hope of convincing her (*J*, 881)."

Having to reorient his pleading was almost like having to start his life's work all over again. His earliest plans, as we find them in his notebooks (published as *Journal des Faux-Monnayeurs* in 1926) envisaged two narrators: one (significantly named Lafcadio) was a young wanderer, a curious but uncommitted observer of men and things; the other was a middle-aged novelist, engaged at the moment in the effort to turn his intelligence of the world into a work of art. This design reveals the familiar topography of Gide's psyche: the division of the self into two beings, the one instinctively seeking freedom and pleasure, the other imposing the restraints of reality.

The principal subject of the novel in this first plan was to be the divorce between reality and consciousness. The story would have two foci, Gide said, the event and the novelist's effort to make a book out of it. "That is the main center, the new center that throws the story off its axis and draws it toward the imaginary. In short, I see this notebook, in which I am writing the history of the book, incorporated in its entirety into the book, forming its principal interest, for the greater irritation of the reader" (*OC*, 13:31).

The shock of losing his assurance of Madeleine's love had driven Gide back to the instability of his childhood and youth, and it was from that base that he had to begin his recuperation. The climactic event of the novel, as he then envisaged it, was to be the meeting of the two narrators. It is not too hard to see in that event a symbol of reintegration and reconciliation.

Gide did recover, more or less, from the destruction of the Catharist illusion on which his adult life was founded, but his recovery, if we may believe the symbolic account of it in *Les Faux-Monnayeurs*, did not reach the desired stage of reintegration. He had to be content with a strategy that involved renunciation, repression, and criticism (the refusal of repression). The first place to see this is in the design of the finished novel.

Very little of the original project found its way to completion. There are two narratives side by side in *Les Faux-Monnayeurs*, but they fall far short of representing the duality of Gide's psyche. In place of Lafcadio there is a conventional narrator who attaches himself to one character after another, reporting what they do, what they say, and what they think. His reportage is predominantly objective and is confined to the present. (His occasional intrusive comments are those of an amused but powerless observer.)

Édouard's journal, which comprises about half the novel, has a more varied content, but a surprisingly large portion of it is narration of precisely the same type as that done by the external narrator. Édouard describes actions and records conversations. His participation in the event does not much alter the tone of his report. The greatest difference between him and the other narrator is that he knows and recalls the past. Incidents and conversations that took place 10 years before the present of the story are fully described and transcribed in his journal.

The remnant of the original project is to be found in a few passages in which Édouard reflects on his own problematical relations with the real world and on the transformation of those relations into a novel. In much of this he appears as an authentic narcissist, alienated from his own being and seeking his real self in someone else's life. "I am anything but what I think I am—and that varies unceasingly. . . . Nothing could be more different from me than myself. . . . My heart beats only in sympathy; I love only through others . . . and never feel more intensely alive than when I escape from myself to become someone else, anyone else" (*RRS*, 987). A little further on he writes: "Nothing has any existence for me except a *poetic* one (and I give that word its fullest sense)—beginning with myself. It seems to me sometimes that I do not really exist, but simply imagine that I do. The hardest thing for me to believe in is my own reality" (*RRS*, 987–88).

It is this disjunction that he feels between himself and reality that Édouard wants to express in the book he is planning. The novelist in his book will try to turn away from reality, but Édouard will constantly bring him back to it. The core idea of the work will be "the rivalry between the real world and the representation that we make of it. The way in which the world of appearances imposes itself on us and in which we try to impose on the outer world our particular interpretation constitutes the drama of our life. The resistance of the facts invites us to transport our ideal construct into dreams, hope, the future life, our belief in which is nourished by all our disappointments in this one" (RRS, 1096).

Even here reason is overcoming neurosis, for what Édouard describes is no more than the common human experience of tension between intellect and imagination, between condition and desire.

Édouard is an antirealist. He wants to write a novel "which would be at once as true and as far removed from reality, as particular and as general, as human and as fictive as *Athalie, Tartuffe,* or *Cinna*" (RRS, 1081). What he would like to create is "something which would be like the *Art of the Fugue*" (RRS, 1084). The one sample of his work that he offers to our view is a short dialogue on the moral risk of casual theft which he shows to his young nephew Georges in an attempt to help him break the habit of stealing. The piece is abstract, analytical, and very self-conscious. It contains multiple references to its own purpose, style, and use.

The project that Édouard describes is very close to the one that Gide initially conceived for *Les Faux-Monnayeurs*. But we now hear this poetic impulse expressed by a *fictional* character who is speaking within a novel that does not remotely resemble the one he wants to write. This can only imply that Gide's narcissistic impulse had been overcome and to a large extent devalued by a different conception of the work.

This change is disclosed in the "Second Notebook" of the *Journal des Faux-Monnayeurs*, where Édouard is visualized more and more as a character in the novel and less and less as a Gidean double. At one point, after writing a brief dialogue in which he has Édouard express impatience with the need for a texture of facts in the novel, Gide inserts a gratuitous critique of the symbolist school, whose adherents, he says, were disenchanted with life, pessimistic, yielding, and resigned (OC, 13:36–37). The suggestion is too pointed to be ignored: Édouard is at heart a symbolist. His hatred of realism derives from his reluctance to examine the texture of human life. Thereafter, Gide treats Édouard's book as something that will never be accomplished. "Each time that Édouard is called on to expose the plan of his novel, he talks about it in a different way. In a word, he bluffs; he is afraid, at bottom, of never being able to get it done" (OC, 13:38). About a year later Gide decided to pass on to Édouard his own thoughts on purifying the novel of the heterogeneous elements that Balzac had added to it, and that have persisted as part of the canon of the genre. He adds the note that Édouard "will never succeed in writing that pure novel" (OC, 13:42). Immediately thereafter he says:

I must carefully respect in Édouard everything that makes him incapable of writing his book. He understands much; but is constantly pursuing himself; through everyone else, through everything else. Real devotion is nearly impossible for him. He is an amateur, a failure.

A character all the more difficult to establish in that I am lending him much of myself. I need to draw back and push him away from me in order to see him well. (*OC*, 13:42)

Having overcome his narcissistic impulse by turning it into fiction, Gide proceeded to write a novel that is aesthetically, more closely related to realism than to symbolism or romanticism. A note written about the time when he was transferring the initial project of the book from himself to Édouard reads: "My novel, rather curiously, is developing backwards. That is, I am constantly discovering that this or that, which happened earlier, ought to be told. Thus the chapters are added, not one after the other, but always pushing further on the one that initially I thought would have to be first" (*OC*, 13:39). This note suggests that Gide was then adding the "social conditioning" that Édouard found so tedious in the novel.

A very striking feature of *Les Faux-Monnayeurs* is the reappearance in its pages of a number of important motifs of *Les Caves du Vatican*. I observed that Gide had originally planned a major role for "Lafcadio" in the novel, but that he had dropped it in the course of writing. What we find instead is the outline of Lafcadio's career in *Les Caves* repeated, more or less, in that of Bernard Profitendieu. Bastardy, vagabondage, moral perturbation, reintegration—everything but the murder is reproduced. In a like manner, the role of the man of letters, which belonged to Julius de Baraglioul in *Les Caves*, is repeated, but enlarged to accommodate both Édouard and Count Robert de Passavant, who inherits Julius's opportunism. Protos is similarly divided, his criminal character being passed to Strouvilhou and his manipulations of the lives of others going to Édouard.

There are also other replications. The Pension Vedel-Azaïs, with its atmosphere of pious Calvinism, controls the action of *Les Faux-Monnayeurs* in much the same way that the Vatican did in *Les Caves*. The counterfeit coin racket is clearly modeled on "the Vatican swindle," and the violent death of Boris is the equivalent of the murder of Fleurissoire.

This deliberate and obvious replication of motifs was no doubt done in order to indicate a special kinship between the two novels. Gide had long ago established the practice of pairing his books, and he always provided some unavoidable clue to their gemination. (In *L'Immoraliste* and *La Porte étroite* it was the Norman locale; in *Les Nourritures terrestres* and *El Hadj*, the desert; in *Saül* and *Le Roi Candaule*, kingship.) These clues in turn point to internal, thematic relations, which are unfailingly ironic.

In the present instance the clues point to Gide's representation of the bourgeois character. From *Les Caves* to *Les Faux-Monnayeurs* it has changed hardly at all. Something like a generation has passed, but the drama of life in the middle-class milieu is fundamentally unaltered: the individual's desire for freedom and autonomy is still frustrated by a social order that demands obeisance to its hierarchical authorities and lip service to its fictitious ideals.

The ironic dissimilarity of the two novels resides in the profound change in authorial tone from one to the other. In 1914 Gide's critique exuded confidence. His extravagant humor was achieved at the expense of the *crustacés*, whose manners and ideas were the principal objects of ridicule. He, Gide, was the most ingenious of the *subtiles.* In 1925 his tone was much chastened. He still accused the lies, the hypocrisies, and the repressions of his class, but his criticism had become sober, judicial, and desperate. The "crustaceans" had triumphed all along the line. In the few years that separated *Les Faux-Monnayeurs* from *Les Caves du Vatican* there had been four years of terrible war that had made the power and the interests of the middle class appear, not petty and ridiculous, but monstrous and perhaps invincible.

The primary reality represented in the images of *Les Faux-Monnayeurs* is (as it was in *Les Caves*) the author's own personality. The social order appears secondarily as what has threatened, restricted, and deformed him. Of the several vehicles of self-disclosure in the work none is more profoundly representative than Édouard. In him Gide draws an ironic (but respectful) portrait of himself as a novelist whose introspective vision can find no adequate means to express itself. Édouard objectifies the neurotic substrate of Gide's personality, the condition of ambivalent indecision that had haunted him since childhood. He represents, as Gide suggested, his author's *poetic* nature. He lacks the countervailing power of Gide's artistry, that practical sense that leads the poet to discover in the literary tradition forms capable of translating his apprehensions of himself and the world. In that deficiency lies the chief irony of the character.

Gide's greatest departure from the model of *Les Caves du Vatican* is in the wealth and variety of images depicting sexual desire and its repression, frustration, and compensation. This subject, as we know, was an essentially poetic one for Gide. It was at the very source of his creativity.

His work reveals a nearly uninterrupted application to the exposure of his erotic complexity and to its sublimation in symbolic figures and strategies. *Les Faux-Monnayeurs* contains the most complete and most explicit of Gide's attempts to make his erotic nature felt and understood. His treatment of the theme is encyclopedic: he presents images of his sexuality in childhood, youth, and manhood. This essentially historical development is represented in the novel simultaneously by a number of characters. In fact *all* of the characters play some role in its exposition. There is no dramatic unfolding of the subject. The conflicts between desire and repression are largely static and circumstantial. They do not serve here, as they did in earlier fictions, as the adversaries in an oppositional strategy.

The underlying reason for this aesthetic difference is no doubt Gide's determination to present his erotic complexity as an effect of social and cultural forces. I have repeatedly observed that the constant and overall tendency of Gide's art is to transform his personal problems into social and intellectual conflicts that involve his class as a whole. That is precisely what we find in the characterizations of eroticism in *Les Faux-Monnayeurs.*

Édouard is the major symbol of the Gidean Eros. We see him, as an adult male, engaged in both heterosexual and homosexual relations. His love affair with Laura illustrates with exemplary clarity Gide's ambivalent ties with womanhood. In the first, or idyllic, phase of their love Laura is an adolescent girl, 12 years younger than Édouard. She is a "Beatrice," a guiding influence in Édouard's life and work. He credits her with having inspired every line he has written and with having made him over in her image—even as he was pretending to educate her. This image of pure love between a man and a girl child is a classic expression of the Oedipus complex. Laura is the ideal image of what Gide's mother had been for him and of what he had at first recaptured in his marriage to Madeleine Rondeaux.

However, the idyll of Laura and Édouard belongs to the past of the novel. Their relations in the present of the narrative are of another order altogether. When Laura reached marriageable age, Édouard refused her, counseling her to marry Douviers; which she obediently did. This was a first degradation of the ideal. Then, in the sanatorium, she became the mistress of Vincent Molinier. As the novel commences, she has emerged from the clinic, pregnant and abandoned by her lover. She appears before Édouard sullied and abject. All of her ideal erotic characteristics have disappeared, leaving nothing but her female nature. Seeing her thus,

Édouard is released from her spell and is able to devote himself, moderately, to her cause, without incurring any erotic obligation toward her. Laura, as an adultress, an abandoned mother-to-be, and finally a repentant wife, offers Édouard an unimpeachable pretext for the refusal of sexual love. And that, of course, is the entire justification of this picture of her in the novel.

At bottom there is no difference between this version of the refusal of sexuality and the many others that we have seen in Gide's work. There is, however, a profound difference in its quality and tone: the image is shocking in its lack of elevation and decorum. Édouard plays a passive and ungenerous role in the affair, and Laura's descent from the ideal to the abject is almost completely devoid of grace. (The love she inspires in Bernard offers some relief from the spectacle of her abandonment.) Gide, in short, made no attempt to sublimate this refusal.

Édouard's affirmative sexual character is homoerotic. He is a cautious, patient pederast, but a persistent one. (The last entry in his journal—"I am curious to meet Caloub"—is an indication of his restless, roving desire.)

He meets his nephew Georges, as a stranger, under circumstances that recall the incident of the theft of the scissors in *L'Immoraliste*. The child is on the point of stealing a book from a bookstall. The incident puts them on a footing of secret complicity and gives Édouard a moral advantage that he tries to exploit. But Georges is not responsive, and the relationship comes to nothing. Much the same thing occurs between Bernard and Édouard. A shady intimacy is established when Bernard takes possession of Édouard's valise and reads his diary. Édouard responds by engaging Bernard as his secretary. Their ensuing intimacy reveals, however, that they have little affinity for each other.

Édouard is more fortunate in his relations with his nephew Olivier. Their first encounters are marked by mutual desire and reticence. Édouard is then obliged to suffer patiently while Olivier is wooed by another homosexual, Robert de Passavant, but in the end he triumphs through his unflagging affection and moral authority. In order to illustrate and emphasize the ideal quality of their love, Gide goes to the extraordinary length of having Édouard's sister, Pauline, bless his union with her son. She is motivated by resentment of her husband's philandering. There is certainly some improbability in this incident but that is its chief interest in this novel where Gide attempts, in general, to give a realistic account of behavior in a certain social milieu. Pauline's conversation with Édouard is one of the most obviously wish-fulfilling scenes in all of Gide's fiction. It condenses in one motif a gentle and harmonious dissolution of the Oedipus complex, a bitter denunciation of heterosexual relations, and an outright assertion of the value of pederasty.

What strikes us most forcefully in the series of Édouard's encounters is their explicitness. Elsewhere we have seen Gide reflect the Oedipus complex, the refusal of sexuality, and the longing for homosexual relations in a number of disguised and sublimated forms. In *Les Faux-Monnayeurs* the whole subject is treated clearly and openly, and along with the wish-fulfilling dream there is an effort to reveal the negative, or unrealized, relations of the pederast.

Gide presents a morbid version of the refusal of sexuality in the character of Armand Vedel. This youth, whose aggressive uncleanliness, bitter outlook, and withdrawal from the world are symptoms of a nagging sense of shame and guilt, is a more or less conscious prisoner and victim of his mother fixation. He attempts to break free by thrusting his sister Sarah, the erotic surrogate of his mother, into the embrace of Bernard Profitendieu. This is both a renunciation and a vicarious satisfaction: Armand's tears and the kiss he bestows on the visible trace of Sarah's defloration offer a concentrated image of his ambivalence. His concern over the fate of his older sister, Rachel, who is burdened with all the charges of the family and the *pension*, represents, on the other hand, a sublimation of his shameful desire. Rachel is a maternal figure, and Armand's devotion to her is an expression of his mother fixation. However, his feelings are of such a nature that they lead him out of the erotic morass and into a moral revolt against the hypocrisy and the callous exploitations of his parents.

Gide does not represent Armand as "cured." He remains an unbalanced figure in the novel. The abrupt reversal of manner that brings him out of untidy seclusion and into the glittery circle of Count Robert de Passavant implies anything but a healthy return to worldly concerns. De Passavant is a diabolical influence, a corrupter of virtue and truth. When Armand goes over to his camp it is a sign of the triumph of cynicism and artificiality. The sore in his mouth that he shows Olivier is an emblem of the corruption that he has chosen to be.

The archetype of Armand Vedel is the adolescent Gide. The gestures are exaggerated and stylized, but what they reveal is a youth struggling against guilt and dependence. The rage within him is seeking an outlet, a use, a justification. It finds an external focus in the hypocritical mystifications and exploitations of his social class. For Armand, the authority of that class is concentrated in his father; his rebellion is, therefore, at bottom an attack upon the father. (His father has been his enemy, of course, in the sexual drama of his infancy.) His accusations against his milieu are just; and he knows they are. But his motive is ambiguous and impure; and he also knows that. He makes a clear acknowledgment of his guilt when he abandons the role of critic—the critic who is committed to the good—and espouses the cause of negation and evil represented by De Passavant.

What Gide objectifies in Armand Vedel is the torment that accompanied, in his adolescence, the revival of the oedipal situation. Having no father, Gide directed his rebellion, of necessity, against the social and cultural authorities to which he was subject. In the explanatory fiction, however, he makes a clearer identification between the social order and the father. That Gide's adolescent revolt also exceeded the limits of criticism to become an espousal of evil is indicated by the expressions of Manicheanism that are visible throughout his mature work.

In the character of Boris, Gide reflects the neurotic narcissism of his childhood. The conversations that Édouard overhears between Boris and Bronja at Saas-Fee demonstrate with painful accuracy the child's ambivalence and indecision. Madame Sophroniska reveals to Édouard that Boris is a compulsive onanist, and that his present acute anxiety was initiated by his mother's discovery of this activity and her severe reprimands. Under the angelic influence of Bronja, Boris overcomes his compulsion, but the threat of its reassertion is contained in the "talisman" that he has relinquished to Madame Sophroniska. She, in turn, unwisely hands it over to the diabolical Strouvilhou and thus sets in motion the events that lead to Boris's death.

The ethereal child Bronja arouses in Boris feelings of reverence and purity that have their model in Gide's love for Madeleine Rondeaux. Bronja's death leaves Boris without an ideal to exert a counterpull against his demonic compulsion. His decline and fall following her death no doubt translate the destitution that Gide felt upon losing his wife's esteem and confidence; and that sentiment, as much as his memories of himself as a child, is the model of his fictional invention. In addition, we can discern in Boris's loss of Bronja the recapitulation of a more pervasive theme of Gide's entire work: the will to be freed of the mother fixation in all its forms, real and symbolic.

Les Faux-Monnayeurs is the most openly confessional of Gide's fictions. It is not surprising, therefore, to find in it an image of compulsive onanism in an adult male. Pastor Vedel, the father of Rachel, Laura, Armand, and Sarah, is saddled with this Gidean demon. His struggles against the compulsion are recorded in his diary under the cover of efforts to give up smoking. Both Sarah and Édouard easily see through this artifice. Gide does not develop the motif beyond this point. It is related, more or less, to the picture of hypocritical piety projected by the minister; but that image would have been sufficient without this particular detail. Such a gratuitous and superfluous disclosure can only point to that poetic determination to reveal himself that often drove Gide to something approaching exhibitionism.

The subject of sexuality and erotic relations is a very large one in *Les Faux-Monnayeurs*. It is presented in a manner quite unlike that of Gide's psychological novels. In those stories the erotic theme was developed logically and dramatically; here it is disclosed episodically. Édouard's history, it is true, exhibits the two essential motifs of Gide's work, the refusal of heterosexual relations and the formation of a homosexual alliance; but they are not shown in contention, and they are not related in a causal or sequential manner. Gide's design is as clear as it was in the conflict strategies of his earlier books. The erotic relations of men and women are everywhere a failure. The old La Pérouse couple are estranged to the point of no longer speaking to each other. The Moliniers and the Profitendieus are divided by infidelities past and present. Laura's history is one of repeated insuccess. Bernard, seeing the sad concern of Rachel over his intimacy with Sarah, is seized with disgust and quits the *pension*. The only heterosexual loves that have value are those of Boris for Bronja and of Bernard for Laura; both are symbolic expressions of the Oedipus complex. Bernard confesses to Olivier that since he has known Laura he has "no desires at all." Thanks to her his "instincts have been sublimated" (*RRS*, 1151).

The only love that ultimately brings joy and satisfaction is that of Édouard and Olivier. This is a victory for Corydon, but it is not by any means an uncomplicated one. Édouard suffers the frustration of seeing Olivier fall into the hands of another homosexual, and then, having won him back, nearly loses him a second time to death. (In Olivier's attempted suicide Gide reveals very forcefully the latent death wish that is implied in the refusal of sexuality. Oedipal love and pederasty are regressive movements of the sexual instinct, away from the prolongation of life, back to infancy and then to prenatal oblivion.)

Paralleling the erotic theme in *Les Faux-Monnayeurs*, there is a similarly loose-knit, episodic exploration of moral attitudes. There is no moral strategy properly speaking, no conflict of interests articulated in moral terms like those that structured the psychological novels and *Les*

Caves du Vatican. In his plan for *Les Faux-Monnayeurs*, recorded on 19 July 1921, Gide said that the work would have three bases, the artistic, the intellectual, and the moral. Under the latter heading he was thinking especially of the insubordination of children and of the refusal of their parents to accord them freedom (*OC*, 13:25).

The theme of insubordination (which echoes distantly Ménalque's campaign to wrest children free of the authority of their parents) persisted in Gide's mind and became a central concern of his book. The company of adolescents—Bernard, Olivier, Armand, Sarah—bear the prestige of moral authority in *Les Faux-Monnayeurs*. They stand between their parents, who have in general lost all sense of honor and dignity, and their younger brothers, who are still living a savage, instinctual life undisturbed by the mutterings of conscience.

Bernard is the most fully developed moral figure in the novel. His moral life begins with revolt against his father. The discovery of his bastardy merely offers him a pretext for the rebellion that had long been brewing within him. Rebellion against what? Against the duplicity, hypocrisy, and mendacity that characterize life in his milieu. Monsieur Profitendieu, by accepting dishonor rather than risk a scandal inimical to his career, concentrates in himself everything that Bernard has come to loathe in his surroundings.

Once Bernard has acted out his rebellion by running away from home he begins to discover the truth about himself, and the truth is that he is at heart a puritan and a conservative. "Do you know what filled me most with horror at home?" he says to Laura. "Luxury. So much comfort, so many facilities. . . . I felt myself becoming an anarchist. Now, on the contrary, I think I am turning into a conservative. . . . Listen, if someone were to ask me today what virtue seems finest to me, I would answer without hesitation, probity. Oh, Laura! I would like, all my life long, to give off, at the slightest blow, a sound that is pure, honest, and authentic. Nearly all the people I have known ring false" (*RRS*, 1093–94).

On his baccalaureate examination Bernard finds in some frivolous verses of La Fontaine the pretext for a tirade against the easygoing, joking, ironic character of "French wit." He pleads for a reaffirmation of the French virtues of seriousness, logic, and patient research. He confides to Olivier that he is thirsting for moral action. Still, when the angel leads him to consider in turn the three ideological positions (Christian, Nationalist, and Socialist) that his culture offers him, he is unable to commit himself to a choice. His nightlong contest with the angel is without issue. The following day he explains his dilemma to Édouard: "It was then that I asked myself how I was to establish a rule of conduct, since I could not envisage life without a rule and yet would not accept that rule from someone else's lips" (*RRS*, 1215). It is nonetheless just such a rule that he is hoping to extract from Édouard. The latter wisely demurs, telling Bernard that only by living can he learn how he ought to live. Bernard's subsequent decision to return to his family and accept Monsieur Profitendieu as a father is the final, and most positive, step in his return to the order against which he had rebelled.

The rebelliousness of Armand and Sarah Vedel is motivated by a climate of hypocrisy more systematically nourished than the one in which Bernard found himself. Édouard, speaking of their grandfather, says in his journal: "Simple souls like Azaïs are certainly the ones I have the greatest difficulty in understanding. If you are a little less simple than they, you see yourself forced to play a sort of game in their presence; it is not very honest, but what can you do about it? You can't discuss or define anything; you have to acquiesce. Azaïs imposes hypocrisy on all of those around him who don't happen to share his belief. When I first began to frequent the family, I was indignant at seeing his grandchildren lie to him. I finally had to follow their lead" (*RRS*, 1015).

Armand, from having grown up in this atmosphere where statements are never in accord with reality and truth, finds himself permanently and consciously divided into two persons: "Whatever I say or do, always a part of me hangs back, watching the other part compromise itself, mocking and hissing it, or applauding it. When you are so divided, how in the world can you be sincere?" (*RRS*, 1229). Armand knows, however, the reason for his division: it lies in the culture of Virtue. "Yes," he says to Olivier, "I think it is the sincerest thing in me: the horror, the hatred of everything that is called Virtue. Don't try to understand. You don't know what an early puritan upbringing can do to you. It leaves in your heart a resentment that you can never get over" (*RRS*, 1231–32). Armand's hatred of virtue is so great that it makes him injure his sister Rachel, the one person in the world whom he respects and loves and who exemplifies true virtue in his eyes. The same perverse sentiment drives him to accept the authority of De Passavant, who is the negation of virtue. Armand's moral rebellion is as useless as Bernard's.

The desperation of the adolescents at not being able to break free of the duplicity of their circumstances is projected into adulthood in the character of Strouvilhou. This archetypal rebel has resolved in his own way the dilemma that Bernard and Armand are facing. The principle of his thought and action is a radical misanthropy. His hatred of mankind is rooted in his hatred of himself. "As a man," he says, "I scorn and hate myself as much as I do others" (*RRS*, 1195). Unable to tolerate the pious platitudes of men concerning their betterment and their ultimate salvation, he can breathe only when he has reversed their propositions. "I like to turn problems upside down. And if I cannot bear the thought of a Christ sacrificing himself for the fruitless salvation of all these frightful people I rub elbows with, I find some satisfaction, and even a sort of serenity, in imagining this contemptible crowd rotting to produce a Christ" (*RRS*, 1197).

Strouvilhou turns the frustrated negativity of Bernard and Armand into a militant negation. His rebellion does not end in surrender. He has made it a consistent program of action that includes the organization of vice among the young, the issuance of false coin, and initiation of an avant-garde movement in literature. In support of his candidacy for the editorship of Count de Passavant's literary review he says:

We are living on hand-me-down sentiments that the reader imagines he feels, because he believes everything that is printed; the author counts on that as he does on the conventions that he believes to be the bases of his art. Those sentiments ring as false as metal slugs; but they pass as currency. . . . I warn you: if I take the direction of a review, it will be in order to puncture illusions, to demonetize all those fine sentiments and those I.O.U.'s, words.

. . . The most wide-awake members of the younger generation are already more than fed up with poetic inflation. They know how much hot air is concealed by learned rhythms and sonorous lyrical clichés. If we propose demolishment we will always find helping hands. (*RRS*, 1198–99)

Strouvilhou overplays his hand in exposing these intentions to De Passavant. The count, as much threatened by this insurrection as any of his fellow *littérateurs*, prefers to entrust his review to the less radical vision of Armand Vedel. This is the price Strouvilhou has to pay for being an "idealist." His nihilistic countermorality is in the last analysis no more efficacious against the prevailing climate of hypocrisy than Bernard's passion for honesty.

The panorama of moral attitudes is enriched by the minor figures of Vincent Molinier and Lady Griffith, an American. Together, they illustrate the ethics of absolute self-interest. Lady Griffith's outlook is summed up in the story she tells of the wreck of the *Bourgogne*, where she saw some passengers driven away from the lifeboats in order to make those already in them more secure. It was not a question of the survival of the fittest, but of the most privileged. Finding herself in the latter group, Lilian never thereafter lost her sense of election. Her life became simply a recapitulation of the lifeboat incident.

Lady Griffith is destroyed, however, by Vincent Molinier, whose self-interest is just as ruthless as hers. Vincent was not on the *Bourgogne* when she sank, but his upbringing has implanted in him the "lifeboat" mentality. He abandons Laura when they leave the sanatorium, her presence having become an obstacle to his ambition. Even the money he had promised her to see her through her confinement he finds can better be devoted to his own ends. He severs his ties with De Passavant as soon as he sees that he has nothing further to gain from their friendship. Lilian's turn comes, we assume, in much the same way. Vincent is reported to have drowned her and to have then sunk into a dementia in which he saw himself as the devil. This epiphany suggests nothing so much as a ridiculous poetic justice. It is as though Gide were mocking his own indignation before an attitude so ingrained and so widespread that no accusation could effectively touch it.

Strouvilhou represents one response to the ambiguous moral climate of the bourgeoisie; Lady Griffith and Vincent Molinier illustrate a response that is diametrically opposed to his. Strouvilhou's nihilism has developed out of his frustrated desire to *be* what his culture told him he should be: principled, consistent, and courageous. Lilian and Vincent have ignored the precepts of their society and looked only at what *is done* in it. They have thereby escaped its contradictions and its cowardice, and they manifest with exemplary openness its real principle.

The figure who stands most in opposition to these extremes is Rachel. She is a living example of Christian virtue made practical and operative. It is not her words but her acts that exemplify abnegation and self-sacrifice. But of what avail is her virtue? It only renders Armand, Sarah, and Bernard more bitter toward a world that makes such inhuman demands of the virtuous. All three are responsive to Rachel's pathetic example, but their response is nothing but revolt and refusal. It is as though they recognized that her virtue serves and justifies the way of the world, that it sanctifies an order in which the meek and gentle are sacrificed to the rapacious and the indifferent.

When all of the attitudes and actions described in *Les Faux-Monnayeurs* are regarded together and the "moral question" is seen in the aggregate, the unavoidable conclusion must be that, within the given conditions and circumstances, no ethical life is really possible. Lilian and Vincent arrive at this knowledge through experience and intuition; they do not seek to controvert the fact or to mask it. Their elders, the Moliniers, the Profitendieus, the Azaïs-Vedels, are not so straightforward. They accept the world as it is and find their advantage in its inequities, but they entertain in themselves and inculcate in their children the illusion that justice and virtue can prevail in that same world. The result is that the young, who believe in the illusion, face an insurmountable contradiction. They cannot live in the world as it is, but neither can they get out of it or change it. Strouvilhou takes refuge in denial. He turns his ideal upside down and tries to realize it in the form of pure negation. Armand is treading the same path. Bernard, on the other hand, has lived so long in a circumstance of contradiction that his being has assumed the form of contradiction. Therefore the only authentic life and the only possible ethics for him are a life and an ethics of contradiction. He reenters the world of hypocrisy and deceit, committed to the ideal of probity but knowing that it is impossible in his time.

More than 25 years after the publication of *Les Faux-Monnayeurs* Jean-Paul Sartre voiced the same conclusion about the same world. In *Saint Genet, Comédien et Martyr* (1952) he wrote: "Thus any ethics which is not presented explicitly as *impossible today* contributes to the mystification and the alienation of men. The moral 'problem' originates in the fact that ethics is *for all of us* at once inevitable and impossible" (177).

This conclusion leads us to what was certainly the overarching concern of Gide in *Les Faux-Monnayeurs*, the theme to which all other themes are ultimately subordinated: his determined indictment of the middle-class culture which he still felt as crippling and binding. *Les Faux-Monnayeurs* is, no less than *Les Caves du Vatican*, a work that derives its principal energy from the critical motive. In *Les Caves* the literary means employed to achieve the ends of criticism were satire and burlesque; in *Les Faux-Monnayeurs* they are realism and understatement. The realism of Gide involves first of all an objective vision of typical personalities and institutions of the petty bourgeoisie. The climate of middle-class family life, of the private boarding school, of the world of letters, is evoked in scene after scene. The irony of Édouard's occasional judgments against realism draws attention to the impersonal tone of the primary narrative. Édouard's consciousness of the disparity between factual reality and ideals, and his desire to write a novel "as true and as remote from reality, as particular and at the same time as general, as human and as fictive as *Athalie, Tartuffe*, or *Cinna*," are among the most tellingly realistic details of Gide's novel, for in Édouard's contradictory aesthetics we see an analogue of the ethical contradictions of his class.

Gide's notebooks reveal that he labored to achieve a "flat," self-effacing narrative voice (*OC*, 13:52), and that he aimed to give his reader the advantage of judgment, allowing him to think himself more intelligent, more moral, more perspicacious than the author (*OC*, 13:45). The unstructured character of the narrative is designed to yield a similarly ironic effect. Gide imposed upon himself the difficult rule of beginning each chapter from scratch, without taking advantage of the "momentum" of the story. He thus stifled any tendency toward the dramatic in his narrative. Things happen with little evidence of causality. Actions, however decisive in appearance, produce no serious consequences, no sequels that might not have occurred as well with different antecedents. The characters of the story, whatever their longings, are as unromantic as possible. In the final analysis they *do* nothing and *are* at the end what they were at the beginning. Édouard's projected book that will never be written is, in a way, the emblem of all the failures that are revealed in the course of the story.

There are, to be sure, horrors in the novel: surrenders, betrayals, violent abuses. But these are disclosed without emphasis and without comment. They are simply the daily fare of a people whose contradictions lead them inevitably into horror. *Les Faux-Monnayeurs* is the completed image of those "marshlands" that Gide depicted in an important book of his youth. The frantic struggles of Bernard and Armand to get out of the middle-class morass of mendacity, duplicity, and abdication of duty and ideals are without avail. At the end they, like Tityre, are learning to nourish themselves on the worms that live in the mud under their feet.

L'École des femmes

Closely related in subject and tone to *Les Faux-Monnayeurs* are three short stories that Gide began writing within two years of the publication of the novel. (His travels in the Congo filled most of the intervening time.) *L'École des femmes* (*The School for Wives*) (1929) was begun early in 1927. Writing at first "joyously and easily" he soon lost interest in the story and finished it, under the pressure of a publication commitment, in November 1928. The sequel, *Robert* (1930), went much faster: it was written in less than a week in September 1929, and published the following year. "The third panel of the triptych," *Geneviève* (1936), was begun on the heels of *Robert* in March 1930, but Gide again lost interest in his work, and this time, having no external goad to drive him to completion, he wrestled with the task until 1936.

These three stories have not been much praised by those who have studied and written on Gide's work. (A notable exception is J.-J. Thierry's qualification of *L'École des femmes* as a "masterpiece of the psychological novel"—*RRS*, 1594.) The reason for this neglect is not difficult to find: the stories do not come up to the expectations aroused by Gide's earlier fiction. Issuing from the hand of a writer who only a few years before had so brilliantly dramatized the intimate conflicts of desire and repression, they are surprisingly, and disappointingly, lacking in passion, violence, perversity, and strangeness. They are written in that low-keyed realistic mode that Gide had developed in *Les Faux-Monnayeurs* with the design of revealing the invisible tensions and conflicts in the commonplace, unchanging life of the bourgeoisie.

Gide had not initially intended to write three stories around the same pretext. The second and third pieces simply grew in response to all that was left unsaid in the first. The idea of *L'École des femmes* dates from the time when he was planning *Les Faux-Monnayeurs*. It is outlined in the second paragraph of the *Journal des Faux-Monnayeurs:*

The story of the two sisters. The elder who marries, against the wishes of her parents . . . , a vain person, without value, but polished enough to charm the family, after having charmed the girl. She, however, while the family is making amends for having doubted the wisdom of her choice and finding in their son-in-law all sorts of virtues which exist only in appearance, is discovering little by little the basic mediocrity of the man to whom she has bound herself. She hides from everyone the contempt and disgust that she feels, rises to the challenge and makes it a point of honor to enhance her husband's glitter, conceal his inadequacies, and repair his social errors; so that she is the only one to know the emptiness of her "happiness." Everywhere, this couple is referred to as a model one, and when finally, exasperated, she tries to separate from this hollow man and live her own life, she is the one society accuses. (The question of the children is to be considered separately.) (*OC*, 13:6)

Even though Gide's execution of the story did not embody all the developments contained in this outline, the strategy is essentially what we read here, and the value, or meaning, is precisely that stated in the project. The underlying motive of the story is the one that I have identified in so many other works of Gide: the refusal of sexuality. The image in which the motive is realized, the dissolution of a marriage, is equally familiar. The particular character of *L'École des femmes* lies in the motivation that Gide invented to justify Éveline's growing disgust with Robert and her desire to be rid of him. The erotic motive is completely sublimated in the strategy of refusal. Éveline's desire for separation is justified by ethical considerations alone. It is her husband's character that revolts her, not his physical presence. Nowhere in her account is there the slightest hint of a sexual disaffection. Nor is there any inclination to celibacy or desire for another man. The story that Éveline tells is that of a young girl who is completely won by the charm and attentions of a serious and gifted young man. She forces the consent of her parents, who are not much taken with her choice. Then, in the years of intimacy that follow, she learns that Robert's attentions to others are not spontaneous manifestations of a gentle nature but are rather calculated designs employed to gain favor and advantage with associates and with persons in power. His intelligence and seriousness are devoted to nothing loftier than financial deals, influence peddling, and party propaganda. In short, the whole person that so dazzled and delighted her at first turns out to be something she could not even imagine before her marriage. Robert is a shadow with no substance. He is not a creation of God and nature, but a product of a particular social environment. His being is contained entirely in his appearance. He is *nothing but* a succession of poses. Were he a hypocrite, she might at least respect the autonomous decision that had made him one, but even that sort of being is lacking in him. "For Robert is not a hypocrite," Éveline writes. "He imagines that he really has the sentiments he expresses. And in the final analysis I think that he even feels them, and that they come at his call, the finest, most generous, noblest feelings, always exactly the ones that it is right to have, the ones that it is advantageous to have" (*RRS*, 1282).

Despite this profound insight into Robert's being, Éveline goes on justifying her alienation in terms of his character, of what he does or does not do. She is incapable of drawing the conclusion indicated by her observation. At one point she writes: "Oh, how I should like to see him just once, defend a cause in which he would really have to compromise himself, experience feelings from which he could draw no advantage, have convictions that would gain him nothing" (*RRS*, 1284). What she would have Robert do is more or less what she herself is doing. She wants him to act out the contradiction between the ideals (screen values) and the actions (real values) of their class. Her utterance makes it clear that, in her thought, authentic causes, sentiments, and convictions must be in opposition to the existing order. The proof of their authenticity lies in what they *cost* the adherent, rather than in what he may gain from them. The corollary proposition is, of course, that he can save *himself* only by losing, or renouncing, everything else. In spite of her religious upbringing, Éveline is far from knowing exactly what to understand by "saving oneself." She is only sure that there must be some sort of evil in a life that is able to accommodate antithetical ends. What revolts her is that Robert can do this so easily and with such success, that he can enunciate, and have accepted, a verbal interpretation of his conduct that is the very reverse of the facts. It does not occur to Éveline—because her education and upbringing have carefully concealed it from her—that this is simply "the way of the world," that, far from being in contradiction with himself, Robert has admirably adapted his life to those modes of action and speech that, in his time and place, lead to the twin goals of wealth and righteousness.

Éveline is a victim of the mystifications of her own class. Not seeing the concrete exploitations of Robert and his associates—which is no great wonder, since they guarantee the ease and plenty of her material life—she locates the evil in Robert's "duplicity," in his indifference to the disparity between his actions and his maxims. "It is not so much his actions I despise," she writes, "it is the reasons he gives for them" (*RRS*, 1309). But this is only an illusion of evil, a phantom created by the mystifications of bourgeois morality. Every event tends to thrust this fact at Éveline's consciousness. Robert continues to prosper. Everything turns to his advantage. He takes an enormous profit from the slim patronage he had accorded to his friend, the painter Bourgweilsdorf. Even while shirking combat service, he manages to be in the right place (Verdun) at the right time to receive a military decoration for heroism. When Éveline confronts him with her desire for separation, he bursts into perfectly genuine tears: he had never suspected that she loved him less than he loved her. There is, finally, nothing that she can accuse him of; he is never really in the wrong. But the sense of his unworthiness persists in her.

Unable to find Robert at fault, Éveline turns—with unconscious perspicacity—against the ideas and institutions that are protecting him. "He has a way of talking about duty that would make me detest any 'duty,' a way of using religion which would make any religion suspect, and a way of playing with lofty sentiments that would disgust you with them forever" (*RRS*, 1281). Another time she writes: "I have badly neglected my religious obligations. The practices that Robert displays have sort of disaffected my heart; the manifestations of his piety have made me doubt the genuineness of my own" (*RRS*, 1287). After an interview in which she had tried to gain the sympathy of her confessor she is forced to conclude that "the Church and he are concerned only with externals. Father Bredel can accept much more easily a simulacrum that is useful to him than my sincerity which embarrasses and aggravates him" (*RRS*, 1289).

Frustrated in every attempt at revolt against her situation, Éveline is finally reduced to a typical gesture of desperation: she seeks a post nursing soldiers afflicted with a contagious disease and dies in their midst. This gesture of self-sacrifice is related, without emphasis, as a sort of foreword to her diary. Gide made no effort, here or elsewhere in the story, to induce the pathetic note that the heroine's problem might well have justified. He was aiming rather at the tone of quiet, restrained desperation that contrasts so sharply with the passion and tears of Alissa's diary in *La Porte étroite* and with the devastation and despair at the end of the minister's journal in *La Symphonie pastorale*. Éveline has nothing of the heroic individualist about her. Her reaction to her situation is in no wise idiosyncratic. Her confession reveals her to be a typical representative of her social class. She illustrates in a very touching and convincing manner the dilemma that we saw manifested in the youths of *Les Faux-Monnayeurs*, the rending drama that Sartre has described as *the inevitability and impossibility of morals in our time.*

The formal arrangement of *L'École des femmes* is designed to produce one major reversal in the story. In the first part, dated 1894, Éveline recounts the period of their courtship and her engagement to Robert. Here she is all naïve wonderment and admiration, unable to believe that Robert has really chosen her to be his wife. Only two things cast doubt upon her judgment: her father's dislike of the young man—which seems to be inspired by their political differences, but is in fact based on a very accurate intuitive assessment of his character—and the deceit that Robert works on her in the matter of their diaries. These were to be kept separately and held in privacy until the death of one or the other released his account of their life together to the survivor. Robert persuaded Éveline to let him read her diary before their marriage and then confessed that he had written nothing in his. Not content with having deceived her trust and abused her generosity, he managed to make her feel guilty for protesting against his conduct. Thus, all at once, with this incident that closes the first part of her diary, the irony of Éveline's choice is revealed.

In the second part of her diary, dated 20 years later, the conditions are exactly reversed. Éveline now knows what Robert is, while everyone else, including her father, is taken in by his apparent probity and generosity. Her situation now strikes *her* as ironic. She wants to punish Robert for his duplicity by leaving him, but she knows that her action will only bring blame upon her.

Éveline's view of things is, however, false. The real irony of her situation derives from her ignorance and confusion. Her alienation from Robert is founded on the illusion that they can *have* the life that is theirs without *being* what they are—what Robert so clearly *is* in her eyes, and what she *is* without really being aware of it. Her duplicity is at least as great as his, and is blind to boot.

L'École des femmes is an admirable piece of ironic dissimulation. The erotic motive, the will to be free (which meant to Gide to be sexually free) of the marriage bond (which meant to him the repressive mother fixation) is too basic, too powerful, and too insistent to disappear from the story; but Gide has turned it into a consequence of separation rather than a cause. The action has been displaced altogether to the ethical plane. Gide's execution of the story is mainly the work of his critical intelligence. Imagination, fantasy, wish fulfillment have little place in it once the initial impulse to liberation is given. His art consists above all in having evoked a convincing and consistent climate of opinions and attitudes to support and justify Éveline's decision.

In this atmosphere, the play of ideologies is an important element. Her father's anticlerical liberalism is opposed to her mother's conservative Catholicism, and then even more to Robert's aggressive and chauvinistic Catholic nationalism. These positions, which seem to those who profess them so irreducibly opposed, are not truly in conflict at all. They are not alternative systems of socioeconomic life. They are nothing more than manifestations of the contradictory content of the middle-class ethos.

Young women of Éveline's class are given to extravagant dreams of self-deprivation and sacrificial service to mankind. By these visions they seek obscurely to expiate a guilt they cannot even articulate. Before meeting Robert, Éveline had "seriously considered becoming a nurse or a Little Sister of the Poor" (*RRS*, 1252). (This design persists in her mind and is realized in the final, defiant challenge that she hurls at Robert.) Her friend Yvonne has the same impulse to self-sacrifice, and she enlists Éveline's aid in acting it out. (It is worth noting that Yvonne's wish is prompted by disappointment in love, and that it turns ironically to her advantage by leading her to a devoted and distinguished husband.)

Éveline again expresses the wish for poverty when she learns, before her marriage, that Robert has inherited wealth. "I am almost sorry for it: I should like to leave fortune to those who need money to be happy"

(*RRS*, 1262). This pretentious statement epitomizes the elaborate illusions fostered and entertained by her class. Gide knew as well as anyone
the implications of such a vain utterance; he had been in thrall to the
same illusions most of his life.

Robert

The fictional illusion is less convincing in *Robert* than in *L'École des
femmes*. The ease and speed with which Gide completed the story would
lead us to think that he took no small pleasure in composing Robert's
self-serving apologia, but that very satisfaction is perhaps the source of a
certain incongruity in the character of the diarist. Éveline's diary was
very well motivated. It began with a girl's desire to keep a record of the
blissful time of her engagement. It was prolonged by a woman's need to
confide to someone, if only to herself, a marital disillusionment that none
of her close associates was able to see or understand. The tone of the latter
account is accusing and self-justifying, but not exaggeratedly so. Éveline
creates little interest in herself by what she writes. The interest of her
story lies, as I observed, in what she unwittingly tells about the mind of
her class. Her value lies in her typicalness.

Robert undertakes his account of his life with Éveline as an act of
self-defense. The motive is convincing. But what he writes is so far from
being a justification of his actions and his reasons that he emerges an even
sorrier figure than he was in Éveline's diary. She denounced the facile
piety of his maxims but stood in some awe of his power and astuteness. In
his own account he appears to be nothing more than a very petty tyrant,
one who is unquestioningly obedient to the authority of church and state
because he derives from them his claim to govern the conduct of his wife
and children. His tone is peevish and defensive as he writes of Éveline's
insubordination and failure to conform to her role as a woman. "I
consider that the role of the woman, in the family and in civilization as a
whole, is and must be conservative," he writes. "And it is only when the
woman assumes complete consciousness of this role that the man's
thought, freed of this responsibility, can allow itself to forge ahead. How
many times have I felt that the position taken by Éveline held back the
real progress of my thought and forced me to assume in our household a
function which should have been hers" (*RRS*, 1324).

In thus acknowledging that he assumed a feminine role in his own
household, Robert seems to have no sense of his ridiculousness. It is the
same when he recounts how Éveline laughed at his overly serious manner

of reading a passage from the biography of Joseph de Maistre that showed the young count's absolute obedience to the will of his parents. Éveline laughed because Robert's tone indicated to her how much he wanted her to find the anecdote edifying. In relating this incident, however, Robert only invites his readers to join in Éveline's amusement.

The second part of the story relates Robert's attempt, together with Father Bredel, to induce Éveline, during a critical illness, to resume her religious practices. Although weak and vulnerable she refused confession and contrition and accepted the host only because it was thrust upon her. When she recovered, she declined to recognize any miraculous power in the sacrament she had received. Robert recounts it thus: "Éveline . . . came through this ordeal failing to recognize the grace of God and more stubborn than before, like those people mentioned in the Scriptures who have eyes to see and do not see, ears to hear and do not hear; so that I almost came to regret that God had not taken her to him at the moment when she had shown the greatest submission and when even in the midst of her disbelief she had accepted Him" (*RRS*, 1340). Robert relates this sentiment with no apparent sense of its horror and grotesque perversity. Reading it, we can hardly fail to see him as a monstrous idiot and Éveline as more of a heroine than her own narrative had led us to believe.

Robert has nothing like the interest and importance of *L'École des femmes*. It betrays no compelling ulterior motive. It is devoid of genuine irony. The chief character is not so much a social type as a caricature of that type. Gide's critical observation of the middle class, so surely and so penetratingly objectified in *L'École des femmes*, is here dissipated in a satire that is neither very keen nor very humorous.

Geneviève

Gide's pretext for writing *Geneviève* was a few paragraphs in Éveline's diary in which she recounted a conversation with her adolescent daughter about Robert. Geneviève despised her father for the same reasons as Éveline and was warmly sympathetic and defensive toward her mother. She saw the drama, however, in sexual terms and embarrassed Éveline by assuming that she had been in love with the painter Bourgweilsdorf. In the course of this conversation, Geneviève announced her intention to seek a free union rather than marriage.

This picture of juvenile revolt had a twofold value in *L'École des femmes*. It served the strategy of the story by intensifying Éveline's moral isolation. Even her most sympathetic ally was shown to be incapable of understanding her real problem. At the same time, Geneviève's outspoken revolt was a means for Gide to express his own lifelong rebellion against morality and paternal authority.

In writing a story from the point of view of Geneviève, Gide's primary design was to amplify the theme and the image of youthful revolt. He took pains to show that the source of rebellion was the latent sexual desire of his adolescent heroine, but that she found ample justification for it in her mother's unhappy marriage and in the condition of women in general in her society. To disclose this interplay of motives, he placed Geneviève first in a homosexual situation and then later in an incestuous one.

Between Sara and Gisèle, Geneviève experiences the full range of erotic feelings without ever being entirely aware of their origin. Everything about Sara conspires to arouse sensual passion: her sultry beauty, the poems of Baudelaire she recites so well, the painting of her in the nude done by her father. When to these lures are added her Jewishness, the marginal social milieu to which she belongs, and her emancipated ideas on love and marriage—all forbidden but terribly desirable attributes—Geneviève barely escapes realizing what it is she desires of her. The attraction of Gisèle, an angelic type who exerts a spiritual and intellectual authority over her, is a restraint of sorts on Geneviève's desire for Sara, but in truth she wants to love both girls and is jealous of their relationship, which is older and more intimate than hers with either of them.

What holds this explosive situation in check is an intellectual sublimation. The three girls channel their erotic energies into a program of feminine independence. By projecting their wish for sexual freedom into feminism and the future, they are able to restrain the desire for immediate gratification. (Some time later when the danger has passed, Gisèle reveals that she had been more wildly in love with Sara than Geneviève had been, but she had concealed her passion better.)

When Geneviève is separated from her two friends, her erotic interest is transferred to Dr. Marchant, a long-time friend of her parents. In her fantasies she has already substituted him for her father, so that when she conceives the design of asking him to father a child upon her she is in truth giving expression to an unconscious oedipal wish. Dr. Marchant's confusion and embarrassment suggest that he has harbored a similar fantasy, which Geneviève's invitation brings into the open.

Again in this instance Geneviève does not recognize her desire and attributes her proposal to a need to protest against social controls:

In truth I had never analyzed the components of my resolve, but in my particular case I think it was again and above all a matter of protest; yes, protest against what my father called "good morals," and more especially still against him, who symbolized those "good morals" in my eyes; a need to humiliate him, to mortify him, to make him blush for me, disavow me; a need to affirm my independence, my insubordination, by an act that only a woman could commit, for which I expected to assume full responsibility, without very seriously envisaging its consequences (*RRS*, 1405–6).

Geneviève could not make a clearer case of her feelings: she is tormented by an ambivalent love-hate for her father, the same emotion that had dominated the childhood and adolescence of Gide.

The real force of *Geneviève* resides in these two episodes, which are quite obviously disguised statements of Gide's own eroticism; they are fantasies like those that his imagination devised to bring a secret joy and fulfillment to his psychic life. They reveal the poetic impulse in one of its purest forms. In addition to fantasy, there were certainly real events in Gide's life that lent substance to his fictional representations. (Geneviève's relations with Dr. Marchant hint very strongly at the relations of Gide with Élisabeth Van Rysselberghe, the daughter of some long-time friends, who bore his daughter Catherine in 1922.) There is the further likelihood that his imagination had been nourished by readings in psychoanalytical literature. (Geneviève cites Freud in her diary [*RRS*, 1385] and Gide, in his *Journal* under the date 29 December 1932, quotes a passage from the work of Wilhelm Stekel.)

The feminine disguise is a work of considerable artistry, comparable to Proust's "Confession d'une Jeune Fille" and to his characterization of Mademoiselle Vinteuil in *À la Recherche du temps perdu*. In *Geneviève* Gide depicts with great delicacy the restraints that modesty and ignorance impose upon the instinctual drives of a young woman of the middle class. The insurgent feminism of Geneviève and her friends is very effective, because Gide makes evident its origin in their latent wish for sexual liberty and its vanity within the context of their social and economic circumstances.

In 1933, at a moment when he was frustrated by the incompletion of *Geneviève*, Gide wrote in his *Journal*:

If I had been able to complete right away this *Geneviève*, which was to be a sequel to my *École des femmes* and in which I proposed to let the new generation speak, I would doubtless have exhausted in the process (I would have purged myself of) a lot of ratiocinations that have taken up residence in me and that I have felt forced to entertain in myself. I have not been able to discharge them upon a "hero," as formerly I had done with the Nietzschean preoccupations in my *Immoraliste* and with the Christian ones in my *Porte étroite*, and I am still stuck with them (or with myself).[2] In entertaining these trains of thought, I was not able to push them to extremes, to absurd limits, as I would have been able to do in a novel which would, all at the same time, have exposed them, gone over them and criticized them, and would finally have freed me of them. The trap, badly set (that I no longer have the power to set well) has suddenly closed on me. (*J*, 1160)

This is an excellent statement of the cathartic function that fiction served in Gide's life. His reluctance—or as he termed it, his incapacity— to push his idea to the limit is the essential factor in that alteration in his style of fictional representation that was noticed first in *Les Faux-Monnayeurs*, and that I called the abandonment of the romantic mode. No doubt what is implied in this loss of power is that the catharsis, which his earlier work so palpably was, had brought about dissolution of the complex. Instead of being a prey to his complexity, he had become master of it. In place of passion there was now understanding. The need for catharsis had in fact become very slight, and his literary imagination had necessarily to turn from the cathartic mode to the mimetic. His own personality and his own life appeared to him no less problematical than they had before. He still harbored the same drives. But a deeper understanding of these drives had made it impossible for him to push his fantasies to the extremes they had once reached.

Self-knowledge had also made Gide more aware of the social nature of his complex and had intensified his already lively sympathy for other victims of societal repressions. The progressive socialization of his personal history is the primary clue to understanding Gide's public activity and the motives of his fiction during this late period of his life.

In this development we can see the reason for the decline in his creative power that Gide so often complained of in these years. Up until his fiftieth year—which coincided with the break in his relations with his wife and the end of the First World War—Gide's fiction had been an essential and absolutely necessary representation of the illusions that his instinctual needs projected in the face of a hostile and contrary reality. His stories and plays afforded him a symbolic release of the tensions created in him by the desperate struggle to maintain those illusions against the denials of reality. His psychic life and his fiction were made of the same dream stuff. With self-knowledge there came submission to reality—for the expression of rebelliousness in Gide's later fiction is just that—and the collapse of illusions.

The mental state of understanding is one of equilibrium and accommodation. It does not *demand* objectivation or symbolic "acting out." Gide had reached the point where his primitive impulses were strong enough to provide the schemata of a story (the feelings of lust, frustration, hatred, and violence) but were no longer powerful enough to override his reason and create fantasies of completion and satisfaction. His understanding of his own drives had to assert itself, and in so doing it drained the impulses of passion and gratification.

This, very simply, is what happened with *L'École des femmes* and *Geneviève*. this is why they are so different from *L'Immoraliste* and *La Porte étroite*. No work of Gide contains a more sophisticated understanding of a social character than *L'École des femmes*, and yet no work, not even *Geneviève*, seems aesthetically less finished.

Oedipe

Although the subject had been in his mind for many years and seemed an inevitable one for him, Gide had to drive himself rather hard to complete *Oedipe* (1931). In October 1930, when he was close to finishing the play, he wrote in his *Journal*: "Certainly I am no longer tormented by an imperious desire to write. The feeling that 'the most important part remains to be said' no longer dwells in me as it did formerly, and I persuade myself, on the contrary, that I no longer have much to add to what a perspicacious reader can glimpse in my writings" (*J*, 1014).

Though it has neither the haunting beauty of *Saül* nor the seductive charm of *Le Roi Candaule, Oedipe* is a play of considerable mettle. It owes this character to a fortunate conjunction of motives in the mind of its author. The essential traits of the legend of King Oedipus were so compatible with those of Gide's personal history that the subject lent itself admirably to the sort of self-disclosure, at once poetic and critical, that he was ready, at this stage of his life, to make. This was a time when he had attained a rather thorough understanding of himself and when he was able to perceive the imperious role that the "Oedipus complex" had played in his destiny. He was therefore able to identify himself easily and naturally with the Theban king and to regard their situation with indulgence and even humor. This is the primary motive and the underlying raison d'être of the play.

The Oedipe of acts 1 and 2 is a creature of pride and self-sufficiency, a man such as Gide had been—not constantly and not entirely, but in his dominant mood, so to speak—during the period of his greatest creative power, from 1896 to 1914. Oedipe feels as though he were "led by a god." He owes his happiness to no one but himself, to nothing but his own manly enterprise and to a fortunate disposition of chance.

Believing himself to be the son of Polybe, he had learned one day from a fortune-teller that he was fated to slay his father. This prediction, far from spelling misfortune, turned to his advantage, for it brought him the knowledge that he was a foundling. When he left Polybe's household to go and ask the god whose son he was, he met with another apparent mishap that turned to his profit: in anger he killed a stranger on the road, and, being unclean, could no longer approach the altar of the god. Chance had thus obliged him to live without the example of a father or the counsel of a god. Ignorance of his past had made him place all his hope in the future. It was in this spirit that he had challenged the Sphinx and won. His victory gave him a kingship, which he thought he owed to his wits alone, and a wife so gentle that he found in her consolation for the mother he had never known.

Oedipe experiences a great satisfaction also in his four children. The two boys, with their emancipated talk and their eager lusts, are just what he was at their age. They seem prepared to challenge the Sphinx and win in their turn. The girls are very dissimilar, but Oedipe is equally delighted with Ismène's lighthearted joy and lyrical turns of speech and Antigone's severe, but entirely genuine, piety. He is, in short, a perfectly happy man, not too much troubled by the plague that is ravaging his kingdom and inclined to dismiss Tirésias's warnings as mere exercises of priestcraft.

Gide's Oedipe, while manifesting objectively the same history as the Oedipus of Sophocles, manages to evoke, with a tantalizing aptness, the conditions of his author's existence in those years when the latter commanded with such exuberant mastery the resources that nature and chance had given him. Gide had by then thrown off the paternal authority of social regulation and the authority of God as represented by the church and the priesthood. He had outwitted the monster that guarded the seat of intellectual authority by seeking a response to its riddle in his own particular humanity. He had moreover married a woman who consoled him for the loss of his mother and had engendered, in his books, children who were pleasing to his eye. Michel and Lafcadio were to Gide what Étéocle and Polynice are to Oedipe; in Alissa he had created his own Antigone; and the joyous voice of Ismène was audible throughout his *Nourritures terrestres*.

Gide's situation at that time, was, of course, full of irony. Underlying his revolt against all forms of paternal authority was the symbolic murder of his father; and his conjugal happiness reposed on the fulfillment, again symbolic, of an incestuous desire for his mother. Nor were the children of his imagination altogether so glorious as they appeared at first to be. They sprang as much from the darkness of his soul—from his destructive anarchism and his frightful sense of impurity—as from the clarity of his artistic purpose.

The irony of Oedipe's happiness is abundantly revealed in the play through Tirésias's preaching about the sin that no man escapes, through Créon's observation that Oedipe owes his crown to the man who murdered King Laïus, and above all to the comical disclosures of the disposition to incest in the royal family, which Gide brought out with such gaiety that he was accused by some contemporary critics of coarseness. Speaking of Jocaste, Oedipe says: "What a wife! What a mother! As for me who never knew my own, I have for her a love almost filial and at the same time conjugal" (*Th*, 263). When he and Créon are eavesdropping on the children, they learn that both of the boys are lusting after their sisters, but Oedipe refuses to be shocked by the impurity of their desire.

At the end of act 2, as Oedipe prepares to assume his new role as the suffering king, he scrutinizes his life to that moment and realizes that it all derives from the crime that he committed in a moment of anger:

When I left the road that led to God, was it really because my hands were no longer clean? I cared little about that, at the time. It seems to me even today that it was my crime which turned my steps first toward the Sphinx. What is to be had from a God? Answers. I felt that I was an answer to a question I didn't yet know. It was the question of the Sphinx. I, being quick-witted, won. But since then, hasn't everything become more obscure for me? But since then, but since then. . . . What have you done, Oedipe? Lulled by my prize I have slept for twenty years. But now at last I hear the new monster stirring in me. A great destiny awaits me, crouching in the evening shadows. Oedipe, the time of repose is past. Awake from your happiness. (*Th*, 288–89)

This song of self-transcending and rebirth might be taken as a lyrical condensation of the prolonged and painful awakening from illusion that Gide experienced in the wake of his estrangement from his wife in 1918. What follows for Oedipe in act 3 of the play is the discovery of what his years of power and triumph were really based on. In interpreting this moment of the hero's life, Gide emphasizes, not the crimes of murder and incest—Oedipe says impatiently to Créon: "Why come confusing me with these problems of kinship? If my sons are also my brothers, I shall only love them more" (*Th*, 294)—but the blind fulfilling of destiny, the denial of freedom implied in the events. What appalls Oedipe in his predicament is the knowledge that he has all the time been the unwitting captive of his own past:

Oh, frightful recompense of the enigma! What! So that is what was hidden beyond the Sphinx! . . . And I who was congratulating myself on not knowing my parents! . . . Thanks to which I wed my mother, alas, alas, and with her all my past. Ah, yes! I understand now why my valor slumbered. In vain the future was calling me. Jocaste was pulling me back. Jocaste, who foolishly tried to suppress what had to be, you whom I loved as a husband and, unknowingly, as a son. . . . It is high time. Leave me! I break the bond. . . . And you, children, companions of my somnolence, opaqueness of my fulfilled desires, it is without you that I must enter my evening and accomplish my destiny. (*Th*, 294–95)

It was no doubt in a mood comparable to that of Oedipe that Gide confronted the knowledge that his years of exalted conjugal devotion were no more than the recapitulation of his infantile desire for exclusive possession of his mother; that his Tristan romance was no magnificent invention of his manhood, but simply a repetition of his emotional life as a child. His greatest books too were born of this illusion and, in a sense, had to die with it.

Beyond this point of recognition and acknowledgment, Oedipe sees only a choice between submission to the God he has offended—which means submission to the priestcraft of Tirésias—and the invention, truly the invention this time, of a future appropriate to his past. He elects the latter course and, putting out his own eyes, inflicts upon himself a punishment that is at once an act of rivalry with the blind priest and a symbolical castration. He leaves his kingdom gladly to his sons, saying: "Freely I leave them, for their misfortune, a kingdom neither won nor merited. But, from my example, they have taken only what pleased them, authorizations, license, letting go restraint, the difficult and the best" (*Th*, 302). Accepting the companionship of his pious and devoted daughter, Antigone, he sets out as a wanderer. "I am no longer a king, no longer anything but a nameless traveler who gives up his wealth, his glory, himself" (*Th*, 303).

There is no element in this resolution of the drama of Oedipe—the will to command his own destiny, the continued defiance of institutionalized religion, the expiatory renunciation of the flesh, the assertion of piety and devotion, and the election of the nomadic life—that cannot be traced to the fantasies that occupied and shaped Gide's spiritual life. Oedipe is a picture of Gide beginning again, reordering his vital resources for a new plunge into the future. Nothing is different from what it was, and yet everything is somehow renewed.

It is with this sort of scheme of equivalencies in mind that we can best perceive and appreciate the poetic quality of *Oedipe*. This is not, however, the value that Gide chose to emphasize in writing the play. According to his practice as an artist, he aimed to provide a more general order of ideas to accompany and overshadow the personal myth. And since, in this period, the tone of his work was primarily critical, that is the tone that dominates the work. A note in his *Journal*, written just after he had finished *Oedipe*, is illuminating on this point: "I think, however, that I might have let myself go more in the third act. No doubt my reason intervenes too much. There is nothing in it that is not willed, motivated, necessary. What I used to call 'God's portion,' reduced to nothing, for lack of confidence, disbelief in inspiration, which makes me no longer dare to write except with a cool head. One ought to be willing to write without knowing what one is saying, and especially what one is going to say" (*J*, 1030).

Nevertheless, the terseness of Oedipe's utterances and the rapidity of the drama's development in the last act correspond excellently to the theme that Gide wanted to put in evidence, "the battle," as he put it in another journal entry, "of individuality against religious morals," "the opposition between the perspicacious antimystic and the believer, between the man blinded by faith and the one who tries to solve the enigma, between the one who submits to God and the one who opposes Man to God." It was a *moral* problem that he was seeking to dramatize, one that was still pressingly current, and not, as one critic had supposed, the perennial metaphysical debate about free will and determinism (*J*, 1106–7).

Oedipe is the hero who acts *as if* he were free, who, even when he learns that his acts were foreordained, assumes responsibility for them just as though they were the acts of his autonomous will—which is what they were when he committed them—and goes on inventing his life as though it were his to make. He ignores the advantage that he might take from Tirésias's prediction that a blessing will fall upon the land that receives his bones and, refusing repose, sets out on the course of restless expiation that his offenses seem to him to merit.

Oedipe is a hero superior in many ways to Sartre's Oreste (for whom he must, in some degree, have served as a model). Oreste had been taught that he was free (a fact later confirmed by the emissary of Zeus) and had only to learn to accept responsibility for his irreversible actions. In other words, he had to decide to become a moral agent. Oedipe, on the other hand, has heard all his life that he is not free, that he is destined to do this and that; and the event seems to bear out the pronouncements of the priests and the soothsayers on this point. Still, he *makes* his freedom by acting as though he were free and by claiming the responsibility for his actions even when others would relieve him of it. With him, moral action discloses freedom.

Oedipe is a hero of the antimystical, anticlerical, freethinking, liberal mind. He is, at first without knowing it, the enemy of the class in power and authority, the class to which he belongs. When he learns that he is a parricide and a regicide, he freely—even eagerly—accepts expulsion from his class and loss of the prerogatives it confers on him. (Sartre's Oreste plays a similar role and follows a similar course.) Gide's *Journal* contains two entries, written after his play had been presented in Paris and abroad (and not too well received in Paris) that betray his concern that the audience grasp the real interest of *Oedipe*, which lay in "the combat of ideas," and that they understand that "the drama was played on another level than that of the ancient tragedy" (*J*, 1129). He had left the pathos, the sublime, the grand style to Sophocles and claimed only to show what the Greek poet had not seen in his subject. I intend to let you see the back side of the stage scenery, even if it must destroy your emotion, for that is not what is important to me nor what I am trying to arouse: it is to your intelligence that I address myself. I propose, not to make you tremble or weep, but to make you think" (*J*, 1150–51).

A hazardous enterprise, to say the least, since what he wanted his public to see and think about most of them would judge to be subversive of consecrated authority and an offense against eternal truth—in other words an attack on the ideology of their class. *Oedipe* was nonetheless a tonic undertaking for Gide because it allowed him to present a moral *action* once again, in contrast to the moral inertia depicted in *Les Faux-Monnayeurs* and his shorter fiction. It marks in his life and his work a resurgence of the heroic spirit of independence and self-assertion. The real beginning of the play may lie in a note in the *Journal*, written in Zurich on 10 May 1927: "Not, *The New Oedipus*—but rather, *The Conversion of Oedipus*" (*J*, 840). This cryptic sentence is followed, two days later, by a more ample entry that seems to indicate—even though it does not explain precisely—why it was possible and necessary for him to write

Oedipe: "The game is lost, the game that I could win only with her. Lack of confidence on her part, and presumptuousness on mine. There is no use in recriminations, or even in regrets. What is not is what could not be. Whoever sets out toward the unknown must consent to travel alone. Creüsa, Eurydice, Ariadne, a woman always holds back, is worried, is afraid of letting go and of seeing the thread that ties her to her past break. She pulls Theseus back, and makes Orpheus turn around. She is afraid" (*J*, 840). After nearly 10 years, Gide, having traversed hope and despair, felt himself alone and free.

Thésée

On 21 May 1944, six months before his seventy-fifth birthday, Gide wrote in his journal: "Today . . . I finished *Thésée*. I still have large portions to rewrite, and in particular the beginning, for which I could not at first find the right tone. But at present the canvas is entirely covered. For a month I have worked every day, and almost constantly, in a state of joyous fervor such as I had not known for a long time and thought never to know again. It seemed to me that I was back in the time of *Les Caves*, or my *Prométhée*" (*J-S*, 269–70).

Thésée is Gide's last work of fiction. It caps his career in a grand style, for within its pages we discover figures and episodes that recall the essential moments of his long artistic and intellectual life. Rarely has a writer ended his work on such a pure and triumphant note.

An important factor in Gide's enthusiasm was certainly the rediscovery, after many years, of his symbolist style. The appearance of mythical and allegorical figures in place of characters and of extraordinary events and scenes in place of introspective analysis reminds us of *Le Voyage d'Urien, Philoctète, El Hadj, Les Nourritures terrestres,* and *Le Retour de l'Enfant prodigue.* The legendary deeds of Theseus were ready-made for this sort of tale, but, as always, it is Gide's inventions and embellishments upon the basic outline that give charm and value to the work. The hero's comments on his amatory adventures, the explanation of the labyrinth, the interviews with Dédale and Oedipe: these are the high points of the story. Gide's imagination was as fertile as it had been 50 years earlier. All he required was the stimulus of certain resonances from the motifs of the legend to the events of his own life.

In spite of its style, *Thésée* belongs to the spirit of this last period of Gide's work. Thésée, the man of bold but practical action, the founder of Athens and of the Athenian democracy, is the final ethical expression of what Gide had been feeling, thinking, and saying since the end of the First World War. In his symbolist decadent years he had projected in André Walter, Urien, Tityre, and Philoctète a sterile, alienated moral idealism. In the time of his romantic rebellion, we saw in Saül, Michel, Alissa, Lafcadio, and the Swiss preacher images of lawless self-assertion, of desire and refusal pushed to excess. Now, in Oedipe (the hero of the play, not the figure who appears in *Thésée*) and again in Thésée we find expressions of that commitment to freedom and progress that is the conducting thread of Gide's later years.

Thésée, looking back over his life, sees it as one of service to men: "I have definitively purged the earth of many tyrants, bandits and monsters; have cleared certain adventurous trails on which even the most daring minds still set foot in trembling; have cleared heaven in such a way that man, his head less bowed down, would be less apprehensive of surprises" (*RRS*, 1417).

When, in his confrontation with the holy man Oedipe, the latter tells him that the inward world, inaccessible to the senses, is the only true one and that "all the rest is only an illusion that deceives us and obscures our contemplation of the Divine," Thésée answers: "I remain a child of this earth and believe that man, whoever he is and however depraved you judge him to be, must play with the cards he holds." And weighing his life of action against the contemplative career of Oedipe, he concludes: "I am content . . . I leave behind me the city of Athens. More than my wife and my son, I have cherished it. I have created my city. . . . It is sweet to think that after me, and thanks to me, men will recognize that they are happier, better, and freer. For the good of humanity to come, I have created my work. I have lived" (*RRS*, 1452–53).

When it came to enunciating a political charter, however, Gide could do no better than voice through his hero an ideology that is most aptly described as "Radical-Socialist." Thésée renounces his hereditary right to rule as king, but he does so in the hope that he will be succeeded by an intellectual elite that will assure the masses that they are free, but at the same time will encourage them to greater productivity. In a way it is disappointing to see that Gide's lifelong revolt took him no further politically than this stale vision of enlightened paternalism. Still, it serves to remind us that his war with the class to which he belonged was, in the final analysis, not a thing of real substance but a symbolical struggle against paternal authority and control. Thésée is a Gidean hero because he displaced his father and fought the "monsters" of tradition, not because he founded the Athenian democracy.

Apart from the moral value that Gide recognized in the figure of the mythical Theseus, there was (there *had* to be!) a poetic value as well; that is to say, an intimate correspondence between the motifs of the legend and the motives of the Gidean psyche. In this case, it is not so deep and direct a bond as that which existed between Gide and King Oedipus. Gide's Thésée, like Prométhée and Lafcadio before him, represents that unchained, spontaneous, joyous agent that Gide dreamed of being, and that, in a certain sense, he had been. It is of great significance that he closes his version of the legend with the encounter at Colonus of Oedipus and Theseus. His Thésée says of this event: "I am astonished that people have spoken so little of that meeting of our two destinies at Colonus, of that supreme confrontation at the crossroads of our two careers. I consider it to be the summit, the crowning moment of my fame" (*RRS*, 1450). Their meeting is the tardy realization of the project originally announced for *Les Faux-Monnayeurs*; the confrontation of Édouard, the contemplative artist, and Lafcadio, the free agent.

This scheme of representing the union of his most radically opposed tendencies had lain in Gide's mind for a long while. In the Oedipe who appears at the end of *Thésée* Gide pictured the fate that deep down he felt to be his. Here is a man, once proud and defiant, now so burdened with guilt that there is no way left open to him but that of total renunciation. Gide had lived this destiny fully at several critical junctures of his life, and he continued to live it in the depths of his being. At the same time he knew there was another being in him, a free, creative force that never ceased defying fate and finding ways out of the most somber despair. This is the being who wrote his books and who continued to battle for enlightenment and self-mastery. This is the being we see under the features of Thésée.

Thésée's outlook and actions are at every turn in opposition to those of Oedipe. He killed his father too, or at least he thought he had secretly wished his death and had let it come about through deliberate negligence. But he did not hide from the deed when it was done. He acknowledged it to himself immediately and, since his motive had been largely unconscious, he dismissed from his mind any thought of guilt. He remained grateful to his father for cultivating in him the ideals of strength and effort, and he set out to improve upon his reign.

In what way had Gide exhibited a conduct like that of Thésée? Certainly not in his intimate relations, where he was thoroughly like Oedipe. But in his relations with the "paternal" culture he had done something like this. He had let it mold his strength and award him his weapons, and then he had set about to overcome it, without hesitation or remorse. Thésée illustrates the ethics of action, of doing, rather than of being. He represents Gide's action, his work as opposed to his conscience.

Thésée's erotic tastes too are radically different from those of Oedipe. Whereas the latter loved only one woman, his mother, Thésée enjoys a number of fleeting love affairs. Of the three best known of these, two were with girls who presented a certain boyish aspect. Antiope, the mother of Hippolyte, was wiry and athletic and fought fiercely to defend her virginity. Phèdre escaped from Crete with Thésée disguised in the clothing of her little brother, Glaucos. Ariane was a more feminine, more possessive type. She wanted to hold the ball of thread, rather than the end, when Thésée entered the labyrinth. He refused her this power, however, and subsequently abandoned her on an island.

It is easy to see in these motifs Gide's affirmation of his pederasty and his estimation of the freedom it brought him from bondage to the maternal-feminine. As I have many times observed, the most powerful motive in his work is the will to dissolve the oedipal marriage and to find freedom and joy in homoerotic encounters.

The risk of enslavement inherent in pederasty is depicted in the figure of the Minotaur in his enchanted lair. Thésée, upon seeing him, is momentarily disarmed by his beauty, but when he detects the stupid look in the animal's eye, he slays him. Gide had never allowed himself to become the captive of a degrading homosexual relationship.

The labyrinth is a highly condensed symbol that evokes other meanings than those associated with Ariane's thread and the Minotaur. The secret of its power to captivate, as its inventor, Dédale, explains it, is not in its complexity, but in the seminarcotic vapors that invite the mind to "flattering errors" and "vain activity." Under the influence of these, each captive, out of the confusion of his mind, invents his own private labyrinth. Dédale's instructions to Thésée for avoiding imprisonment are, first, to remain master of himself, even under the influence of the fumes, and, second, to return to his past, to himself, to what he is at present. In this whole episode Gide was recounting symbolically the great exploit of his youth: his escape from symbolism. For five years or more his work was written under the spell of symbolist idealism and its metaphysical yearnings. André Walter, Urien, the author of *Paludes*, all entertained those "flattering errors" and indulged in that "vain activity" that Icare illustrates in his monologue on first causes. Gide's return from the labyrinth of symbolism was precisely a return to himself, to his nature and its conflicting demands, and to the problems arising out of his childhood.

Icare is André Walter, long ago destroyed by the conflicting forces within his being, but he is also, as Dédale explains, the spirit of restless seeking that remains to haunt the world. In the immortality of this "continuous symbol" Gide acknowledged the persistence in himself of those unsatisfied demands of childhood and youth that are the inexhaustible springs of his poetry.

Dédale demonstrates, on the other hand, the power of reason that knows how to invent the labyrinth and how to escape from it. He too is a "continuous symbol," the embodiment of the inventive imagination, whether it be technical or artistic. Dédale admires Thésée, not for his heroic feats of arms, but for his devotion to duty, for his enterprise and temerity, and above all for his joy. In the complicity of these two legendary figures, Gide pictured the coexistence and cooperation, in his own personality, of a painstaking, clear-sighted literary craftsman and a bold and impulsive challenger of monsters and superstitions.

The value of *Thésée* resides principally in the aptness of its symbolisms and in the detailed image they afford of Gide's self-awareness at the end of his life. In addition to this excellence, however, there is that of the story's tone, which is as close to perfection as anything in Gide's work. Thésée himself recounts the exploits on which his fame rests, and he does so in a voice that is wonderfully natural, unpretentious, and good-humored. At the same time there is no self-deprecation in his story. He speaks of his own destiny always with a little awe, and as he contemplates his whole career at the end of the tale, his voice rises to a lyrical note. It is his easy, confident voice, as much as anything else, that creates the image of Thésée—which is also the image of Gide—just as, many years before, it was the haughty and self-deluding tone of Michel that told us just who and what he was.

Chapter Five
Conclusion

Gide's preeminent position in twentieth-century letters is amply attested by the mass of critical and scholarly writing addressed to his literary work, to his person, and to his influence that has appeared in the last 50 years. To consider the number of entries under his name in the annual bibliography of the Twentieth-Century French Literature Section of the Modern Language Association is cause for both wonderment and gratification to his admirers and probably of chagrin to those who continue to regard him as a subversive influence.

It was not always so. For the first 20 years of his career, the years that are the most remarkable for imaginative invention and formal innovation, Gide's books were known only to a handful of fellow writers who expressed their admiration, and sometimes their cautions, in private letters. Gide voiced some irritation at being ignored and neglected by the larger public, but in truth that neglect seemed only to stimulate him to greater and more daring efforts.

The fact is that a number of things stood between Gide and the professional chroniclers of literature. First of all there was the unorthodox character of his writing with its emphasis on deeply personal motives, its unworldly forms—myths, parables, and the like—and its polished style, which he invented anew for each new work. The era in which Gide wrote was dominated by novels of a historical and sociological character. Critics whose ideas about literature had been formed by familiarity with Balzac and Stendhal, then Maupassant and Zola, were prepared to discuss Bourget, Barrès, Martin du Gard, Jules Romains, Duhamel, even Proust; but Gide left them largely nonplussed.

Symbolism had been very nearly a salon literature, discussed in a few reviews of limited circulation that were dedicated to its particular aesthetic values. The sensuous beauty and the mystery of Gide's early work would have been illuminated by a close acquaintanceship with symbolist values, but lacking that, the literary chroniclers of the popular press would have had little grasp of his "treatises" and poetic dramas. His satire and humor were even less to the taste of the time.

Gide began to be noticed by the critics of the major journals only after the publication of *Les Faux-Monnayeurs*, which the author had labeled a "novel." With this genre the professional commentators were on familiar ground. But even here Gide perplexed them. The revolutionary form of the work, part traditional narrative, part authorial journal, and Édouard's critique of "the novel" as a literary form made *Les Faux-Monnayeurs* essentially indigestible. The judgment of the famous critic and historian Albert Thibaudet was fairly typical. He called it "a monstrously intelligent novel which Gide, with his genuine art as a novelist, has rendered . . . intelligently monstrous."[1]

But it was not only the form and style of Gide's literature that constituted an obstacle to the critics. The author himself was rather "indigestible." His status as a member of the wealthy landowner class was more than a little offensive to the literary establishment, which was a closely guarded province of the petty bourgeoisie. This was certainly no small factor in the neglect that Gide experienced from the commentators until the 1920s, when the notoriety that accompanied his denunciation of France's colonial exploitation of the Congo made it impossible for the press to ignore him. This event coincided with the publication of his "novel" and thus became a second cause for breaking the silence surrounding his name.

Even more distasteful to the critics than his social status was Gide's religious affiliation. The petty bourgeoisie, and thus the literary press, was either mildly anticlerical or officially Catholic. In both *L'Immoraliste* and *La Porte étroite* Gide had depicted with a deep understanding the thoughts and feelings of a Protestant milieu. This in itself was an alien world to most of those who encountered his books, and in addition he had recounted in the former a young man's rebellion against the strictures of that mentality and his election of a frankly immoral style of life, and in the latter he had gone to the opposite extreme and showed how the atmosphere of Calvinist austerity could lead two young lovers to a mystical renunciation of their sexual instincts. Not even the exquisite art with which they were written could overcome the distaste, and probably the perplexity, that these stories aroused in the literary commentators. It is no wonder that the first serious appraisal of *La Porte étroite* was written by an English critic, Edmund Gosse.

It was only in the 1920s that Gide began to receive any serious critical attention, and even then it was directed far less at literary values than at his perceived influence. The major cause of this breakthrough was certainly the generational confrontation that followed the terrible war of

1914–18. Some of the young men who had been called up to defend the political and social order that had promoted the carnage were in open revolt against the establishment they had been forced to serve. They were seeking among their elders for voices that seemed to authorize and support their rebellion. In the opposite camp were the defenders of the old order—the empire, the nation, the family, the Roman Catholic church, the capitalist bourgeoisie and its minions—who were reacting militantly to the threat of revolution and looking for scapegoats and whipping boys.

Gide was admirably positioned to serve both groups. The book in which he had celebrated his own emancipation from the constraints of family, church, and class, *Les Nourritures terrestres* (1897), had finally been discovered by a younger generation, and in 1923 its message was made known to a large reading public by a page in one of those multivolume novels that were enjoying the kind of critical acclaim that Gide had never known. Roger Martin du Gard (1881–1958), who was a friend and in some sense a disciple of Gide, described in a part of his family chronicle, *Les Thibault*, the crucial effect of reading *Les Nourritures terrestres* on a restless and rebellious youth named Daniel de Fontanin. This mention not only directed the attention of a public of young readers to Gide, it also confirmed the judgment uttered by two reactionary journalists, Henri Béraud and Henri Massis, that he was a dangerous suborner of public morals and a vicious influence on the youth of France.

Gide had knowingly invited this sort of attack by his publication in 1914 of *Les Caves du Vatican*, where his great gift of humor is deployed to ridicule the Catholic church and the French Catholic bourgeoisie. He counted upon that book to undo what he regarded as the misconceived and ill-founded success that *La Porte étroite* was enjoying in some pious, right-thinking milieus. He achieved that end and in so doing forced the literary scribes to notice him. As he himself observed, even adverse criticism advanced the public's awareness of his work. Furthermore, *Les Caves du Vatican* was discovered after the war by the young surrealist group, who promptly installed Lafcadio Wluiki in their pantheon. His open contempt for public order and for all forms of literature made him a model and an inspiration for their own revolutionary action.

Gide's Socratic dialogues on homosexuality, entitled *Corydon*, were published in 1924, and in 1926, the year of publication of *Les Faux-Monnayeurs*, his account of his childhood and youth appeared under the title *Si le Grain ne meurt*. These two books amply confirmed what Gide's earlier fictions had made readers suspect about his sexual orientation, and he was thenceforth fully exposed, by his own choice, to the public view. This was undoubtedly a good thing for the ultimate appreciation of his work, since his disclosures constituted a rationale for the immoralism, as well as for the Catharism, of his earlier books.

The 1930s saw a significant elevation of tone and value in the critical appreciation of Gide's literary work. In 1931, for example, Ramon Fernandez published a study of Gide's fiction in which he based his analysis on the psychological motives that the author had made clear in his autobiographical books, most notably the very complex erotic motive. Gide was grateful for the seriousness and the perspicacity of Fernandez's book. In 1938 there appeared an important aesthetic evaluation of Gide's fiction by Jean Hytier, then a professor in Algiers. This was the first of a number of valuable works on Gide written by university scholars.

In 1947 Gide's international reputation was considerably enhanced by the award of the Nobel Prize for literature. This recognition, which followed closely the publication of *Thésée*, had the effect of canonizing Gide and his entire body of work. Several important critical studies of Gide were published near the end of this decade, among them a long article (in *La Part du Feu*, Paris: Gallimard, 1949) by Maurice Blanchot on the experiential and experimental nature of Gide's fiction. Gide had himself insisted a number of times on this source of his work, but it was a significant event to have a major critic of the day emphasize and attribute supreme value to that aspect of his creation. Also, in 1949, a very important study of the role of German literature and thought in Gide's writing was published by Renée Lang, an academic scholar.

Gide's death in 1951 marked the beginning of the most fruitful decade of critical and scholarly writing on his life and work. In that year Roger Martin du Gard published his *Notes sur André Gide*. This was followed in 1952 by the excellent biography written by Léon Pierre-Quint. The following year there appeared in the United States the critical biography of Justin O'Brien, who devoted many years of his life to translating and elucidating the work of Gide. In the realm of criticism, important studies by three American professors, Germaine Brée, Albert Guerard, and Harold March, were published in the early 1950s. The year 1956 saw the publication of Dr. Jean Delay's masterful psychobiography of Gide. In 1958 Gallimard brought out the Pléiade edition of Gide's fiction and lyrical prose works with its valuable scholarly and critical apparatus written by Maurice Nadeau, Yvonne Davet, and Jean-Jacques Thierry.

In the 1960s it became clear that Gide had captured the admiration and critical interest of many academics, especially in the United States. A great many articles on his person and his work began to appear in the scholarly journals. A number of books that had their origin in dissertations were published in these years. For this audience Gide was not the controversial figure that he had been during his lifetime. His work was regarded as a set of problems and puzzles demanding critical explanation. His stand on morals had become an element of his poetic art. The dissolution of empires; the tense, sustained confrontation of the nuclear powers; and the increasing irrelevance of class conflict in an economic order ruled by faceless boards of financial specialists had obliterated much of the worldly context of Gide's literature. What remained, then and now, was a creative personality with a long history of trials, undertakings, and overcomings.

By the year 1969, the centenary of Gide's birth, his work had long been an international property, and he had become a national monument. There was an Association des Amis d'André Gide, two university centers of Gidean studies, one at Montpellier III, the other at Lyons II, a serial publication at Gallimard called "Les Cahiers André Gide," and a similar series at Les Lettres Modernes. These institutions have been publishing for more than two decades not only critical evaluations of Gide's works but above all documentation of his wide-ranging activities and his relations with others. Gide was one of the great letter writers of his era, and he preserved with care the record of his vast correspondence. Some of its important elements, such as his exchanges with Francis Jammes, Paul Claudel, Paul Valéry, and Roger Martin du Gard, were published before or soon after his death, but more recently—from 1979 onward—the Lyons Center and the "Cahiers André Gide" have brought out several important collections of letters. Of particular interest are his correspondence with Dorothy Bussy, the Englishwoman who translated much of his work into English, and the publication by the Lyons Center of his general correspondence under the editorship of Claude Martin, whose scholarly career has been devoted almost exclusively to Gide since the early 1960s.

No event in the realm of documenting Gide's life, however, has been so important as the publication, beginning in 1973 in "Les Cahiers André Gide," of the record of close personal friendship maintained from 1918 to his death by Maria Van Rysselberghe. Though not so meticulous as James Boswell's record of Samuel Johnson's daily life or Eckermann's conversations with Goethe, these notes have the greater value of being the observations of an intimate friend and equal who was a participant in many episodes of Gide's life, and who was able to elucidate details that might otherwise have remained obscure or ambiguous.

The other notable publications of recent years include Auguste Anglès's multivolume history of the formation and early years of *La Nouvelle Revue française*, of which Gide was a primary moving spirit, and Alain Goulet's thesis on the social context of Gide's fiction.

The shift in the last 30 years from polemic to scholarly criticism and documentation should not lead us to forget how daring and provocative Gide's work was during his lifetime. Of all the judgments that have been uttered on the man and his writing, two stand forth in my eyes as exemplary. One is that of Leon Trotsky, who wrote in April 1937: "André Gide is a man of absolutely independent character who possesses a very great perspicacity and an intellectual honesty that permits him to call each thing by its true name. Without that perspicacity one may mumble about the revolution, but not serve it."[2] Trotsky was of course not displeased with the criticisms of life in Stalinist Russia that Gide had voiced on his return from the U.S.S.R. the year before, but nonetheless it was to Gide's character that he addressed his praise. He thus went to the heart of the matter. Instead of carping about his status as a *grand bourgeois*, as some of Gide's compatriots had done, he recorded his view that Gide's honest portrayal of the traits of his class had in fact advanced the idea of social revolution.

The other exemplary judgment was that of the Roman Catholic church when in 1952, a little more than a year after Gide's death, the Suprema Sacra Congregatio Sancti Officii placed his entire work on the *Index Librorum Prohibitorum*. What better proof than this might one hope to find of Gide's authority as an "immoralist"?

No one will suppose that these opinions were inspired solely by literary taste. Still, they do bear witness to the power of Gide's art. Unquestionably his books had moved his readers and forced them to respond to his words with their deepest and hardest convictions. The thing that we find constantly before us in surveying the critical opinion of Gide is the fact of his *moral authority*. Gide's artistry consisted above all in his having convinced his own generation and the two that followed that his work was a confrontation with the most pressing moral problems of the times. Those who attacked him did so because they considered him to be an evil and disruptive voice, a perverter of ideals, a suborner of the nation's youth. Those who praised him did so for the courage and honesty of his revolt against the restrictions of an oppressive society. In the most enlightened judgments of his work there is a universal tendency to regard Gide's genius as essentially critical. Thomas Mann, in a brief tribute written on the occasion of Gide's death, spoke of the "curiosity" and "creative doubt" that drove him to employ "all the means conferred upon him by Intelligence and Art" in the infinite quest for truth."[3] Writing also in the shadow of Gide's death, Archibald MacLeish recognized in him the guiding consciousness of his era: "In the great generations, the generations which bear the mark of transition and choice, there always arises a man who lives for all the others the life of his times, a man who is aware of the world around him in a way that others are not, who, more than other men, recognizes its profound significance. Gide, out of all the men of his generation, was one of those" (*Hommage*, 29).

There is an evident paradox in the case of Gide, for we know that his work proceeded from the most personal, the most intimate of motives. Just two years before his death he wrote: "An extraordinary, insatiable need to love and be loved, that is what I believe has dominated my life, what drove me to write" (*J-S*, 330–31). It was the injury of his childhood, the deprivation and repression ceaselessly demanding redress, that gave strength and purpose to his imagination. The charges lodged against the world, the efforts to abandon the old tormented self and to be reborn without the crippling sense of injury and guilt, the search for a different love, one untouched by the old guilt and discontent—these drives that are the enterprise of Gide's life, the essence of his work, and the source of his moral authority all spring from the dismemberment of his early years.

Gide was fully aware that his strength lay in his difference—in his "complication"—and that it was grounded in weakness and imbalance. In his essay on Dostoyevski, having pointed to the presence of an epileptic in each of his major books as evidence of the importance that the Russian novelist attributed to his own malady "in the formation of his ethics, in the trajectory of his thought," Gide went on to say: "At the source of every great moral reform, if we look carefully, we will always find a little physiological mystery, a discontent of the flesh, an uneasiness, an anomaly." The reformer, suffering from an inward imbalance, seeks a new disposition of things; "his work is nothing but an attempt to reorganize, according to his reason, his logic, the disorder that he feels in himself" (*OC*, 11:292–93).

Gide's strength was in the "logic" of his nature, in that vital dialectic of desire and restraint, of instinct and culture, that marked the progress of his life from neurotic childhood to the stormy conflicts of his late years. His power as an artist began with his intense preoccupation with himself, with his search for that "superior, secret reason for living" (*OC*, 11:163) that each man bears hidden within his being.

For every impulse he found an equally authentic counterimpulse. The search for love led him to the delight of the senses *and* to the passionate refusal of the sensual. His Christian education implanted in him the seeds of an ascetic moralist and a lyrical enthusiast. He could renounce neither, and therefore became both. He touched the extremes of his culture and experienced in the most intimate and positive way its tensions and contradictions. It was his recognition of the *typicalness* latent in his "complication" that completed his artistic power and assured his genius of its grasp on the minds of men. That, plus the determination reached at the time of *André Walter* to reveal his personality in all its complexity, to hold back nothing, and to make his work coextensive with his being; to make it the consciousness of his life and the validation of his hesitancies as well as of his desires.

From being the defender of his own autonomy it was only a step to becoming the advocate of every effort to preserve authenticity. "The only drama which really interests me and which I am always ready to relate anew is the debate between every being and what prevents him from being authentic, with what is opposed to his integrity, to his integration. All the rest is merely incidental" (*J*, 995). He had found that the secret of health lay in the sickness itself. It was a matter of choosing to be *all* that his impulses—be they the result of nature, chance, or the will of God—told him he could be. This insight placed Gide in the company of those other great "sick men" of modernity—Kierkegaard, Dostoyevski, Nietzsche—who saw, through sickness, what health might be. In spite of his doubts, depressions, dejections, Gide was deeply and continually inspired by the certitude that he had grasped the secret of life. And with that truth came the imperative to make it manifest, to place it before other men as the possibility of their liberation. "I mean to give those who read me," he wrote in 1924, "strength, joy, courage, wariness, and perspicacity—but I am careful not to give them directions, believing that they must find these only by themselves" (*J*, 785).

The sense that his work, arising thus out of necessity, would find its destiny in the hearts of future men was for Gide one of the most compelling motives of its creation. In 1943, as the great battle for North Africa drew near to Tunis where he then was, he wrote in his *Journal*: "To create a lasting work: that is my ambition. And as for the rest, success, honors, acclaim, they count for less with me than the tiniest particle of true fame, which is to bring comfort and joy to the young men of tomorrow. Oh, not to limit life to oneself, but help to make it more beautiful and more worthy of being lived! I believe in no other survival than that in the memory of men; just as I believe in no other God than the one that is formed in their spirits and their hearts; consequently each of us must contribute to his reign" (*J-S*, 223).

Notes and References

Chapter One

1. "Et nunc manet in te," *Journal, 1939–1949; Souvenirs* (Paris; Gallimard, 1954), 1157; hereafter referred to parenthetically in the text as *J-S*.
2. "Littérature et Morale," *Journal, 1889–1939* (Paris: Gallimard, 1948), 94; hereafter referred to parenthetically in the text as *J*.
3. Jean Delay, *La Jeunesse d'André Gide* (2 vols., Paris: Gallimard, 1956–57, 2:518–20.
4. Jean Paul Sartre, *Saint Genet, Comédien et Martyr* (Paris: Gallimard 1952), 536.
5. Denis de Rougemont, in *L'Amour et l'Occident* (Paris: Plon, 1939), advanced the thesis that the concept of love expressed in the lyrics of the troubadours and in the legend of Tristan and Iseult originated in the doctrines of the Catharist "Church of Love," which flourished in the south of France during the twelfth century. In a later book, *Comme toi-même: Essais sur les Mythes de l'Amour* (Paris: Albin Michel, 1961), the same writer identified one of Gide's erotic tendencies with the Tristan archetype ("The Two Souls of André Gide").
6. Corydon, in Virgil's *Bucolics*, is the lover of Alexis. His name has an emblematic significance in Gide's work, appearing notably as the title of Gide's four Socratic dialogues on homosexuality (*Corydon*, Paris: Gallimard, 1924).
7. Henri-Frédéric Amiel, *Fragments d'un Journal*, 2 vols (Geneva, 1882–84).
8. Letter to Marcel Drouin, 10 May 1894, quoted in Yvonne Davet, *Autour des "Nourritures terrestres"* (Paris: Gallimard, 1948), 65–68.
9. *Oeuvres complètes* (15 vols., Paris: Gallimard, 1932–39), 2:161; hereafter referred to parenthetically in the text as *OC*.
10. See De Rougemont, *L'Amour et l'Occident*, book 2.

Chapter Two

1. Quoted by Mario Praz in *The Romantic Agony* (London: Oxford University Press Humphrey Milford, 1933), 455.
2. Paul Valéry, "Existence du Symbolisme," *Oeuvres* (2 vols., Paris: Gallimard, 1957), 1: 691, 694.
3. *Romans, Récits et Soties; Oeuvres lyriques* (Paris: Gallimard, 1958), 7; hereafter cited parenthetically in the text as *RRS*.
4. The mythical Orion was blinded by his fiancée's father, but regained his sight and served as huntsman to Artemis, who finally slew him. As a victim of the feminine, he is an appropriate emblem for Gide's story.

5. The tension that Gide creates in this first section of the story between the desire for purity and virtue and the stifling atmosphere of sensuality is unquestionably rooted in authenticity. In *Si le Grain ne meurt* he disclosed that during the composition of *Le Voyage d'Urien* he was possessed by "onanistic frenzies": "At La Roque, summer before last, I thought I should go mad; almost the whole time that I spent there I was shut up in the bedroom where work alone should have retained me, trying in vain to work (I was writing *Le Voyage d'Urien*), obsessed, haunted, hoping perhaps to find some escape in excess alone, to reach the blue heaven on the other side, to wear out my demon (I recognize his counsel in that thought) and only wearing out myself, I spent myself maniacally to the point of exhaustion, to the point of seeing before me only imbecility, only madness" (*J-S*, 593).

6. *Littérature engagée* (Paris: Gallimard, 1950), 79–80.

7. Gide later wrote in a paper entitled "Souvenirs littéraires et problèmes actuels": "In reaction against the Naturalist school and desirous to give to Symbolism the novel that it seemed to me to lack . . . I had just written a certain *Voyage d'Urien*" (*Feuillets d'Automne*, Paris: Mercure de France, 1949, 188).

8. Paul Claudel et André Gide, *Correspondance, 1899–1926* (Paris: Gallimard, 1949), 46.

9. Yvette Louria, "Le Contenu latent du *Philoctète* gidien," *French Review* 25 (1952): 348–54.

Chapter Three

1. In his article "L'Anti-Barrès" (1932), quoted in Davet, 53.

2. "The dissolution of the personality brought about by a too passively receptive attitude is the very subject of my *Saül* . . . which I wrote right after my *Nourritures*, as a sort of antidote and counterweight," Gide wrote to Pastor Ferrari on 15 March 1928 (*OC*, 15:532).

3. Justin O'Brien, *Portrait of André Gide, A Critical Biography* (New York: Knopf, 1953), 165. (The letter also appears in *Nouvelle Revue française, Hommage à André Gide*, Paris: Gallimard, 1951, 381.)

4. *Théâtre* (Paris: Gallimard, 1942), 77; hereafter cited parenthetically in the text as *Th*.

5. "Lettres à Christian Beck," *Mercure de France*, no. 1032 (1949), 621.

6. "Un Esprit non prévenu" (1929), in *Divers* (Paris, 1931), 61–62.

7. Gide gave the following definition of sensuality in 1898: "Sensuality . . . consists simply in considering as an end and not as a means the present object and the present minute." ("Lettres à Angèle, 10," *OC*, 3:220).

8. "My *Immoraliste* was already half-written and entirely composed in my head when I encountered Nietzsche. I can say that at first he bothered me a lot; but thanks to him I was able to rid my book of all sorts of adventitious ideas which were obscurely tormenting me, which no longer had any need to be

expressed, since I found them much better said by him than I should have been able to do," (*OC*, 13:441).

9. Albert J. Guerard, *André Gide* (Cambridge: Harvard University Press, 1951), 102.

10. Claudel-Gide, *Correspondance* (18 June 1909), 103–4.

11. Charles Du Bos, *Le Dialogue avec André Gide* (Paris: Au sans Pareil, 1929), 162–63.

12. In *Journal,* following 1916. (Published anonymously in Bruges in 1922).

13. An account of this relationship may be found in Harold March, *Gide and the Hound of Heaven* (Philadelphia: University of Pennsylvania Press, 1952), chapter 11.

14. M. H. Fayer, *Gide, Freedom and Dostoevsky* (Burlington, Vt.: Lane Press, 1946), 2.

Chapter Four

1. Claude Naville, *André Gide et le Communisme* (Paris: Librairie du Travail, 1936).

2. The French text reads at this point: *". . . pris au jeu (ou au je)."*

Chapter Five

1. Quoted in Michel Raimond, ed., *Les Critiques de notre temps et Gide* (Paris: Editions Garnier Frères, 1971), 54.

2. Léon Trotsky, *Littérature et Révolution* (Paris: Les Lettres Nouvelles, 1964), 345.

3. *La Nouvelle Revue française, Hommage à André Gide* (Paris: Gallimard, 1951), 11–12; hereafter cited as *Hommage.*

Selected Bibliography

PRIMARY WORKS

Collections

Journal, 1889–1939. 1939. Reprint. Paris: Gallimard, Bibliothèque de la Pléiade, 1982. (Referred to in the text as *J.*)

Journal, 1939–1949. Souvenirs. 1954. Reprint. Paris: Gallimard, Bibliothèque de la Pléiade, 1984. (Referred to in the text as *J-S.*) (*The Journals of André Gide.* 2 vols. Translated by Justin O'Brien. Evanston, Ill.: Northwestern University Press, 1987.)

Oeuvres complètes. 15 vols. Paris: Gallimard, 1932–39. (Referred to in the text as *OC*, 1–15.)

Romans, récits et soties: Oeuvres lyriques. 1958. Reprint. Paris: Gallimard, (Bibliothèque de la Pléiade, 1980.) (Referred to in the text as *RRS.*)

Théâtre. Paris: Gallimard, 1942. (Referred to in the text as *Th.*) (*My Theater.* Translated by Jackson Matthews. New York: Knopf, 1952.)

Théâtre complet. 8 vols. Paris: Ides et Calendes, 1947–49. (Referred to in the text as *TC*, 1–8.)

The edition cited for individual works listed below is generally the first edition. If the work is included in one or more of the collections given above, a brief parenthetical indication of where it may be found follows the entry. The parenthetical English translation cited after the entry is the most recent known to me.

Novels, Tales, Lyrical Works in Prose

Les Cahiers d'André Walter. Paris: Librairie Académique Didier-Perrin et Cie, 1891. (*OC*, 1.) (*The Notebooks of André Walter.* Translated by Wade Baskin. Chester Springs, Pa.: Dufour Editions, 1986.)

Les Caves du Vatican. Paris: Gallimard, 1914. (*OC*, 7; *RRS*.) (*Lafcadio's Adventures.* Translated by Dorothy Bussy. New York: Random House, 1980.)

L'École des femmes. Paris: Gallimard, 1929. (*RRS*.) (*The School for Wives; Robert; Genevieve.* Translated by Dorothy Bussy. Cambridge, Mass.: Bentley, 1980.)

El Hadj. In *Philoctète; Le Traité du Narcisse; La Tentative amoureuse; El Hadj.* Paris:

Mercure de France, 1899. (*OC*, 3; *RRS*.) (In *Return of the Prodigal, Preceded by Five Other Treatises; Saul*. Translated by Dorothy Bussy. London: Secker and Warburg, 1953.)

Les Faux-Monnayeurs. Paris: Gallimard, 1926. (*OC*, 12; *RRS*.) (*The Counterfeiters*. Translated by Dorothy Bussy. New York: Random House, 1973.)

Geneviève. Paris: Gallimard, 1936. (*RRS*.) (In Bussy, trans., *The School for Wives*.)

L'Immoraliste. Paris: Mercure de France, 1902. (*OC*, 4; *RRS*.) (*The Immoralist*. Translated by Richard Howard. New York: Bantam Books, 1970.)

Isabelle. Paris: Gallimard, 1911. (*OC*, 6, *RRS*.) (In *Two Symphonies*. Translated by Dorothy Bussy. New York: Random House, 1977.)

Les Nourritures terrestres. Paris: Mercure de France, 1897. (*OC*, 2; *RRS*.) (*Fruits of the Earth*. Translated by Dorothy Bussy. New York: Knopf, 1949.)

Les Nouvelles Nourritures. Paris: Gallimard, 1935. (*RRS*.) (In Bussy, trans., *Fruits of the Earth*.)

Paludes. Paris: Librairie de l'Art Indépendant, 1895. (*OC*, 1; *RRS*.) ("*Marshlands*" and "*Prometheus Misbound*." Translated by George D. Painter. New York: McGraw-Hill, 1965.)

La Porte étroite. Paris: Mercure de France, 1909. (*OC*, 5; *RRS*.) (*Strait Is the Gate*. Translated by Dorothy Bussy. Cambridge, Mass.: Bentley, 1980.)

Le Prométhée mal enchaîné. Paris: Mercure de France, 1899. (*OC*, 3; *RRS*.) (In Painter, trans., "*Marshlands and "Prometheus Misbound*.")

Le Retour de l'Enfant prodigue. Paris: Vers et Prose, 1907. (*OC*, 5; *RRS*.) (In Bussy, trans., *Return of the Prodigal*.)

Robert. Paris: Gallimard, 1930. (*RRS*.) (In Bussy, trans., *The School for Wives*.)

La Symphonie pastorale. Paris: Gallimard, 1919. (*OC*, 9; *RRS*.) (In Bussy, trans., *Two Symphonies*.)

La Tentative amoureuse. Paris: Librairie de l'Art Indépendant, 1893. (In Bussy, trans., *Return of the Prodigal*.)

Thésée. New York: Pantheon Books, 1946. (*RRS*.) (In *Two Legends: Oedipus and Theseus*. Translated by John Russell. New York: Random House, 1958.)

Le Traité du Narcisse. Paris: Librairie de l'Art Indépendant, 1892. (*OC*, 1; *RRS*.) (In Bussy, trans., *Return of the Prodigal*.)

Le Voyage d'Urien. Paris: Librairie de l'Art Indépendant, 1893. (*OC*, 1; *RRS*.) (*Urien's Voyage*. Translated by Wade Baskin. New York: Philosophical Library, 1964.)

La Symphonie pastorale. Paris: Gallimard, 1919. (*OC*, 9; *RRS*.) (In Bussy, trans., *Two Symphonies*.)

Plays

Several items—translations, adaptations, incomplete works—have been omitted here.

Bethsabé. Paris: Bibliothèque de l'Occident, 1912. (*OC*, 4; *TC*, 2) (In *My Theater*. Translated by Jackson Matthews. New York: Knopf, 1952.)

Oedipe.. Paris: Editions de la Pléiade, 1931. (*Th*; *TC*, 4.) (In Russell, trans., *Two Legends*.)

Perséphone. Paris: Gallimard, 1934. (*Th*; *TC*, 4.) (In Matthews, trans., *My Theater*.)

Philoctète. Paris: Mercure de France, 1899. (*OC*, 3; *TC*, 1.) (In Matthews, trans., *My Theater*.)

Robert, ou L'Intérêt général. Paris: Ides et Calendes, 1949. (*TC*, 6.)

Le Roi Candaule. Paris: Revue Blanche, 1901. (*OC*, 2; *Th*; *TC*, 1.) (In Matthews, trans., *My Theater*.)

Saül. Paris: Mercure de France, 1903. (*OC*, 2; *Th*; *TC*, 1) (In Matthews, trans., *My Theater*.)

Le Treizième Arbre. In *Théâtre*. Paris: Gallimard, 1942. (*Th*; *TC*, 5.)

Poetry

Les Poésies d'André Walter. Paris: Librairie de l'Art Indépendant, 1892. (*OC*, 2.)

Autobiography, Journals, Travels

Ainsi soit-il, ou Les Jeux sont faits. Paris: Gallimard, 1952. (*J-S*.) (*So Be It, or The Chips Are Down*. Translated by Justin O'Brien. New York; Knopf, 1959.)

Amyntas. Paris: Mercure de France, 1906. (*OC*, 2, 3.) (*Amyntas*. Translated by Richard Howard. New York: Ecco Press, 1988.)

Et nunc manet in te, suivi de journal intime. Paris: Ides et Calendes, 1951. (*J-S*.) (*Madeleine*. Translated by Justin O'Brien. Salem, Oreg.: I. R. Dee, 1989.)

Journal, 1889–1939. Paris: Gallimard, Bibliothèque de la Pléiade, 1939. (In *The Journals of André Gide*. 2 vols. Translated by Justin O'Brien. Evanston, Ill.: Northwestern Univesity Press, 1987.)

Journal, 1939–1942. Paris: Gallimard, 1946. (*J-S*.) (In O'Brien, trans., *The Journals of André Gide*.)

Journal, 1942–1949. Paris: Gallimard, 1950. (*J-S*.) (In O'Brien, trans., *The Journals of André Gide*.)

Journal des Faux-Monnayeurs. Paris: Editions Eos, 1926. (*OC*, 13.) (In Bussy, trans., *The Counterfeiters*.)

Numquid et tu . . . ? Paris: Editions de la Pléiade, 1926. (*OC*, 8; *J*.) (In O'Brien, trans., *The Journals of André Gide*.)

Retouches à mon "Retour de l'U.R.S.S." Paris: Gallimard, 1937. (*Afterthoughts on the U.S.S.R.* Translated by Dorothy Bussy. New York: Dial Press, 1938.)

Retour de l'U.R.S.S. Paris: Gallimard, 1936. (*Return from the U.S.S.R.* Translated by Dorothy Bussy. New York: McGraw-Hill, 1964.)

Le Retour du Tchad. Paris: Gallimard, 1928. (*OC*, 14; *J-S*.) (In *Travels in the Congo*. Translated by Dorothy Bussy. Harmondsworth, England: Penguin Books, 1986.)

Si le Grain ne meurt. Paris: Gallimard, 1926. (*OC*, 10; *J-S*.) (*If It Die.* Translated by Dorothy Bussy. Harmondsworth, England: Penguin Books, 1977.)

Voyage au Congo. Paris: Gallimard, 1927. (*OC*, 13; *J-S*.) (In Bussy, trans., *Travels in the Congo.*)

Essays; Social and Literary Criticism

L'Affaire Redureau, suivie de faits divers. Paris: Gallimard, 1930.

Corydon. Paris: Gallimard, 1924. (*OC*, 9.) (*Corydon.* Translated by Richard Howard. New York: Farrar, Straus and Giroux, 1983.)

Divers. Paris: Gallimard, 1931. (A selection from this work appears in *Pretexts.* Edited by Justin O'Brien, translated by Angelo Bertocci and others, New York: Delta Books, 1964.)

Dostoïevsky. Paris: Plon-Nourrit, 1923. (*OC*, 11.) (*Dostoevsky.* Translated by Arnold Bennett. Westport, Conn.: Greenwood Press, 1979.)

Essai sur Montaigne. Paris: Editions de la Pléiade, 1929. (*OC*, 15.) (In *The Living Thoughts of Montaigne.* Translated by Dorothy Bussy. New York: Longmans, Green and Co., 1939.)

Feuillets d'automne. Paris: Mercure de France, 1949. (*Autumn Leaves.* Translated by Elsie Pell. New York: Philosophical Library, 1950.)

Incidences. Paris: Gallimard, 1924. (In O'Brien, ed. *Pretexts.*)

Interviews imaginaires. Lausanne: Editions du Haut Pays, 1943. (*Imaginary Interviews.* Translated by Malcolm Cowley. New York: Knopf, 1944.)

Littérature engagée. Paris: Gallimard, 1950.

Nouveaux Prétextes. Paris: Mercure de France, 1911. (*OC*, 4, 5, 6.) (In O'Brien, ed. *Pretexts.*)

Oscar Wilde. Paris: Mercure de France, 1910. (*OC* 3, 4.) (*Oscar Wilde.* Translated by Stuart Mason. London: Kimber and Co., 1951.)

Prétextes. Paris: Mercure de France, 1903. (*OC*, 2, 3.) (In O'Brien, ed., *Pretexts.*)

La Séquestrée de Poitiers. Paris: Gallimard, 1930.

Souvenirs de la Cour d'Assises. Paris: Gallimard, 1914. (*OC* 7; *J-S*.) (*Recollections of the Assize Court.* Translated by Philip Wilkins. London: Hutchinson and Co., 1941.)

Correspondence

"Lettres à Christian Beck." *Mercure de France*, nos. 1031–32 (July and August 1949).

Correspondance André Gide–Dorothy Bussy: 1918–1951. 3 vols. Edited by Jean Lambert. Paris: Gallimard, 1979–82. (Cahiers André Gide, nos. 9–11.) (*Selected Letters of André Gide and Dorothy Bussy.* Edited by Richard Tedeschi. New York: Oxford University Press, 1983.)

Paul Claudel and André Gide. *Correspondance: 1899–1926.* Paris: Gallimard,

1949. (*The Correspondence of Paul Claudel and André Gide*. Translated by
John Russell. New York: Beacon Press, 1964.)
Lettres de Charles Du Bos et réponses d'André Gide. Paris: Corrêa, 1950.
André Gide. *Correspondance générale (1879–1951)*. 6 vols. Edited by Claude
Martin, with Florence Callu, et al. Bron, France: Centre d'Etudes Gidi-
ennes, Université de Lyon II, 1984–85.
Francis Jammes and André Gide. *Correspondance, 1893–1938*. Paris: Gallimard,
1948.
André Gide and Roger Martin du Gard. *Correspondance, 1913–1934*. Paris:
Gallimard, 1968.
André Gide and Paul Valéry. *Correspondance, 1890–1942*. Paris: Gallimard,
1955. (*Self-Portraits: The Gide-Valéry Letters*. Abridged and translated by
June Guicharnaud. Chicago: University of Chicago Press, 1966.)

SECONDARY WORKS

Biographies, Iconography

Album Gide. Pictures chosen by Philippe Clerc. Text by Maurice Nadeau. Paris;
Gallimard, Bibliothèque de la Pléiade, 1985.
Boisdeffre, Pierre de. *Vie d'André Gide, 1869–1951: Vol. 1. André Gide avant la
Fondation de la "Nouvelle Revue Française" (1869–1909)*. Paris: Hachette,
Essai de Biographie critique, 1970.
Delay, Jean. *La Jeunesse d'André Gide*. 2 vols. Paris: Gallimard, 1956–57. A
valuable psychoanalytical study of Gide's childhood and youth.
———. *The Youth of André Gide*. Abridged and translated by June Guichar-
naud. Chicago: University of Chicago Press, 1963.
Martin du Gard, Roger. *Notes sur André Gide*. Paris: Gallimard, 1951. Recol-
lections of Gide by a longtime friend and disciple.
O'Brien, Justin. *Portrait of André Gide: A Critical Biography*. 1953. (Reprint.
New York: Octagon Books, 1977.)
Pierre-Quint, Léon. *André Gide: L'Homme, sa vie, son oeuvre*. Paris: Stock, 1952.
Documented judgments by Gide's contemporaries are included.
Van Rysselberghe, Maria. *Les Cahiers de la Petite Dame: Notes pour l'histoire
authentique d'André Gide*. 4 vols. Preface by André Malraux. Paris; Galli-
mard, 1973–77. (*Cahiers André Gide*, nos. 4–7.) A record of conversations
with Gide from 1918 to 1951 kept by one of his most intimate friends.

Critical Monographs

Ames, Van Meter. *André Gide*. 1947. Reprint. New York: Kraus Reprint,
1972. A probing analysis of Gide's personality, character, and work.
Blanchot, Maurice. *La Part du feu*. Paris: Gallimard, 1949. Contains the very

important essay "Gide et la littérature d'expérience." (Translated in David Littlejohn, ed., *Gide*.)

Brachfield, Georges I. *André Gide and the Communist Temptation*. Geneva: Droz, 1959. Discusses Gide's political thought and activity in the thirties.

Brée, Germaine. *André Gide, l'insaisissable Protée: Etude critique de l'oeuvre d'André Gide*. 1953. Reprint. Paris: Les Belles Lettres, 1970. A penetrating reading of the entire poetic work.

————*Gide*. 1963. Reprint. Westport, Conn.: Greenwood Press, 1985. A somewhat different English language version of her 1953 work.

Cocteau, Jean. *Gide vivant*. Paris: Amiot-Dumont, 1952. A memoir by a famous contemporary.

Davet, Yvonne. *Autour des "Nourritures terrestres": Histoire d'un livre*. Paris: Gallimard, 1948. Illuminates a turning point in Gide's career.

Du Bos, Charles. *Le Dialogue avec André Gide*. Paris: Au sans Pareil, 1929. Intimate, understanding, but negative.

Ellmann, Richard. *Golden Codgers: Biographical Speculations*. London: Oxford University Press, 1973. Contains a penetrating essay on Gide's relations with Oscar Wilde.

Fernandez, Ramon. *Gide, ou Le courage de s'engager*. Paris: Klincksieck, Bibliothéque du XXe Siècle, 1985. Contains his 1931 book plus other papers on Gide. An outstanding study of Gide's psychology.

Fowlie, Wallace. *André Gide: His Life and Art*. New York: Macmillan, 1965. A study of the development of Gide's art.

Goulet, Alain. *Fiction et vie sociale dans l'oeuvre d'André Gide*. Bibliothèque des Lettres Modernes, vol. 35. Paris: Minard, 1984. A detailed study of the implicit social context of Gide's fiction.

Guerard, Albert J. *André Gide*. 2nd ed. Cambridge: Harvard University Press, 1969. An important study of Gide's use of psychology in the novel.

Holdheim, W. Wolfgang. *Theory and Practice of the Novel: A Study of André Gide*. Geneva: Droz, 1968. A study of Gide's poetics.

Hytier, Jean. *André Gide*. Algiers: Charlot, 1938. A perceptive aesthetic study.

————. *André Gide*. New York: Doubleday, 1962. An English translation by Richard Howard of Hytier's French work.

Ireland, G. W. *André Gide: A Study of His Creative Writings*. Oxford: Clarendon Press, 1970.

Lang, B. Renée. *André Gide et la pensée allemande*. Paris: Egloff, 1949. A very important study of the Germanic influence on Gide.

Lafille, Pierre. *André Gide, Romancier*. Paris: Hachette, 1954. Discusses Gide's intentions and projects. Massive documentation.

Levin, Harry. *Grounds for Comparison*. Cambridge: Harvard University Press, 1973. Contains an interesting essay on Gide.

Littlejohn, David, ed. *Gide: A Collection of Critical Essays*. Englewood Cliffs, N. J.: Prentice-Hall, 1969.

McClaren, James C. *The Theater of André Gide: Evolution of a Moral Philosopher.* 1953. Reprint. New York: Octagon Books, 1971.

Mann, Klaus. *André Gide and the Crisis of Modern Thought.* 1953. Reprint. New York: Octagon Books, 1978. Intimate and laudatory.

March, Harold. *Gide and the Hound of Heaven.* Philadelphia: University of Pennsylvania Press, 1952. Important study of the obsessive motive in Gide's life.

Martin, Claude. *Gide.* 1963. Reprint. Paris: Editions du Seuil, Ecrivains de Toujours, 1974. Biography, iconography, critical evaluation. An excellent all-purpose volume.

————.*La Maturité d'André Gide: De "Paludes" à "L'Immoraliste."* Paris: Klincksieck, 1977.

Mauriac, Claude. *Conversations avec André Gide.* Paris: Albin Michel, 1951. Gide's influence on an important writer of the post-1945 generation.

————.*Conversations with André Gide.* New York: Braziller, 1965. English translation by Michael Lebeck of Mauriac's book.

Nobécourt, R.-G. *Les Nourritures normandes d'André Gide.* Paris: Editions Médicis, 1949. Documentation of the role of Normandy in Gide's work.

O'Neill, Kevin. *André Gide and the roman d'aventure: The History of a Literary Idea in France.* Sydney, Australia: Sydney University Press, 1969.

Perry, Kenneth I. *The Religious Symbolism of André Gide.* The Hague; Mouton, 1969.

Planche, Henri. *Le Problème de Gide.* Paris: Téqui, 1952. A psychoanalytical study of Gide.

Raimond, Michel, ed. *Les Critiques de notre temps et André Gide.* Les Critiques de notre temps, vol. 6. Paris: Editions Garnier Frères, 1971. A useful and illuminating compilation.

Rivière, Jacques. *Etudes.* 1911. Reprint. Paris: Gallimard, 1948. Contains an important early essay on Gide's work.

Schlumberger, Jean. *Madeleine et André Gide.* Paris: Gallimard, 1956. The conjugal drama viewed from the side of Madeleine.

Thierry, Jean-Jacques. *André Gide.* Paris: Hachette Littérature, 1986. A critical evaluation by an important Gide scholar.

Weinberg, Kurt. *On Gide's "Prométhée": Private Myth and Public Mystification.* Princeton: Princeton University Press, 1972. Eccentric but interesting.

Bibliographies

Cotnam, Jacques. *Bibliographie chronologique de l'oeuvre d'André Gide (1889–1973).* Boston: G. K. Hall, 1974.

————.*Inventaire bibliographique et index analytique de la correspondance d'André Gide (publiée de 1897 à 1971).* Boston: G. K. Hall, 1975.

Martin, Claude. *Bibliographie chronologique des livres consacrés à André Gide*

(1918–1986). Bron, France: Centre d'Etudes Gidiennes, Université de Lyon II, 1987.

Periodicals

André Gide, Published irregularly, but more or less annually by Les Lettres Modernes (Minard), Paris, 1971–   . Mainly critical articles addressed to a particular subject.

Bulletin des Amis d'André Gide. A quarterly journal published by the Association des Amis d'André Gide. Montpellier, France: Section André Gide du Centre d'Etudes Littéraires du XXe Siècle de l'Université de Montpellier III, 1968–   . Articles, letters, etc.

Cahiers André Gide. An annual. Paris: Gallimard, 1969–   . Correspondence, memoirs, articles, etc.

Although they bear no series title, the publications of the Centre d'Etudes Gidiennes of the Université de Lyon II belong in this category.

OTHER WORKS CITED

Fayer, Mischa Harry. *Gide, Freedom and Dostoevsky.* Burlington ,Vt.: Lane Press, 1946.

Louria, Yvette. "Le Contenu latent du *Philoctète* gidien." *French Review* 25 (April 1952): 348–54.

Naville, Claude. *André Gide et le Communisme, suivi d'Etudes et Fragments.* Paris: Librairie du Travail, 1936.

Nouvelle Revue Française. Hommage à André Gide. Paris: Gallimard, 1951.

Praz, Mario. *The Romantic Agony.* London: Oxford University Press Humphrey Milford, 1933.

De Rougemont, Denis. *L'Amour et l'Occident.* Paris: Plon, 1939.

————.*Comme Toi-même: Essais sur les Mythes de l'Amour.* Paris: Albin Michel, 1961.

Sartre, Jean-Paul. *Saint Genet, Comédien et Martyr.* (Vol. 1 of Jean Genet, *Oeuvres complètes.*) Paris: Gallimard, 1952.

Trotsky, Léon. *Littérature et révolution.* Paris: Les Lettres Nouvelles, 1964.

Valéry, Paul. *Oeuvres.* 2 vols. Paris: Gallimard, Bibliothèque de la Pléiade, 1957–60.

Index

The Author

Thomas Cordle was born in Atlanta, Georgia, in 1918. His early years were spent in the Deep South and in central Virginia. He attended McDonogh School, near Baltimore, Maryland, and later the University of Virginia. After wartime sevice in the U.S. Navy he received the M.A. and Ph.D. degrees from Yale University. From 1950 to 1985 he taught French language and literature at Duke University, specializing in twentieth-century literature. In 1955–56 he was a Fellow of the Fund for the Advancement of Education. He has published articles on Gide, Proust, and Malraux. Now professor emeritus of Duke Univesity, he lives in retirement in Durham, North Carolina.

The Editor

David O'Connel is professor of foreign languages and chair of the Department of Foreign Languages at Georgia State University. He received his Ph.D. from Princeton University in 1966, where he was a National Woodrow Wilson Fellow, the Bergen Fellow in Romance Languages and a National Woodrow Wilson Dissertation Fellow. He is the author of *The Teachings of Saint Louis: A Critical Text* (1972), *Les Propos de Saint Louis* (1974), *Louis-Ferdinand Céline* (1976), *The Instructions of Saint Louis: A Critical Text* (1979), and *Michel de Saint Pierre: A Catholic Novelist at the Crossroads* (1990). He is the editor of *Catholic Writers in France since 1945* (1983) and has served as review editor (1977–79) and managing editor (1987–90) of the *French Review*.